THE ISMAY LINE

THE ISMAY LINE
The Titanic, the White Star Line and the Ismay family

Wilton J Oldham

CHAPLIN BOOKS

www.chaplinbooks.co.uk

First published in 1961 by *The Journal of Commerce and Shipping Telegraph*. Published as an ebook in 2013 by Chaplin Books. This paperback edition published 2018.

Chaplin Books
Gosport PO12 4UN
www.chaplinbooks.co.uk

ISBN: 978-1-911105-41-1

Copyright © Wilton J Oldham

All rights reserved. No part of this publication may be reproduced, stored in any retrieval system or transmitted in any form or by any means, electronic, mechanical, photocopying, recording or otherwise, without the prior written permission of the copyright holder for which application should be addressed in the first instance to the publishers. No liability shall be attached to the author, the copyright holder or the publishers for loss or damage of any nature suffered as a result of reliance on the reproduction of any of the contents of this publication or any errors or omissions in its contents.

DEDICATION

This book is dedicated to the memory of Joseph Bruce Ismay,
born December 12th 1862, died October 17th 1937,
aged 74 years.

*They that go down to the sea in ships: and occupy their business
in great waters:*
These men see the works of the Lord: and his wonders in the deep

Psalm 107, verses 23, 24

CONTENTS

FOREWORD

AUTHOR'S NOTE

CHAPTER 1
Birth of Thomas Henry Ismay, his early childhood in Maryport, schooldays at Brampton, Carlisle, and apprenticeship in Liverpool

CHAPTER 2
Diaries of T H Ismay's South American voyage

CHAPTER 3
Shipbroking partnership with Nelson, T H Ismay's marriage, the birth of Joseph Bruce Ismay, dissolving the partnership with Nelson

CHAPTER 4
Buying of the White Star Line, its early history, founding of the Oceanic Steam Navigation Company

CHAPTER 5
The Company's first disaster, the Atlantic, Bruce Ismay's schooldays, the buying of the Dawpool Estate

CHAPTER 6
Growth of the White Star Line, the building of the new Dawpool House, presentation of the gilt dinner service

CHAPTER 7
Bruce Ismay's New Zealand tour, the collision between the Britannic and Celtic, founding of the Liverpool Seamen's Pension Fund, T H Ismay's Indian tour

CHAPTER 8
Bruce Ismay's marriage, the Teutonic - first armed merchant cruiser, Bruce Ismay made a partner and comes to live in England

CHAPTER 9
Disappearance of the Naronic, T H Ismay refusing a baronetcy, T H Ismay's last illness and death at Dawpool

CHAPTER 10
Sale of the White Star Line to the International Mercantile Marine

CHAPTER 11
Bruce Ismay president of the IMM Company, the death of Mrs T H Ismay

CHAPTER 12
Salvage of the Suevic, opening of the new Southampton route, loss of the Republic, building of the Olympic and Titanic

CHAPTER 13
Olympic's maiden voyage

CHAPTER 14
Circumstances of Bruce Ismay's retirement

CHAPTER 15
Titanic's maiden voyage

CHAPTER 16
The inquiries and the aftermath

CHAPTER 17
The White Star Line under Harold Sanderson, the war years and after

CHAPTER 18
Sale of the White Star Line to the Royal Mail group, the amalgamation of the Cunard and White Star Lines, the death of J Bruce Ismay

EPILOGUE

APPENDICES
Rules and Regulations of the White Star Line
Affidavit made by A H Weikman

ACKNOWLEDGEMENTS

FOREWORD

Wilton J Oldham – known to his friends as John - was my father. He became very involved with the *Titanic* and the Bruce Ismay story through his other passion - Rolls-Royce cars.

Having met the Ismay family, he embarked on what was to become a 'mission' to prove that the rumours surrounding the behaviour of Bruce Ismay on that fatal night were untrue and at best exaggerated: this he set out to do with full cooperation from the family.

I remember as a six-year-old, when we were living in Cornwall, being woken by a rather fraught mother at 5am to be informed that we were going to stay with Aunt Margaret Cheape (Bruce Ismay's daughter) at Duncrieve, her lovely house in Scotland. My father was already in the car, revving the engine. This happened on a number of occasions - whenever there was an opportunity to continue with his research. He was an absolute stickler for facts. Eventually the book was published, in 1961, but it has been out of print for many years.

I am sure my father would be delighted that people are now being given another chance to read about this infamous event from another point of view - speaking up for Bruce Ismay.

I hope that you enjoy reading it.

Victoria Jervis

AUTHOR'S NOTE

Sixty years ago there was probably no more successful steamship company than the Oceanic Steam Navigation Company, better known as the White Star Line. Its importance and prosperity were almost entirely due to the foresight of one man, Thomas Henry Ismay.

In April 1912 the White Star Line's latest and largest vessel collided with an iceberg and sank while on her maiden voyage from Southampton to New York, with a loss of over 1,500 lives. Amongst the passengers was J Bruce Ismay, eldest son of the founder of the line. He was saved in the last lifeboat to leave the starboard side of the sinking vessel and was bitterly attacked by certain sections of the press in Britain and the United States of America, as they held him largely responsible for the disaster; they also severely criticised his personal behaviour that night. The *Titanic* disaster ruined his life.

It is a quarter of a century since the White Star Line became part of the Cunard Steam-Ship Company; all the achievements of T H Ismay and the interesting early history of the company are more or less completely forgotten. Only the story of the *Titanic* is told and retold, usually with very unjust comments on J Bruce Ismay.

I have always felt that he was one of the most misunderstood and misjudged characters of the early part of the century. So I made it my business to discover the whereabouts of his family; to them I put my proposition, to write a history of the White Star Line (a thing that has never been done before) and the biographies of Thomas and Bruce Ismay, with the intention of trying to give a true picture of these two men as they really were. Mrs Bruce Ismay and her elder daughter, Mrs Ronald Cheape, received me with great kindness and courtesy, and fully approved the project.

During one of my many talks with the family, I discovered a curious coincidence; the house in which I spent my childhood, at

27 Chesham Street, London SW1, was once rented by Mr and Mrs Bruce Ismay, and his sisters later occupied it, and whenever he went to stay with them Bruce Ismay himself slept in the room which was to become my nursery.

This has not been an easy book to write by any means, as everyone I approached has been so kind, that I have been overwhelmed with information. Fortunately Bruce Ismay was a very meticulous person and kept carefully a great many private papers to which Mrs Bruce Ismay has allowed me full access. I have used these old records and letters extensively, in order to allow the main characters in this history to speak for themselves.

Although some may be disappointed with the results of my labours, I hope that this book will give pleasure to most of my readers. I have tried to concentrate on what I call genuine White Star vessels, by which I mean those built by Harland & Wolff; although the others do figure occasionally in the text.

Wilton J Oldham

CHAPTER 1

Birth of Thomas Henry Ismay, his early childhood in Maryport, schooldays at Brampton, Carlisle, and apprenticeship in Liverpool

Thomas Henry Ismay has been described as the most 'Victorian' of the great shipowners of the last century, inasmuch as his life spanned practically the whole of the Victorian era; he was born in 1837, the year the Queen ascended the throne and died in 1899 only two years before her long life drew to its peaceful close at Osborne House, Isle of Wight, where she had spent so much of her time in her last years.

The Ismay family had originally come to Maryport in Cumberland from Uldale, a small hamlet twelve miles away,

Ropery House, Maryport, the boyhood home of T H Ismay

where they were known as 'statesmen', (a North country expression meaning small farmers). The earliest date on which the name Ismay can be traced is on the Rolls of Dun draw, also near Maryport, in 1646.

At the beginning of the century Maryport was a clean well-built seaport on the mouth of the River Ellen, 28 miles southwest of Carlisle. It was a modern town built in the Georgian style with well-designed squares and terraces. Pennant wrote in 1774 "Maryport is another new erection, the property of Humphrey Senhouse, Esq., and so named by him in honour of his Lady. The second house was built in 1750, now there are 100 houses and 1,300 souls all collected together by the opening of a coal trade on their estate".

Ships varying from 30 to 300 tons were built there and there were wooden quays and piers where ships were overhauled and received their lading. In 1841 the Chapelry consisted of 1,195 houses and 5,311 inhabitants and there were 121 vessels using the port, their principal employment being the import of timber from America and the export of some 3,800 tons of coal weekly to Ireland, from the neighbouring collieries, some of which ran under the sea. The port originally came under Whitehaven, but in 1838 the power of registering vessels was granted to Maryport.

There were three shipbuilding yards and, owing to the narrowness of the river, it was one of the few places where vessels were launched sideways. They were built of wood for the American, Baltic and West Indian coastal trades. Also in the town were three brass and iron foundries as well as a rope works.

One of the first shipbuilding yards was owned by Joseph Middleton and one of his ships was captained by a certain Henry Ismay. In 1800 this young man married Charlotte, Joseph Middleton's eldest daughter. When Henry Ismay retired from the sea he and his wife took a small grocery shop in the High Street; their second son, Joseph, was employed as a foreman shipwright in the Middleton shipyard, which was now owned by his uncle, Isaac Middleton.

He married Mary Sealby, daughter of John Sealby who also lived in the High Street and who was described as 'gentleman' in Maryport's Parson and White Directory. Joseph Ismay took his bride to live in one of a row of cottages in what was known as Whillan's Yard, which he had bought in 1833. This was a narrow thoroughfare forming a right of way between two other roads; the houses were very small and cramped together and overlooked the graveyard of a nearby church. It was here that their first son, Thomas Henry Ismay, was born. This boy was destined to become one of the foremost shipowners of his day, who years later entertained royalty on board the splendid ships owned by the firm he founded and made great, the Oceanic Steam Navigation Company, known to the world as the White Star Line.

Four years later the family had increased to four children, as Thomas was followed by twin girls, Charlotte and Mary, and three years after them another sister, Sarah. They now found the little house in Whillan's Yard rather overcrowded, so they bought a double-fronted Georgian house down by the shipbuilding yard. It had a curious name, Ropery House, so called because it was on the road which ran in front of it that all the ropes connected with the shipyard were laid out. It had four main bedrooms and three attics and so made a comfortable home for the expanding family. It was here that their fifth child, John Sealby Ismay was born, when Thomas was ten years old.

Shortly after moving, Joseph started business on his own account, as timber merchant and shipbuilder. He also became Maryport's very first shipbroker, and had a share in some four ships which traded with the port. It is interesting to note here that he dealt with the firm Imrie, Tomlinson, with which his son, Thomas, was one day to be apprenticed. Here is an early letter to Joseph Ismay from them:

> Liverpool.
> To Jos. Ismay Esq,
> Maryport.
> July 11th, 1840.
> Sir,
> We were favoured with yours of the 21st June, The *Middleton* ought to be in, but we suppose she has met with the northerly gales, the *Chalco* that sailed after her is up some time since. But another vessel that sailed with the *Middleton* also keeps out, which is well - we are sorry that the vessel is ordered to London.
> What has Captain White done with his new ship? We should recommend him to take a River Plate voyage, it would season his vessel well and surely, and we could fix him out and home, if he wished. We also want a vessel to load a cargo of coals at a Cumberland port to proceed to Barbary and there load a cargo of sugar for Liverpool freights for this run. The coals £3 10s. 0d. per ton and 5/- extra for sent to London 60 days' abroad. How would this suit her? We could do better for her here, but then it may prevent her changing ports.
> We are, Sir,
> Your obedient Servant,
> IMRIE, TOMLINSON.
> P.S. We could take the vessel as a packet to Rio to sail in August for about £525. Will you or Capt. White write us.

As the young Thomas grew into a sturdy boy, he spent many hours with his friend John Cockton, the son of the local chemist. The two boys loved to go down to the quayside to talk to the sailors and watch the ships coming and going. With his knife Thomas would carve model ships from pieces of driftwood and he showed, even at this age, his keen interest in everything to do with the sea and ships.

When he was twelve, his father was very ill and went to the fashionable spa of Malvern for treatment, leaving the boy at home to look after his mother and younger brother and sisters. During this time he received this letter from his father.

Malvern, June 30th 1849
My dear son,
I received yours and was glad to receive it, and hope you will improve in writing. This letter is very well wrote and spelled. I am very glad there is going to be plenty of fresh herrings as they will assist the working people, work being so slack. I notice Jos. Middleton sale day and should like to be at home that day, but they say I am to stay eight weeks. The illness being so long on me, it will require time to remove it. But it is so expensive, eight weeks will cost £40. Rather over much but my health is above all consideration else. I shall try to make a shorter time serve here, and try to carry it out at home. I have been a fortnight here and am sometimes like to lose heart. I hope you are assisting Mr. Fearnon to take and calculate stock up, so as all may be ready on my return. Hope you have a good crop of potatoes and that you are using them. Also you water the flowers and plants every night. Francis can help you in keeping the garden in good order. Remember me to all my friends, your mother, Sarah and John, and you can say if you have had any letters from C. Jackson. Hoping you are all enjoying yourselves at home, I remain, my dear son,
Your affectionate father,
Jos. Ismay.

He was a bright, intelligent boy, on whom it was obvious both parents relied and they soon realised, that, if he were given a good education, there were great possibilities for his future. So, when he left the local school, they sent him in the following autumn, to Croft House School, Brampton, Carlisle, some 40 miles from Maryport. This was considered, at that time, to be one of the best boarding schools in the North of England and drew pupils from all over the North of England, from Scotland and Ireland. It was run by a Mr Joseph Coulthard, his wife, two sons a daughter, and four assistant masters. It comprised two large houses standing about 300 yards apart. In one were the residential quarters and in the other the classrooms.

The curriculum of subjects taught was progressive for that time and consisted of English, Classics, Modern Languages,

Deportment, Mathematics, Philosophy, Penmanship, Drawing and Music. Philosophy included Astronomy, Geology, Botany, Chemistry and Physiology. Deportment included Dancing, Drill, and Gentlemanly Bearing. By 1852 the number had risen to 128 pupils.

The new boy from Maryport no doubt travelled to school on the newly opened Maryport-Carlisle Railway, the building of which was started the year he was born. It had only been running since 1841 and was considered by many people to be 'new fangled'.

Thomas was small, with a dusky complexion, and intelligent dark eyes which were deeply penetrating. He was thoughtful and kind, very friendly and had a keen sense of humour. His peculiar gift of being at ease with everyone was a characteristic which was to help him greatly in later life. He did well at school and was very popular. He was an individualist even at that age. He chewed tobacco, after the habit of sailors back at home in Maryport, and quickly gained the nickname 'Baccy' Ismay.

When he had been a year at school, his father died quite suddenly aged only forty-six. Thomas' great-uncle, Isaac Middleton, then took a great interest in the boy and it was he who arranged to apprentice him in Liverpool to his own agent, the ship brokers, Imrie, Tomlinson, whom he knew well and with whom Thomas' father had had business. He continued at school and took special studies in navigation. Although he joined in games of cricket and 'prisoner's base', owing to his love of the sea and ships which was in his blood on both sides, he spent all his spare time in building model ships, rigging them too, according to their class, and sailing them on the pond of the new town of Irthington, which was about a mile from the school.

When he was sixteen he started his apprenticeship as arranged at 13 Rumford Street, Liverpool. There was a sailing vessel, the *John Glaister*, which was built in 1846 to a 100 AI Lloyds specification, especially for travelling between Maryport and Liverpool, which it did every alternate Tuesday. It is most likely that the ship-loving Thomas chose to travel by this route. In 1853, when he arrived, the city was an extremely busy and very important seaport, for it not only handled an enormous quantity of exports and imports, but was also a busy shipbuilding centre. Two of the better-known shipyards, which have long since disappeared, were those of Potter and of Evans.

Some idea of the size of the Liverpool docks in those days can be gained from the following. There were 880 acres total area of the estate and 207 acres total area of water. Exports were valued at £50,699,668; tonnage of vessels entering the docks was 4,005,016.

William Imrie, the senior partner of the firm, had a house called Claremont a few miles out of the city, at West Derby. His son, also called William, was exactly the same age as Thomas and was also serving his apprenticeship in his father's business. It is not known where Thomas lived while in Liverpool, but it can only be assumed that he lived at Claremont, as the two boys formed a friendship which was to last a lifetime. The second partner, John Tomlinson, who lived at Fulwood Park, Aigburth was more of a sleeping partner, leaving the active business to William Imrie.

CHAPTER 2

Diaries of T H Ismay's South American voyage

Whilst serving his time with this firm, Thomas gained a good reputation with Liverpool merchants generally, because of the prompt and efficient attention he gave to their affairs. After three years with them, he wished to gain more experience of the world and decided that to improve his practical knowledge of ships, it would benefit him to go on a sea voyage. So he arranged with Jackson & Co of Maryport to sail to Chile as supercargo on board their vessel *Chas. Jackson,* a barque of 352 tons, built in 1852, commanded by Captain Metcalf.

On January 4th 1856 this vessel sailed from Liverpool for South America with Thomas Ismay on board. He was away from his homeland for nearly a year, and during this time he had many adventures and thoroughly enjoyed the experience. Whilst on this voyage he kept daily diaries, which are still in existence although he did not complete them. They give a very good idea both of life on a sailing vessel in those days and of the personality of Thomas Ismay, aged nineteen years; consequently I have included extracts from them in this chapter: -

January 4th, Friday, 1856. Slept on board last night, so that I might not be called up until they were really sure of sailing. The morning very dull, and a slight mist overhanging the Mersey. The Pilot stepped on board, and away we went from the Albert Pierhead at 7.30 a.m. in tow of the steamer, and one sailor short of our complement. At 10 a.m. the steamer left us with letters for a few friends left behind. Here we are in a good vessel, and I hope a fair set of men as seamen, with a very long voyage before us. At 3 p.m, passed the Great Ormes Head. At 8 p.m, sighted Holyhead on which I looked with a kind of sadness, feeling only now the reality of being about to bid farewell to old England, with this as the last link between home with all its associations of love and happiness and the unknown welcome of strange faces in far off Chile. But I began here also to experience an unpleasant commotion within my own frame, evidently caused by the somewhat heavy rolling of the vessel, I gladly retired to bed about 8.40, and as to what occurred there, the result of the above feeling it is needless to write here.

January 6th, Sunday. I had a very good night's rest, although it had been blowing very strong, especially towards midnight, when by some unaccountable misadventure that important article the Cook's Galley Funnel was lost overboard, however, I am happy to state that a sufficient quantity of material of the right sort was on board to replace the lost one, and further that our dinner was not the worse for the loss. This is my first Sunday at sea, and very different it is to those on shore where everyone looks his best, here everything is quite quiet and in harmony with my feelings. The crew are all clean and some are reading, no work done except attending to the working of the vessel. Lightfoot, one of the apprentices, playing on the flute in the forecastle.

January 7th, Monday. This is the 19th anniversary of my birthday, and a beautiful day it is, being almost calm, remained on deck nearly all day shooting gulls. The crew in the forecastle had a bottle of brandy given them to drink, and if I judge from the songs I heard them singing, they enjoyed the contents. During the evening Rapp, the Captain and myself were amusing ourselves with singing, Home Sweet Home, etc. Of course, the performance would have elicited great applause from an audience endowed with taste. I do hope I may enjoy every anniversary as well.

January 9th, Wednesday. After dinner I was reading below, when I heard cries of a steamer close on our weather bow. I immediately hurried on deck and found her to be the Screw Transport *Sarah Sands* No. 233 from the Crimea bound to Liverpool, our number 8024 was hoisted but it was scarcely necessary for she came within hailing distance. There seemed to be a great many officers (Military) and soldiers on deck. The steamer herself presented anything else than a shipshape appearance caused partly, by her being so light having consumed a great portion of her coal, and also pitching and rolling considerably. We felt well pleased at having seen the steamer for our friends at home will have the satisfaction to learn of our safety so far. It caused no small excitement for a short while on board.

January 11th, Friday. I feel somewhat better to-day, and I am confident that once I get quite better of this Liverpool cold, I will gain strength rapidly. At dinner struck by a heavy sea, which created quite a commotion among the dishes for the contents were all mixed up together, and as Rapp truly remarked, it would have taken the celebrated Sayer to have given a name to the various ingredients so mingled together. You have to hold on to your plate to keep it near you, to hold on to your glass of water to avoid the unnecessary luxury of a shower bath; to hold on to the table to keep yourself off the top of it, and keep away from your neighbours. Besides this, to dodge or defend yourself as the case may be, from the flying dishes that occasionally make little excursions on their own responsibility. A man that can get his victuals at sea on board a ship in a storm can get his living anywhere, he can have no fear of the future so far at least as eating is concerned.

January 15th, Tuesday. During the night another gale has sprung up with a disagreeable cross sea. Very little sail set, while on the main deck got several drenchings for the sea is coming right over the rail on the main deck where I was amused by seeing the Pig (the only one on board) washed right along the deck by a sea, fortunately it did not go overboard.

January 17th, Thursday. After dinner while sitting in the cabin I heard the cry from the Chief Officer of "Land ho". Land ho I muttered to myself as I hurried on deck fearing it might vanish ere I could get a glimpse of the welcome object said to be in view. He alone who is at sea can appreciate and describe the sensation that tingles through the veins at the shout of "Land ho". It was decidedly the pleasantest sound that has reached my ears since my departure from Liverpool.

January 21st, Monday. I have taken advantage of this fine day to get my clothes dried for the best of vessels are somewhat damp.

January 24th, Thursday. The Captain is suffering severely from toothache, after much persuasion I induced him to get a little salt heated, and put into a flannel stocking and tied round the jaw. The Captain found relief from it.

January 25th, Friday. Before 6 o'clock I went and had a good cooling in the cask (like Diogenes in his tub) which we use as a bath.

January 27th, Sunday. At 10 a.m. passed the island of Bonavista on our right, its name implies an island of great beauty, but owing to the fog the outlines were scarcely visible, and so the world has lost the advantage of my opinion, whether its appearance gives the lie to its name or not. We have the awning spread over the quarter deck so as to keep the deck cooler.

January 28th, Monday. We are becalmed. We begin to feel the heat especially to-day, there being no wind. Many porpoises about, had the Harpoon sharpened and tried our best to secure one, but without success.

January 30th, Wednesday. After enjoying a bath, which is quite a luxury in this latitude, also a good breakfast, which is also equally essential, I commenced some Manifest of the vessel's cargo which are to be delivered to the Customs Officials in Valparaiso, this employed me until nearly noon. I find considerable difference between settling down to work on a long four legged stool in an office, and on board a ship. Oh, for the days of Good Queen Bess or any other Queen during whose reign offices were not in existence.

(THIS DIARY IS NOT COMPLETED)

April 8th, Tuesday. The date of our arrival in Valparaiso, Chile, at 6 a.m. a reef was taken in the topsails which I am told is a necessary precaution before entering the Bay owing to the heavy squalls blowing down from the hills, which surround the town except that part facing the Bay. About 7.30 a.m. four Whale Boats rode alongside and offered to tow the vessel to the anchorage ground which we were then about two miles distant from. The

Captain engaged the services of the four boats each of which contained four Chilenas as rowers and well they rowed, if they put a little more spirit into their movements. The Captain of the Ports Assistant came on board, he took charge of the vessel to her moorings, and seemed to hold a similar position to what our Pilots do at home ports. The vessel was moored with two anchors ahead and one astern, almost sufficient to hold her until Doomsday. I learnt, however, that this is quite a requisite precaution owing to heavy gales blowing here from the North and termed Northers and are very dangerous to shipping in the Bay for they are accompanied by a heavy swell or roll. I then went on shore and received my letters which had only arrived by the mail yesterday. I was somewhat disappointed as to the number I received, perhaps the next mail will bring more. However, I learn all are well at home. A Mr. Nixon to whom I was introduced invited me to accompany him to the theatre, and to which I readily assented. Had a walk round a portion of the town. My opinion I postpone until I have had a better opportunity of seeing and judging correctly. On our way to the theatre called in at a French shop to purchase a pair of gloves for the theatre and for which I paid a Dollar and a half equivalent to 6 /- English, this was my first outlay in Chile. A remarkably good looking French girl fitted me on with a pair and was highly amused at my trying to make myself understood in French. At the theatre door we found Nixon waiting for us when he got our tickets. On our entrance and paying the entrance money you receive a scrip of paper on which is the number of your seat. You pass across a large room where refreshments can be obtained, and where it is customary to retire to during the intervals of the scenes and smoke or get ices of which there is an abundance. The theatre you find to be an exceedingly comfortable place, and the Pit where I had taken tickets for was exceedingly comfortable and quite a different place to that at home. Each person had a chair (arm) to himself so that overcrowding was prevented and no ladies are allowed in the Pit. The Boxes when taken must be taken by one person and cost about £2 10s. 0d., they are capable of accommodating about eight persons. I armed myself with an opera glass, so I had a good view of the Fair Chilenas of whom I had heard much respecting their beautiful appearance. The performance consisted chiefly of four sisters dancing, which was excellent, and they received frequent applause, from the audience not such as the English Theatres audience greet their favourite performers with.

April 9th, Wednesday. After having slept tolerably well at the hotel, considering the accommodation, which was not so good as I could have wished, rose at 6 a.m., to go on board with the Market Boat to breakfast. The Captain and I had a long ramble to the top of some hills which surround Valparaiso on the land side and on some of which a considerable part of the town is built. At 8 o'clock I met Nixon and accompanied him to his father's house where I was very kindly received. There was also another English lady and gentleman present, the gentlemen present were continually smoking, before tea, at tea and after tea in the drawing room, in fact everywhere they keep up a continual cloud. There was dancing until towards 12 o'clock when I betook myself off to the hotel where I proposed sleeping.

April 14th, Monday. The breakfast here differs much from an English one. It is generally soup, fish, steaks, and some joint cold, with light French wine then coffee.

April 27th, Sunday. After breakfast a party of us mounted on horseback went for a very pleasant ride. We spent a very pleasant day in the plains, and about 5 o'clock started on our way back. We rode very quickly for the heat of the day was over. On our arrival there we were as usual saluted by the infernal dogs, which infest this port. One of which received a cut which he will keep in mind for a few days to come.

April 30th, Wednesday. During the evening after dinner at a cafe, I danced a native dance with a native lady. The dancing is usually accompanied by two or three singers. It consists of a good deal of advancing and retiring, and no little waving of handkerchiefs. They prefer it to our English Quadrilles, Polka, etc., and will dance it all night without change.

On May 9th 1856 Thomas was invited to stay, whilst in Valparaiso at the home of a Mr and Mrs Mouat.

May 16th, Tuesday. Last night I slept on shore, and on

getting up, I find I have been quite a savoury dish during the night to some mosquitoes, for I am very much bitten.

During this visit, he spent much time on horseback, exploring Valparaiso and the surrounding countryside, and at night enjoying a social life, dancing, parties, theatres, etc. He observed that most of the merchants were well-to-do and had lovely houses on the heights above the city, from which they had a splendid view. On the other side of the city there were apparently picturesque dwellings, overhanging the steep hillside. These were the homes of the poorer people and, in spite of their attractive appearance from a distance, on closer examination "the habitations consist of wretched clay huts, fireplaces outside of the doors, impurities of all sorts taint the air, and dark wild looking, loathsome faces peep forth here and there".

He also objected to the numbers of stray dogs, which roamed Valparaiso, which were the scavengers of the city, and for the way trivial offences, such as "going at more than a trot in the city" were heavily fined, while greater crimes went almost unnoticed.

Thomas noticed that the reconstruction work of the city was done by offenders against the law, "chained by a large shackle, two together, and guarded by a party of soldiers, I have seen 200 march through the city to work". The South American women also came under the observation of the nineteen-year-old traveller as is seen below:-

May 19th, Monday. As I write up my journal, there are a couple of ladies in the room, so I may as well jot down a few notes respecting the countrywomen in general. Between the ankles and chin, the Chilean women are said to be the best formed race of women in the world. The Chilenos are invariably short, but exceedingly well formed, and in walking are very erect, especially the lower class. They have very beautiful and long hair, and of which they are very fond, and when young wear it in two long braids divided at the back towards the centre. Their complexion is the red and white greatly improved by the good human smiles with which the face of one of my fair companions is at present glowing. They are possessed of an easy natural manner, and I fancy are generally devoid of affectation. They have an extremely disagreeable habit of spitting, which is most prevalent among the poorer order, and elderly ladies. They are exceedingly fond of smoking, although it is not so openly indulged in as formerly. They are very fond of music, and I believe, there are more pianofortes in Valparaiso than in any town in England with the same population, although nearly the whole of the pianofortes are imported from England, and after paying freight, and duty, cost a considerable sum. Some of the ladies play exceedingly well, and when requested to favour the company do so with a willingness which would startle young English ladies.

On May 30th Thomas booked a passage on the steamer *Bogota* bound for Caldera. Two days later Mr and Mrs Mouat and some friends accompanied him to the port and saw him sail at 1pm. The *Bogota* arrived at Caldera on June 3rd, where he transferred his baggage to the *Conrad*.

June 3rd, Tuesday. Had dinner on shore, wrote a letter home, then took it on board and bid my steamboat acquaintances goodbye, when on returning, it was quite dark, I made a spring for the *Conrad* and missed her, and down I went into the water some few feet. I rose and luckily caught hold of a piece of wood attached to the quay. I held on there and attempted to make myself heard, but without success for my throat was full of salt water. I then commenced splashing, and was eventually heard by a man on the pier, who cried out in Spanish saying there was a man in the water. They heard it on board of the ship, and passed me a rope, which I caught hold of and got on board. My hat had floated off, and was picked up some time after. My watch stopped at 5 minutes to 7. My pocket book spoiled. Cigar case, etc. However, if in my descent I had knocked my head against the quay, I might have become senseless and have drowned, for no one heard my fall; once in a lifetime is rather too often to have the above, but I have had them too often.

He was to spend ten days aboard this vessel, during which time he occupied himself with sailing in a small boat in the harbour, and going ashore and exploring the town. On June 13th he took a train to Copiapo.

June 13th, Friday. Rose early and cleaned firearms, etc.,

went to the Station and took ticket and seat for Copiapo. (N.B. Caldera to Copiapo 55 miles.) Found a Mr. Levert a passenger to whom I had been introduced, he is an American and I find a very agreeable companion. The railroad pays 15 per cent per annum. Arrived at Copiapo at half past 12. The carriages are very comfortable on this line, and you can pass from one to the other. Took my baggage to the Commercial Hotel, but did not like the place, so I moved to the French hotel, which I find tolerantly comfortable.

Young Ismay wanted to see over the many mines in the district especially the copper mines. On horseback he had a good look round the mines and countryside of Copiapo and then left in another steamer for Cobija, where he was to rejoin the *Chas. Jackson*. When he arrived at 2pm the ship was lying some way out and he was taken out to her in a whale-boat. On the following morning the *Chas. Jackson* set sail for Liverpool via Islay!

July 9th, Wednesday. We reached Islay about 9 o'clock and truly thankful we were.

July 12th, Saturday. Turned out about 7 a.m. not quite so early as I should wish. Busy getting the vessel ready for sea. At 10 a.m. went on shore to settle the Agent's account. When I returned on board the vessel was got under way, and we are homeward bound with two hands short, and the second officer ill. Unbounded hospitality. The evenings are passed in music and dancing; one finds nothing but gaiety, good breeding, and amiability, also elegance. They dress with taste especially taking much pains with their hair and feet, but they do not seem to be good housewives according to my English idea. One hears a great deal about the laxity among married women in Chile. The cause of this may be traced to the inattention of the women to their domestic duties, and partly to the loose morals of the men, and discontent at home. Another cause assuredly is the indifference to religion, which unhappily prevails throughout the whole of South America. If the higher classes were possessed of pleasing manner and exhibit a certain amount of intelligence, the lower classes are a complete contrast to them. If they can get a little dried meat, and some water melons they are satisfied, and are content to sleep beneath bare walls in rude huts.

July 14th, Monday. Got the carpenter to partition the long boat for the livestock, 12 sheep, 8 pigs, 4 ducks, 4 geese, one goat, and some 40 fowls.

July 15th, Tuesday. Slept comfortably, had a bath, fed the livestock, which I intend doing before I have my own breakfast so I am more likely not to forget them. The goat I find is getting considerably tamer. When first brought on board she ran about the deck so much that I was compelled to fasten her up.

July 16th, Wednesday. This evening, while reading in the cabin the steward brought a light, when he informed me that he was in possession of three more candles only. I thought it was very pleasant information to receive at sea, when we have the prospect of not looking on a tallow chandler's establishment for some three months or so. It is a gross piece of neglect. The steward should have informed the captain of the state of supplies before leaving Islay. He will in all probability get what he merits when the captain is informed of it. He informs me so that I may tell the captain and by so doing escape the first of the spirit of vexation.

July 17th, Thursday. It is very monotonous on board ship at times. I manufactured a sort of gangway for the fowls up to the place where they roost. After luncheon fell asleep with a book and did not wake until 5 p.m. - much to my annoyance for I am frequently instilling into the captain that he sleeps too much, and overmuch sleep is injurious to the system.

July 22nd, Tuesday. A strong squall struck the vessel and carried away the royal and split the top mast and lower studding sails. The wind being right aft, we were carrying studding sails on both sides. I expected some of the spars going but the sails went instead, and so much the better. About 1 a.m, I got up and dressed and went on deck for I was unable to coax sleep, although I tried to secure it on some new approved principles, which I had just read about. Went on deck and found the water making a clean breech over the vessel. I went below and turned in and was just on the point of going to sleep when I heard a smash in the after cabin. I got up to see what was wrong, found all lights out and the water was coming into the cabin, when a sea struck the vessel and sent me leeward and my foot struck on a piece of glass and nearly cut off my large toe on the right foot, when a light was procured I found the cabin floor almost covered with my blood. The captain put some dressings on to try to stop the bleeding, but it continued bleeding for a considerable time.

July 23rd, Wednesday. The captain dressed my foot by bathing it, they tell me if it had occurred in the tropics I should very probably have had lockjaw. I am unable to put my foot to the ground.

July 24th, Thursday. The vessel is making considerable quantities of water and they pump her out every two hours. It is rather dismal more especially when you are lame. I much prefer being on deck during a storm. The captain says he never recollects seeing such a sea running.

July 31st, Thursday. It is regular dismal weather this, and I shall not be sorry when we get round the Horn and into pleasant latitudes. It is just a year gone to-day on a Sunday morning at 8 o'clock when I had the extreme misfortune to lose my very dear twin sister, Charlotte, so little thought I that I should be here then, what changes ere another revolution around the sun.

August 1st, Friday. About 3 a.m, I heard a strange noise on the main deck, and got a light and found the goat in great pain, so I got some sacks and grass and laid her on top of it for I have for several days back been in expectation of her bringing forth a young one, and I already congratulated myself on milk to coffee. I turned in again at 4 a.m. leaving word on deck to attend to the goat. At 8 a.m, I turned out and asked whether there were one or two kids, when to my astonishment, I was told it had killed itself by eating too much bread, when cut open they found an immense quantity, and that it was not with kid, such is life, they are great swindlers in Islay. The carcass was thrown overboard.

August 7th, Thursday. This morning we have our old friend Cape Horn in sight, we have a heavy swell and head wind. The watch on deck are all on the poop for it was out of the question to remain on the main deck for the water was waist deep on the lee side. The seas were coming right over the poop. Occasionally shipped green seas all over us. At 4 a.m, I turned out and as I was going up the gangway I got regularly wet through, the vessel having shipped a sea. It was I found anything but pleasant just getting out of a warm bed, and getting wet through, and so to remain for hours, but everyone generally enjoys a laugh when another gets wet, and it is best for the sufferer to laugh too, besides it is only a wetting with salt brine.

August 8th, Friday. True life on the ocean wave sounds very pleasant when in the tropics but when the cold and sea come over to an excess, then life on the ocean wave is all very fine especially off Cape Horn with such a night as last (which is by far the wildest we have experienced since leaving England), it is another thing. At 3 p.m. the wind died away, and changed, when I thought she would have rolled her masts out for the sea was running heavily.

August 9th, Saturday. At 2 p.m, we had a good view of the Falkland Islands, and after dark we could distinctly see the light of Stanley Harbour.

August 11th, Monday. Early this morning the wind lulled until it became a dead calm. Owing to the thick fog we could not see 20 yards on any side. The vessel was rolling very heavily and it was impossible to sit or stand anywhere with the least comfort. These fogs rise the sea in this part of the world, quite as much as a heavy gale of wind.

August 12th, Tuesday. During the night the vessel prevented me and the rest on board from sleeping owing to the heavy and incessant rolling. I got the carpenter to put a plank alongside my berth to prevent my rolling out during the night, which I stand a good chance of doing, if we have any more nights like the last.

August 14th, Thursday. To-day we are going along at a good speed under reefed topsails. I with my usual luck got a good wetting. They tell me on board I get more than my share, but I don't feel any ill effects, so I don't care.

August 20th, Wednesday. This is our third calm day, I say confound the calm, this is the longest we have had since leaving England. I would rather be soaked through twenty times a day with a fair wind.

August 25th, Monday. Strong gale with a heavy head sea, and the ship labouring heavily. About 10 o'clock the fore topgallant mast carried away and the fore royal yard. If anyone had been aloft they would have had a good chance of getting severely lamed if not killed.

September 2nd, Tuesday. Last night I slept on the sofa, for it is much too hot in the berths. The steward and I had a rat hunt this evening, we caught six with our hands, and the remainder nine in the trap, some of them were of a large size.

September 6th, Saturday. While sleeping on the sofa a large rat walked over my face.

September 14th, Sunday. I went to have my usual bath, but as it was a deal calm, I thought I would have a swim overboard. I let my self down with a rope, and had requested one of the boys to give me another line to take hold of before I plunged in. They commenced shouting "Shark, Shark!" but I thought they wished to startle me, so I let myself further down into the water, and gave a look round to see all was clear for a dive, when I saw a shark not more than a couple of feet clear of my feet. I used a little expedition and got out of reach. I looked round and saw no less than three sharks playing about. They followed the vessel all day.

September 19th, Friday. Last night a rat kept running over where I was sleeping on the sofa. They have eaten through the deck into the cabin. Also into a large pumpkin into which they got by a hole, and which I have plugged up with two of them in it.

September 24th, Wednesday. Very busy painting ship. I was painting the boats and had a gangway erected to prevent my falling when down I went right amongst the paint and oil jars. Most fortunately I escaped without injury although it was a wonder, not a drop of paint lost.

September 25th, Thursday. Three vessels in sight. Two barques and one brig. Painting outside the ship. Narrowly escaped a good ducking for I was only supported, when over the side by one strand.

September 26th, Friday. Before sunrise sighted the barque *Godavery* from Caldera for Liverpool 62 days out. It was too warm to sleep last night. I had half a mind to take my bed into the main top and sleep there.

October 1st, Wednesday. Caught ten rats in the trap.

(THE DIARIES ARE UNCOMPLETED).

CHAPTER 3

Shipbroking partnership with Nelson, T H Ismay's marriage, the birth of Joseph Bruce Ismay, dissolving the partnership with Nelson

On arrival back in Liverpool on board the *Chas Jackson* in the autumn of 1856, Thomas set about putting his affairs in order. As he was only 13 when his father died, Joseph Sealby, his mother's brother, was made trustee for Joseph Ismay's estate.

Apparently Joseph Sealby had delegated some of his business to his son John, and one of the things he had taken over was the management of two of the ships part owned by Thomas Ismay; *Mary Ismay* and *Charles Brownell*. Thomas visited the latter in Liverpool; he was very shrewd even at nineteen-and-a-half years of age and he did not consider his cousin a suitable person to manage the ship, and said so in no uncertain terms (to the captain of the vessel). This brought an angry letter from John Sealby, which is reproduced here:-

> Saddle Hotel, Dale Street, Liverpool.
> October 30th, 1856
> To Thomas H. Ismay Esq.,
> Sir,
> On my arrival in Liverpool I find that you were aboard of the *Charles Brownell,* in the presence of Mr. Jackson and Captain Metcalf, a party in no way interested in the vessel.
> You put what I consider a very impertinent and improper question to Captain Bexfield, viz.:- Did he consider me a fit person to have the management of the vessel? Until I have your reply, I refrain from making any comments upon.
> Hoping to hear from you immediately, and an explanation of what you meant.
> Yours, etc.,
> John Sealby.

On getting no reply he sent off another letter, even more indignant.

Liverpool.
November 1st, 1856.
To Mr. Thomas H. Ismay.
Sir,
I wrote to you on Thursday last to which you have not replied, as a man of business leaving common courtesy aside I consider you ought to have answered it.

I now beg to inform you that unless I have what I consider a sufficient explanation I decline holding any further communication with you either personally or by letter, as the manner you have conducted yourself in ever since I have had anything to do with the *Charles Brownell* has been in plain terms sneaking and underhanded.

I did intend when I last had an interview with you in our office that on my return from Liverpool to have so arranged matters that we would in future have worked together in the matter of the *Charles Brownell,* but now I am sorry to say that from what has transpired I never can work with you as from what I have seen and heard my confidence in you is so shaken that I would never know how to believe you.

You may and most likely will consider the tenor of my letter too strong, but in my opinion I have not said one word too much, in fact, scarcely sufficient for the manner in which I have been treated. But allow me now to tell you so that it may cause any further annoyance on your part to cease, that so long as the vessel is in the position that she now is, that I cannot on any consideration (so long as I am so interested in her myself and on behalf of my father and Joseph) give her into your hands, as I know perfectly well that is what you are fighting for.

A copy of this letter I have sent to my father not wishing to keep anything I have said from him.
I remain,
Yours obediently,
John Sealby.

Thomas's reply was brief and to the point:-

Maryport.
November, 5th, 1856.
To John Sealby, Saddle Hotel, Dale Street, Liverpool.
Sir,
Your letter bearing the date 30th October was duly received by me. I put the question to Captain Bexfield as to whether he considered you fit to manage the vessel.

You ask an explanation of what I meant by what you consider a very impertinent and improper question. By a fit person I mean one, who if the Captain requests to have the vessel supplied with Sails, Ropes, etc., can judge they are actually wanted or not.

In my opinion you are not capable of judging. Your letter of November 1st came duly to hand with contents duly noted.

I remain,
Yours, etc.,
Thomas H. Ismay.

This was received and acknowledged by John Sealby as below: -

Liverpool.
November 7th, 1856.
To Mr. Thomas H. Ismay.
Sir,
I am in receipt of your letter of the 5th, and am obliged to you for your opinion, at the same time I will thank you if you have any charges to lay against me as to my unfitness to manage the vessels to favour me with them, so as I may lay them before the owners at the next meeting along with the letter I have just received, as I cannot succumb to your individual opinion.

The said charges I will therefore thank you to favour me with in writing against my return home.

I remain,
Yours, etc.,
John Sealby.

And followed up on November 25th by another letter from John Sealby, enclosing a copy of the letter his father had sent to the owners of the *Charles Brownell*:-

Maryport,
November 25th, 1856.
To Mr. Thomas H. Ismay, Messrs. Imrie, Tomlinson, Liverpool.
Sir,
Your letter of yesterday's is to hand enclosing Bond in favour of the Cumberland Union Banking Company for your attention I am much obliged.

The owners could not be liable solely for their own individual share, I certainly thought that you would have known that each and every owner is liable so long as he is worth anything whether he signs or not. By placing a mortgage upon the ship it would improve our position as our liability would be the same. With respect to an advance by the owners the means adopted was deemed the best.

The sum you offered is too little, therefore I cannot entertain it at that money, as soon as we have our account from Imrie, Tomlinson, a statement showing the position of the ships will be forwarded to each of the owners.

I beg to enclose you a copy of letter forwarded this day to each of the owners of the Barque *Charles Brownell*.

I am requested by my father to inform you, that it is his intention to sell the Brig *Mary Ismay* on her arrival in Liverpool, and from the tenor of the letter sent to the owners of the *Charles Brownell* you will see that his intention is the same in respect of her.

On accomplishing the sale of the two vessels to withdraw from the Trusteeship, it is needless to make any comment as to his reasons for so doing, as you well know the cause.

I remain,
Yours obediently,
John Sealby.

Maryport.
November 25th, 1856.
Dear Sir,
On the other side I hand you copy of letter received by my son from Mr. T. H. Ismay (one of the owners of the Barque *Charles Brownell).*

I must explain that although the management of the *Charles*

Brownell is still and all along has been in the hands of myself as Acting Trustee for the Estate of the late Mr. Ismay, for some time my son has taken an active part in looking after her, I finding myself unable to look after her as I like.

I think it quite unnecessary to offer any remarks upon the letter as it speaks for itself, but I have to inform you that on account of the annoyance I have had from Mr. Ismay for some time back, (he having tried all in his power to get the vessel into his own hands, which of course, I could not allow particularly taking into account the position the vessel is in), and as I find that there is going to be nothing but unpleasantness with him.

I have after mature deliberation decided with the sanction of the owners representing the majority of shares to sell on her arrival in Liverpool.

In conclusion I beg to state that I offered my shares to Mr. Ismay for the purpose of his buying me out, but his offer being inadequate, I have now determined upon adopting the beforementioned steps.

Injustice to myself I must state that at the time I offered him my share, it was with the distinct understanding that I had the sanction of all the owners before I could sell, as I deemed it wrong to sell out myself without the sanction of all concerned.

Hoping the steps decided upon may meet with your approval.
I remain,
Yours obediently,
Joseph Sealby.

As can be seen from these letters Thomas successfully rid himself of his trustees. While Thomas continued to work for Imrie, Tomlinson, he met a retired sea captain, Philip Nelson, whose home town was also Maryport and who had retired from the sea some years previously. He now 'dabbled' in anything to do with ships; he owned a vessel called the *Anne Nelson,* named after his wife, a model of which is preserved in the Liverpool Maritime Museum. He had already been a partner in a shipbroking business and was also a canvas merchant. His firm was known as Nelson & Company.

The friendship developed between young Ismay and Nelson with the result that in the latter part of 1857 the two decided to start a shipbroking business together. They took new offices in

Drury Buildings, 21 Water Street but, owing to the fact that Ismay was under 21, they had to wait till January of the following year before they could sign the articles of agreement; during this time Thomas was living in the village of Huyton, seven miles out from the city, and he usually rode in on horseback.

The partnership was not however to last very long; Nelson was extremely cautious in all he did, and Ismay was full of youthful enthusiasm for the very latest design in ships. Iron in shipbuilding was not yet very popular, but he was convinced that the day would come when practically all ships would be built of this material. Two years after the founding of the new company, they commissioned the well-known Scottish shipbuilder, Alexander Stephen, to build them their first ship, the *Angelita*, a brigantine of 129 tons, and Thomas had his way in that it was built of iron.

After another two years they found they really could not work together and agreed to part company early the following year, 1862. In the meantime in the November of 1861 the *Angelita*, under command of Captain Peter Gardiner Dow, was loading a cargo of mahogany at Honduras with which she was to sail direct to Liverpool. On November 26th she left Honduras for her home port and had a fair passage until she reached the Southern Irish coast. On January 22nd the weather became very thick and a tremendous storm arose, forcing her into Dunmanus Bay. One of the crew was very ill and Captain Dow wanted to get him ashore for medical treatment but he died some hours before this could be effected.

On entering Dunmanus Bay at about 2am on January 24th the captain anchored off Furze Island with the object of riding out the storm; about 4am the cable parted and the vessel drifted straight on to the rocks off Horse Island. All the crew could do was to abandon the ship to her fate and take to the long boat; they were all saved, but the *Angelita* herself slipped off the rocks into six fathoms of water, where she began to break up and a good deal of her cargo was washed ashore. So after three years, Thomas Ismay lost the first ship he had been responsible for building, but the loss was not as severe as those which were to come when T H Ismay's business became known the world over as the White Star Line.

A few months after the loss of the *Angelita* the partnership with Nelson was dissolved. Thomas moved his office to 10, Water Street, and his firm became known as T H Ismay & Company; this was to be the head office of his firm until 1898 when the new 30 James Street offices, built to the design of Norman Shaw, were completed. This fine new office block was really the first modern block of offices to be built in Liverpool and created a sensation when they were opened as the headquarters of the White Star Line.

Mrs T H Ismay around 1895

At the same time as the *Angelita* was first commissioned by Nelson, Ismay & Company, a great change had come about in T H Ismay's personal life. He had met Miss Margaret Bruce, the elder daughter of Luke Bruce of 36 Dexter Street, Liverpool, and on April 7th, 1859 the wedding anniversary of Thomas's father and mother, he married her at St Bride's Church, Percy Street.

Unfortunately in compiling this history it has been quite impossible to ascertain all the facts connected with the early life of T H Ismay and the circumstances in which he met his wife will probably have to remain unknown for ever.

In the Liverpool street directories of the time Luke Bruce is given as a master mariner, ships' surveyor and shipowner; there is no doubt that in some such capacity Thomas Ismay was introduced to him. Another point which may throw some light on T H Ismay's life at the time is that in 1861 the vessel named *Ismay* was captained by a man named Thomas Leslie. Capt Leslie married Mary Bruce, Mrs. Margaret Ismay's only sister, so it may have been through Capt Leslie that Thomas first met Margaret.

To say that the marriage was a happy one would be an understatement. In Margaret, or 'Maggie,' as he called her, he had found a wonderful partner, who always took a great interest in all he did, and encouraged and supported him all his life. They were utterly devoted and each lived for the other. In all, they were to have nine children, including two pairs of twins, of whom two died in childhood.

Thomas had moved to Enfield House, Great Crosby, some months previously; this was a medium-sized Regency style house standing in its own grounds just off the main road (pulled down in 1928 to make way for shops). It was there that he took his bride to live and there the following year their first child was born, a daughter, whom they christened Mary, always known as 'Polly'. She was followed on December 12th 1862 by their eldest son, Joseph Bruce, who like his father was destined to have a brilliant career in shipping, although tragically marred to some extent by the *Titanic* disaster in 1912. Although his character was to be quite different from his father's, he inherited his high qualities of integrity.

T H Ismay was now in business on his own and was proving most successful. His ships were chiefly employed in general cargo trading to South America.

In 1864 he became a director of the successful National Line of steamships which had been founded by a group of Liverpool business men the previous year. The original idea was to run steamers carrying cargo and steerage passengers to the Southern States of America, and all the ships were given Southern names. At the end of the Civil War they were transferred to the New York route instead, and their names were tactfully changed.

In this year, too, some prominent Liverpool businessmen decided to found a training ship for the sons of seamen and other boys of good character, to fit them for a career at sea. This was called the *Indefatigable,* and was stationed in the Mersey. Most of the boys who trained in her joined the Merchant Navy. The fees were £30 a year, or whatever the parents could afford; T H Ismay was a founder member of this organisation and always took a great interest in the boys' welfare. He was later treasurer and became chairman of the board of directors in 1878, remaining so until he died in 1899.

Although as can be seen T H Ismay was already successful and had laid the foundation stones of his remarkable career, he never forgot Maryport, the town of his birth. If he could ever help a Maryport man he did. A sailor from there could always find a berth in one of the Ismay ships. Nor did he forget his childhood friend, John Cockton, from whom all medical supplies for the ships were obtained; if any parts or interior fittings were needed, they too came from Maryport.

In 1865 the Ismays moved to Beech Lawn House, Waterloo, (now known as Winchester House, 13 Beech Lawn, and converted into flats). This was a large, three-storeyed Georgian house, with a lovely view overlooking the Mersey to the Wirral, with the Welsh hills beyond. There was a large garden behind and beyond that ran a lane, with stabling and coach houses. Thomas Ismay's opinions were very decided on all things, and his ideas on gardens were unorthodox. He never cared for conventional flowerbeds, but as he was fond of peaches and grapes and other exotic fruit, he grew these under glass.

It was here also that he built his 'Grotto'; the remains of this curious garden are still to be seen today. At the bottom of the lawn, near the carriage houses, he had the ground excavated, and the soil was replaced by large boulders of red rock, which were faced with mirrors, over which miniature waterfalls ran. There were rare plants growing between these rocks, and the whole had the effect of a sunken garden, with walks of iron spiral staircases to the top and down again to a paved well in the centre, where there were seats. The Grotto was covered by a glass roof, which was swept away in the blitz on Liverpool during the Second World War.

Once the White Star Line was established, whenever one of their steamers passed the house, she would sound her siren in salute.

CHAPTER 4

Buying of the White Star Line, its early history, founding of the Oceanic Steam Navigation Company

There was at this time trading between Liverpool and Australia a fleet of sailing vessels which had been founded in the early 1850s by two partners, Pilkington and Wilson. Their ships had been built of wood, mostly in America. They had done a tremendous business during the gold rush to Australia, and had acquired a first-class reputation as carriers of emigrants and cargo to the Antipodes.

The names of some of these ships, such as *Red Jacket, Shalimar,* etc, are now legendary amongst the clippers of the last century. *Red Jacket* carried as a figurehead an Indian chieftain, with a five-pointed white star on his chest. From this Pilkington & Wilson adopted their house flag, mounting the white star on a red burgee and the line popularly became known as the White Star Line. When Pilkington retired, Wilson was joined by James Chambers and the firm was known as Wilson and Chambers.

The main object of all the shipping lines carrying gold prospectors to Australia was speed, to get them there in the shortest possible time, before the gold fields were worked out. Wilson was determined to beat all his rivals, and he built larger and finer ships, borrowing on mortgages from the Royal Bank of Liverpool. He always advertised a ship as being under penalty to make the passage in 68 days. His partner James Chambers, was so alarmed at this that he retired from the firm in December 1865. In the following year Wilson was joined in partnership by Mr. John Cunningham; two years later Wilson & Cunningham owed the bank £527,000, when the bank failed. Consequently Wilson and Cunningham dissolved their partnership and the firm went into liquidation.

So in 1867 T H Ismay bought the White Star flag and the goodwill for £1,000 from Wilson, and he then introduced his own iron ships into the Australian and New Zealand trade.

After two years' trading under these conditions, he was invited one night to dine with Gustavus C Schwabe, a prominent Liverpool merchant, who lived at Broughton Hall, West Derby. (The house still stands as a convent). After dinner, over a game of billiards, Schwabe put a proposition to Ismay. He explained that his nephew Wolff had recently entered into partnership with Mr Edward Harland, in a shipbuilding enterprise at Belfast. Their firm had already built some iron ships of revolutionary design for Bibby's Mediterranean trade. Schwabe was a fairly large shareholder in this company, but had been told there were no more shares available. He was anxious to invest more capital in shipping, so he now suggested to Ismay that he was the man to start a new company of steam powered vessels for the North Atlantic. Schwabe said that if Ismay would agree to have the steamers built by Harland & Wolff he would back the scheme to the limit, and get other Liverpool businessmen he knew to do likewise.

On September 6th 1869, the Oceanic Steam Navigation Company was formed, with a capital of £400,000 in £1,000 shares. It is significant to note that of this amount Thomas Ismay subscribed a very large sum; he was only 32 years old and 12 years before had started business with £2,000 capital. The first list of shareholders included the names of Edward James Harland, engineer and iron shipbuilder, and Gustav William Wolff, iron shipbuilder.

Immediately on the founding of the company Harland & Wolff were commissioned to build four ships to Mr. Harland's design; the first one being the pioneer *Oceanic,* to be followed by the *Atlantic.* The original steamers were all of similar design, with such improvements in each case as were found necessary through the experience gained by their use in service. The original order was increased to six ships, the additional two being the *Adriatic* and the *Celtic,* which were 17ft longer. The old letter book of the firm still exists and one of the earliest letters reads as follows:-

 4th October, 1869.
 To Messrs. Harland & Wolff, Belfast.
 Sirs,

We think it would be well for your Mr. Harland when he comes over with model specification and drawings, to come prepared to have an interview with the Surveyor to the Board of Trade, and with this object in view would suggest he brings over copy of correspondence he had regarding the application to pass Messrs. Bibby's boat for the carrying of emigrants, also copy of the recent correspondence he had with the Board of Trade; for we think it may possibly be more politic and courteous to consult them before finally deciding as they would perhaps the more readily give their approval. We are quite anxious to have the models, etc. fixed upon and may mention that the spa deck vessel *Prussian* is now here.

We are, dear Sirs,
Yours Truly,
T. H. ISMAY & CO.

In 1870 William Imrie, of Imrie, Tomlinson, died and his son William, T H Ismay's friend and erstwhile fellow apprentice, then transferred the whole of his business to T H Ismay & Company, and the firm became Ismay, Imrie & Company. The two friends were working together again, in a business they both thoroughly understood. Together they built up one of the finest shipping companies the world has ever seen. Ismay took charge of the steam vessels and Imrie those under sail, the sailing vessels being operated under the name of North Western Shipping Company.

William Imrie, born at Bootie in the same year as Thomas Ismay, was quite a different personality. He was just as capable as his partner, but he was extremely shy and retiring, while Thomas had tremendous drive and energy and was equally at home with persons from all walks of life. He had the knack of choosing people to work for him who were particularly well suited to their positions. He used to say "Never do a job yourself,

if you can get someone to do it for you as well as you can, it leaves you free to get on with more important things". Another of his sayings was "Never let a weak man in the trade in which you are engaged go under, it will make room for a stronger man to replace him and the newcomer might be able to do you down too". He always took misfortune as a challenge to be overcome, and never appeared discouraged. At this time there were six persons employed in the offices in 10 Water Street, Liverpool.

The Oceanic Steam Navigation Company never held a launching ceremony; the vessels were simply put into the water, having been named long before they left their slips. Some of the principals of Ismay, Imrie & Company would journey over to Belfast to see the new ships safely launched.

Another curious fact was that all steam-powered vessels had a gold band on the hull, but those under sail had not. There was no recognised position for this band until 1915, when it was put quarter-way down the black hull below the name, on all ships of the line. Another unusual feature of the White Star Line was that, unlike most other ships which usually flew the ensign from the gaff while at sea, their steamers always flew it from the stern to avoid it becoming soiled by the smoke.

While Edward Harland was drawing the plans of the first vessel to be built for this new steamship company, Thomas Ismay and his partners were drawing up the rules and regulations for their vessels. The original rules and regulations are given in Appendix A.

In February 1871 *Oceanic* (I), the first of the four original sister-ships appeared in the Mersey for her maiden voyage on March 2nd. As the ships of the White Star Line had always sailed to Australia under the former management, the public was quite convinced that the new ship was going to do the same, but this idea was dispelled when the following advertisement appeared in the *Liverpool Daily Post*, March 1st 1871:-

WHITE STAR LINE, OCEANIC STEAM NAVIGATION CO. LTD.

The new first class, full powered screw steamships *Oceanic, Baltic, Atlantic, Pacific, Arctic, Adriatic.* Sailing on Thursdays from Liverpool, and calling at Queenstown on Fridays to embark passengers. Will sail as under for New York, via Queenstown. *Oceanic,* 4,500 tons, 3,000 H.P., Capt. Digby Murray, to sail tomorrow, Thursday, March 2nd, 1871. These steamships have been designed to afford the very best accommodation to all classes of passengers, and are expected to accomplish quick and regular passages between this country and America. The State Rooms, with Saloon and Smoking Rooms, are placed amidships, and the passengers are thus removed from the noise and motion experienced at the after part of the vessel. Passengers are booked to all parts of the States, Canada, and Newfoundland, Nova Scotia, India, etc. at moderate through rates. A Surgeon and a Stewardess carried on each ship. Drafts issued at New York for sums not exceeding £10 free. Parcels will be received at the Company's Offices until 6 p.m. of the day before sailing. Bills of Lading to be had from Messrs. Benson & Home, and Mawdsley & Son. Shipping notes at the Company's Office. Loading berth, South West corner Bramley Moore Dock. Saloon passage £18 18s. 0d. and £16 16s. 0d. Return Ticket 27 guineas. Steerage as low as by any other first-class Line.

Rates of Freight, etc., may be obtained by applying to J. K. Sparks at the Company's Offices, 19, Broadway, New York; in Belfast to Samuel Gowan & Co., 4, Corporation Street; or to 7, East India Avenue, London, E.C. or ISMAY, IMRIE & CO., 10, Water Street, Liverpool.

The names *Republic* and *Celtic* were substituted for those of *Pacific* and *Arctic* owing to the disasters to the two steamers of the Collins Line which were so named. With the appearance of the first *Oceanic* in the Mersey the old shell-backs were incredulous, as the ship was long and narrow more like a yacht than an Atlantic liner. The design was completely revolutionary; the old high bulwarks had disappeared and iron railings were substituted, so that the sea could flow freely from the deck. The deckhouses had gone and the decks were built out to the full width of the ship for the first time.

The designs were Edward Harland's, but on seeing them for the first time Thomas Ismay suggested various alterations which Harland & Wolff incorporated. These were really the success of the enterprise. He moved the main saloon and all first class accommodation amidships where the vibration from the engines was least felt. The cabins had a larger porthole than before and in consequence were bright and airy. The *Oceanic* and her sister ships rendered all other Atlantic steamships obsolete overnight and the other companies had to take counter measures.

This was the start of the wonderful relationship which existed between the White Star Line and Harland & Wolff. The heads of each of the firms became personal friends and with the exception of *Laurentic* (II), the ships were all built on a 'cost plus' basis. Harland & Wolff were given absolute *carte blanche* to produce the finest possible ships, which they did. To the total sum spent was added a percentage, which was their profit. No other builder ever received a White Star contract, as the managers undertook not to employ any other firm to build ships for them, while Harland & Wolff agreed not to build ships for any firm in direct competition with the White Star Line.

On taking a vessel over White Star commanders received the following letter from Ismay, Imrie & Co:-

February 1871
To Captain Digby Murray
Dear Sir,

When placing the Steamer *Oceanic* under your charge, we endeavoured to impress upon you verbally, and in the most forcible manner we were capable of, the paramount and vital importance above all other things of caution in the navigation of your vessel, and we now confirm this in writing, begging you to remember that the safety of your passengers and crew weigh with us above and before all other considerations. We invite you also to bear in mind that while using due diligence in making a favourable passage to dismiss from your mind all idea of competitive passages with other vessels, concentrating your whole attention upon a *cautious, prudent,* and ever watchful system of navigation, which shall lose time, or suffer any other temporary inconvenience, rather than run the slightest risk which can be avoided. We are aware that, in the American Trade where quick passages are so much spoken of you will naturally feel a desire that your ship shall compare favourably with others in this respect, and this being so we deem it our duty to say to you most emphatically that, under no circumstances, can we sanction any system of navigation which involves the least risk or danger.

We request you to make an unvariable practice of being *yourself on deck* when the weather is thick or obscure, in all narrow waters, and whenever the ship is *within* 60 *miles of land;* also to keep the lead going in either of the last mentioned cases, this being, in our opinion, a measure of the greatest importance, and of undoubted utility.

We attach much importance also to giving a wide berth to all headlands, shallow waters, and other positions involving possible peril, and we recommend you to take cross bearings where practicable when approaching the land, and where this is not feasible you will then do well to take casts of the deep sea lead, which will assist in determining your locality.

The most rigid discipline on the part of your officers, should be observed, whom you will exhort to avoid at all times convivial intercourse with passengers, or with each other, and only such an amount of communication with the former as is demanded by a necessary and businesslike courtesy. We must also remind you that it is essential to successful navigation that the crew be kept under judicious control; that the look out be zealously watched, and required to report themselves in a loud and unmistakable voice after each bell sounds, as in this way you have a check upon their watchfulness.

We have full confidence in your sobriety of habit, but we may nevertheless exhort you to abstain from stimulants altogether, whilst on board ship (except in so far as the requirements of health may demand) endeavouring at the same time to imbue your officers, and all those about you, with a due sense of the advantage which will accrue not only to the Company, but to themselves, by being strictly temperate, as this quality will weigh with us in an special manner when giving promotion.

The consumption of *coals, stores* and *provisions* and indeed all articles constituting the equipment for the voyage should engage your daily attention, and so far as possible at a *regular fixed hour,* in order that you may be forewarned of any deficiency which may be impending, and that waste may be avoided, and a limitation in quantity determined on while it is yet time to avail of this expedient. The vessels of the Company have always been hitherto, and will be so long as the direction is in our hands provided with a full and complete outfit under these various heads, but where waste and thoughtless extravagance occur on the part of those in charge of any of the departments, it will be your duty to check such reckless and dangerous proceedings, and take measures to bring about an immediate change. We count upon your reporting to us without fear or favour all instances of incapacity or irregularity on the part of your officers or others under your control, as in this way only can we determine upon their respective merits, and hope to surround you with an efficient and reliable staff.

After having thus dwelt somewhat minutely upon matters of

detail connected with your command, it may not be unprofitable to impress you with a deep sense of the injury which the interest of this Company would sustain in the event of any misfortune attending the navigation of your vessel:-

First. From the blow which such would give to the reputation of the line.

Second. From the pecuniary loss which would accrue the Company being their own insurers to a very large extent: and

Third. To the interruption of a regular service upon which much of the success of the present organisation must depend.

We may also state that, if at any time you have any suggestions to make, bearing upon the steamers; their outfit; or any matter connected with them and the trade, we shall at all times be glad to receive, and consider such.

We have alluded to such points as have occurred to us regarding this subject of safe and watchful navigation, and we need scarcely say to you, in conclusion, how deeply the question affects not only the well being, but the very existence of the Company, and how earnestly we ask for your co-operation in achieving that success which can only be obtained by prudence and watchfulness at all times, whether in the presence of danger, or when by its absence you may be lured into a false sense of security.

It is the opinion of many that, where there is apparently least peril, there is most danger, and we incline to think that this remark is nearer the truth than is often thought to be the case.

Wishing you every success in your new command, we are,
Yours faithfully,
Ismay, Imrie & Company.

Liverpool had always been a busy seaport and there had been difficulty in docking all vessels. The Oceanic Steam Navigation Company, a new company, had great difficulty in securing suitable facilities for the uploading and unloading of their vessels, as can be seen by the letter below. (Many of the letters written in the company's old letter book are in T H Ismay's own handwriting.)

March 9th 1871
To Thomas Dyson Hornby, Esq.,

Chairman of the Docks and Quays Committee,
Mersey Docks and Harbour Board.
Sir,

We are in due receipt of your Committee's communication of the 2nd instant, relative to our request for the appropriation of a berth in the North Docks for the steamers of the Oceanic Steam Navigation Company, which will, we expect, in the course of a short time sail weekly between this port and New York; we extremely regret to learn that you are unable, so far, to arrange for their use a suitable berth. We are aware that the space at the North end is already well occupied, but think, nevertheless, that some arrangement could be made, without detriment to other Companies as to admit of our steamers loading and discharging on this side.

With respect to your suggestion as to a berth being set apart for us, on the South side of the Morpeth Dock, at Birkenhead, we can only say that such would neither be convenient nor suitable for the steamers, although at the same time, we are fully alive to the advantages, both pecuniary and natural, with which such a step should be followed. We may further observe that the Company alluded to, has no opposition to contend with hence their loading in the Birkenhead Docks.

In conclusion, we must again urge upon the Committee the necessity of the Company's steamers loading and discharging in the Liverpool Docks, and we, therefore, trust that such arrangements may be come to, as will admit of our application meeting with success in obtaining the accommodation sought for.

We are, Sir,
Your most obedient servants,
Ismay, Imrie & Co.

It was not until September of the following year that the dock question was finally settled, the Harbour Board granting the West Waterloo Dock with an area of 2,772 square yards as a permanent berth for White Star steamers.

Ever since Ismay, Imrie & Company had originally been formed as Nelson, Ismay & Company they had run sailing ships to South America. On October 12th 1871, they despatched Mr Henry Griffin as an agent to South America to ascertain whether the sailing vessels needed supplementing with steam ships. Nearly

12 months later he was back in Liverpool to report his findings, and he was quite certain that there was an opening for steam vessels in this service.

On November 30th 1871, the *Atlantic* left Liverpool half an hour ahead of the Inman Liner, *City of Paris,* which overhauled her; the letter below explains what happened then:-

December 8th, 1871
To William Inman Esq.,
Tower Buildings.
Dear Sir,

We deem it only right, and for our mutual interests, to bring under your notice the following facts in connection with your s.s, *City of Paris* in order that you may take such steps as you think advisable to prevent the recurrence of an act, which we conceive to have been fraught with considerable danger.

The s.s. *Atlantic* left Liverpool on the 30th ult, passing the Bell buoy at about 2.10 p.m., her Commander having instructions to proceed as far as Queenstown at a reduced speed, and to carry no sail. The *City of Paris* left Liverpool about half an hour after the *Atlantic,* and when outside the Bar, was observed to make sail, and, as might have been expected, she gradually overhauled the *Atlantic,* and at about 5 o'clock was on her quarter; your boat then made more sail, setting her top-gallant and main trysails, and when abeam was very close to our ship, the Skerries also being abeam, and unpleasantly close to her port side.

Whilst in this position, the helm of the *City of Paris,* which had forged ahead on the *Atlantic* starboard bow, was put astarboard, thus, deviating from her own straight course, and deliberately steered *across the bows* of the *Atlantic,* at a distance of about 50-60 yards. The speed at which the two vessels were going must have been from 10-12 knots, and had anything, unfortunately, gone wrong on board your vessel at that moment, she would, in all probability, have been run down; a calamity, we may observe, the consequences of which, would have been truly deplorable.

We feel convinced that you cannot be aware of this very unwise and hazardous course on the part of the officer in charge of your boat; and we are likewise sure that you will take prompt

and decisive measures to prevent the recurrence of such a proceeding
on a future occasion; at the same time, we consider it but just to ourselves to state that, we have enjoined the Masters and Officers under our charge, to act on all occasions even in excess of mere prudence to avoid the possibility of danger, regardless of any loss of time thereby involved, which, in comparison with the safety of life and property, we deem to be wholly unimportant. Awaiting your esteemed communication, we remain, dear Sir,
Yours truly,
Ismay, Imrie & Co.

Unfortunately the outcome of this dispute is not known, but Ismay, Imrie had clearly stated their case.

The following year the third of the original quartet, the *Republic,* appeared in the Mersey. Captain Digby Murray, who had been in command of the *Oceanic* and the *Atlantic* was transferred to her. She sailed in extremely bad weather from Liverpool to New York; below is his report to the company of the maiden voyage and a copy of the engineer's log.

REPORT OF CAPTAIN OF STEAMSHIP 'REPUBLIC'
Steamship *Republic* at sea, February 3rd, 1872.
Gentlemen,
Since leaving Liverpool we have had nothing but bad weather.

In my letter to you from Queenstown, I told you of the detention from leakage in upper between-decks, forward of saloon; I am sorry to say it still continues, and we have many other difficulties to contend with; the saloon and state-rooms have been flooded through the new ventilation; the windows of wheel-house have been dashed in by a sea, and compass unshipped and broken, thermometers broken, etc.; the stanchions of the bridge and bridge compass carried away, gangway abreast of saloon unshipped and carried aft, chocks of two boats washed away, and keel of No. 4 boat started; wooden cover of forward ventilator washed overboard, a great deal of water washing down companion-way into women's quarters aft; said hatch companion is a nuisance, and if the ship is to continue to use it a proper cover should be furnished, though that will never make it tight. Work has so multiplied on our hands since leaving, that we have not been able to do all that is even absolutely necessary. We had great difficulty in getting our yards down, lift blocks being too small in the mortice; we had to give up the attempt the first night. Main-hatch tarpaulins are too small; and I think the officers had better join the next ship a little sooner, so as to attend to their own details of work; the officers and men are getting worn out; Mr. Steele and the boatswain are both laid up. I think the ship is too deep for the time of year. I should much like to see a fixed rule as to the loading draught of the ships from either November or December to April, and from that month for the rest of the year; loading, also, to the last minute in the river, and then survey, stops the officers and crew from getting the ship into proper sea-going order. I have not been able to swing my quarter-boats in yet, and we have had all hands on deck the best portion of the time since we left. Mr. Williams hardly leaves the deck, and I was compelled to order him below this morning, fearing I should have him knocked up. Mr. Whittle had a very narrow escape this morning while securing the forward ventilator; I thought at one time he was gone. The ship dips her stern in pretty frequently and very heavily; at the same time has so much weight in her fore end that it gives her no chance to rise, and, though I have the will, I am quite unable to drive her. Boats chocks had better be a hollow iron frame, so as to show but little resistance to sea. Seamen's forecastle should be thoroughly cemented off from cargo, as it is simply impossible to keep scuppers in water-ways from choking. I have represented this every voyage.

The iron bulkhead forward of saloon has been cut right through to the deck, and then a piece of angle iron bolted to the deck for a door-sill, instead of leaving part of bulkhead to form it; and water consequently runs under it into saloon.

Passengers complain of difficulty of seating themselves at table; settee should have an extension stool, and be the width of the stool apart.

The turtle back has completely caved in; the beams from the hatch forward all gone, most of them, in two or three places; the riveting has gone more or less. To give the present turtle backs sufficient strength, I think a pitch pine stringer, about 3 feet wide, should be introduced on each side, fitted to admit the beams and lie close to the deck, and then thoroughly stanchioned, as also a good iron thwart-ship stringer on the plate forward from anchor to anchor. We have cut up all boats and awning spars, and have a complete forest of shores under it. The new ventilators, as before mentioned, are a perfect failure, drowning the passengers out, nor can we make them tight.

February 7th - It is still blowing a heavy gale; but, the ship having lightened, there is no longer any difficulty in driving her. Mr. Fair and I have carefully gone over the bunker plates together, and we can come to no other conclusion than that 900 tons was the extreme quantity of coal we had, leaving 885 tons, calculating 45 cubic feet to the ton. Mr. Fair seems to be a very first-class man. Everything is very satisfactory in the engine room.

Ventilator covers forward want altering; there should either be a top to screw on or a deep tight fitting plug to drive in. I fear a great deal of water has gone down them. We have had several times to ease to dead slow, and even then men have worked at them at the risk of their lives. I have been fearful of the effect on the bleaching powder, as much water has undoubtedly gone down.

February 8th - We encountered a terrific gale in about lat. 47° and long. 42° W., our decks were swept, all boats but two entirely destroyed, one of the two left open right out, the engine-room skylight smashed and driven down on top of the cylinders; this skylight had never been properly bolted or secured. Mr. Williams the second officer, whose pluck and endurance has been beyond all praise, was securing a sail over fidley (great quantities of water having gone down and put out the lee fires), was caught by No.4 boat as it was dashed a perfect wreck inboard, one of the davits unshipping and coming with it, and crushed against the railing round the funnel; his left thigh broke a little above the knee; his left ankle was dislocated; we fear some of the ribs broke. We trust the accident may not prove fatal, but time only will tell us; he shows amazing pluck, and is at present doing well; if he does not recover, he will be a very great loss to the company, for men like him are very few and far between. No canvas was set during the gale; it was ordered at one time but the utter worthlessness of the crew, skulking and stowing away, crying like children, made it difficult to do anything; it was as well it was not set, as it would only have blown away. A sea struck the mizzen boom, and broke it clean in two; imagine where a sail would have been! We steamed against the gale about twenty revolutions, making from one-and-a-half to two knots. I tried her slower, but could not keep her up to the sea; having previously burnt 400 tons of coal; the ship herself behaved well, shipped no heavy water forward, and consequently did not increase damage to turtle back; the rails on promenade deck have been mostly swept away, telegraphs broken and thrown down, top of standard binnacle washed overboard, forward gangway ditto, large ventilator, three davits, ditto, doors and windows, shutters and all, smashed in bodily.

The ships, with their present doors, are not seaworthy, and if they are not altered we shall yet lose a ship by them; had we been running instead of hove to, I doubt if we could have prevented the fires from being put out. Our carpenters are precious little account in bad weather, and a very slow lot at any time; our crew often a lot of curs; to have got a sail up, or cut away for use, I should have had to ask assistance from the passengers; to have got one from below, would have been impossible. I feel rather discouraged in again applying for stronger doors; and if I have expressed myself strongly, I feel very strongly on the subject; there ought also to be proper protection to fidley, gratings, iron shutters, and I think also a proper cover to engine-room skylight, with three ring-bolts on each side of deck to pass overhaul lashings to. I fear Mr. Harland will say this is an exceptional gale; these ships, during their career, will run long enough, I hope, to encounter many exceptional gales.

I am not satisfied with the manner in which boats are secured, but will go into it with Captain Spear and yourselves on my return; they are now over-secured; a sea strikes them, and they are torn asunder; the only boat we have saved was insecurely lashed, and that, strange to say, proved her salvation; there was something to give. I shall enclose a catalogue of damage on arrival, so will not say any more about it at present. We were unable to cook for two days, indeed not properly for two-and-a-half. No communication with the icehouse, and for a considerable time with the storeroom; the after door being broken in, water came down the hatches in large quantities, and we could not get to them; the quadrant was half the time entirely under water, the ship dipping occasionally to the wheel-house. It is useless my saying more till my return. I should like, however, to see all windows built up; charts, books, and clothes are wet all the time; windows are not fit for the trade. Pray condemn bad weather ventilators;

passengers will stand a little closeness, but not wet; and it has fairly ruined carpets, paint, cushions, etc., etc. Smoking room ventilators are worse still. The crew (excepting only the seamen), officers, engineers, and stewards, firemen and coal trimmers, have behaved splendidly. When the lee fires were put out, the watch below turned out without being ordered, kept below, and worked like men. We have much to be thankful for in the performance of both the engines and the men.

I had one seaman (so-called) rope's-ended for stowing away in the coal bunkers for the fourth time; it had become really a serious question; we could only get four men of the starboard watch the other night; I therefore consulted with the officers and chief engineer, and we have decided that the safety of the ship requires decisive measures, and that after this we will strip and flog every man stowing away while on watch; the crew were mustered and notified, and an entry made to that effect in the official log. We are making some water in No. 5 hold; I do not think it can be serious, but I shall carefully watch it. I think it would be a great advantage if three-cornered, i.e. jib-headed trysails, of storm canvas, were fitted to the mizzen and jigger-masts of these ships during the winter; there would then be but little difficulty in getting after canvas on the ship, which enable engines to be slowed more than on this occasion. I have found practicable the cut-away forefoot, allowing the bow to be easily knocked to the leeward by a sea.

The *Atlantic* is so soon after us, that I question if it would not be better for this ship to return without passengers; but I shall consult Mr. Sparks, and the result you will hear by him long before you receive this.

Anchored off the bar at 3 p.m. this day, Wednesday 14th.

Some of the coal on board, Mr. Fair complains bitterly of; full of sand and dirt; the passengers appear to be satisfied with the voyage; and though I do not generally lay much stress on their letters, owing to the very exceptional weather, I have requested the Purser to forward a copy to the office.

I know of nothing further to add at present; we shall not arrive at quarantine till midnight, and cannot dock till 1 p.m. on Thursday.

I remain, etc.
(Signed) Digby Murray.

Messrs. Ismay, Imrie & Co.
New York,
Wednesday, February 14, 1872.

I have omitted, I see, urging the necessity of a communication with engine-room; perfectly independent of telegraph, there should be bells or gongs from forward wheelhouse; during a great portion of the gale, we had no communication with the engine-room, and when, though the wind moderating more rapidly than the sea, it became necessary to still further moderate the speed of the engines, the only way we could communicate was by shouting down the fidley to the firemen. It made Mr. Fair, too, very uneasy, as he could not tell what was happening on deck, or at what speed he was required to drive; indeed he expressed an unhappy uncertainty as to whether we might not all have been overboard.

I regret to have to add, that while docking the *Republic,* although nearly half-an-hour after high water, the ship's bow, when close to the pier, was caught by a strong eddy from the south, i.e. flood; she was instantly reversed full speed, but struck the wooden piles at the end of the pier; the ship had very little way on at the time, and the pier suffered hardly any damage, but owing to the severity of the frost the iron had become so brittle that two bow plates have gone in the wake of the rivets. I cannot blame myself, as I do not think the accident was attributable to any lack of judgment on my own part; but as Mr. Sparks was fortunately on board at the time I trust he will frankly give you his impression as to the accident.

The New York agent had written to the head office on several occasions regarding complaints he had received from steerage passengers. So Thomas Ismay conceived the idea of sending someone out, travelling steerage, with whom the officers and crew of the ship were totally unacquainted. This was in order to satisfy himself exactly what conditions in the steerage were like. So in September, the following letter was despatched to the New York agent:

Per *Oceanic,* s.s. Liverpool.
September 25th, 1872.
To J. Hyde Spark, Esq., New York.

Dear Sir,

Referring to your remarks regarding the complaint from Steerage Passengers, we are of the opinion that much as we have already done for their comfort, there is still room for further improvement without incurring additional expense, and being anxious to have some report upon which we can depend and act, we have decided to send Captain Hinds out in the present steamer as a Steerage Passenger, so that on his return he may be able to report to us from actual experience, and from his report we may be able to judge what are the best means to adopt in the future.

His trip is unknown to anyone in the office here, you will, therefore, please keep the knowledge of his visit from any of your staff. Captain Hinds is a stranger in New York. You will therefore please advise him as to where he should stay, and advance him what money he may require up to £20, debiting the same to us.

As to his return, we leave it with you to send him back either by one of our own boats, or in such manner as you think best.

We are, dear Sir,
Yours truly,
Ismay, Imrie & Co.

It was as a result of this experiment that Ismay, Imrie decided on drastic steps, and conditions in the steerage were greatly altered.

Mr George Prince commented on this when he retired from the position of Southampton manager of second and third class passenger departments. At a gathering on June 28th 1926, on board the *Olympic,* he was presented with a watch by his colleagues, after 58 years' service with the company.

In thanking everyone, he spoke of the sensation created by the *Oceanic* in 1871 on her first voyage and of the enlightened foresight of Thomas Ismay and William Imrie in breaking the tradition of placing passengers aft, as had always been the custom, thus involving them in discomfort and vibration. T H Ismay, Mr Prince stated, could justly claim to be a pioneer, for it was he who later fitted up rooms for married couples and their families in the third class quarters. Formerly they had been berthed in large rooms holding 20 to 30 people, which was a disgrace. Moreover, it was the White Star Line which abolished the necessity of passengers providing their own beds, blankets and eating utensils.

It was indeed a revolution in the carrying of emigrants and the scenes witnessed of passengers carrying their own beds were gone forever.

During the first 18 months of the company's existence they experienced troubles with the steam vessels. The propeller blades kept breaking, so just before Christmas they sent the following letter to the builders:-

December 20th, 1872.
To Messrs. Harland & Wolff, Belfast.
Dear Sirs,
Constant breakage of the propeller blades is becoming a question of the most serious importance to us, not only on account of the great expense entailed thereby, but also as affecting the prestige of the Line, which must suffer if these accidents continue. You have already been advised, and have doubtless heard with the same amount of concern as ourselves, that in addition to the *Oceanic, Baltic* and *Atlantic* we now learn per *City of Washington* that she passed the s.s. *Adriatic* on the 13th inst., when about 1,500 miles

from New York *with two blades of her propeller broken.* This makes a total of *nine* blades broken within *two months,* and it behoves us, therefore, at once to take the matter into most serious consideration, and if possible to ascertain the cause of, and devise a remedy for, these mishaps.

With this end in view, we should be glad if you will help us with your experience and advice on the subject, and to our mind the questions appear to be:

1. The cause of the breakage, whether attributable to any extraneous circumstances such as the screw fouling any wreckage, or timber, or whether from any fault in the construction of the blades themselves.

2. Does already obtained experience warrant the continuance of cast steel as the material to be used? Being thinner and lighter than cast-iron are they not therefore weaker and is not steel a more uncertain metal?

3. Are loose blades as strong as solid propellers?

4. Gunmetal being almost universally used in the Royal Navy in this particular would it not be suitable for us? Though the first cost is heavy, yet from the strength and toughness of

the material, they would be less likely to break and therefore be cheaper in the long run.

These are all questions which we ask ourselves, and on which we would also seek your opinion, and would suggest whether it would not be as well - at your convenience - to have a general conference for the purpose of duly considering and weighing the several points in detail, as regards this question, in the hope that by doing so some satisfactory conclusion may be arrived at. Meanwhile we have requested Mr. Horsburgh, our superintendent engineer, to confer with the several superintendent engineers of the other lines, with a view to obtain information on the same subject.

We are, dear Sir,
Yours faithfully,
Ismay, Imrie & Co.

It is not known what Harland & Wolff had to say to this letter but troubles with shafts and propellers breaking continued until the introduction of twin screws.

CHAPTER 5

The Company's first disaster, the 'Atlantic', Bruce Ismay's schooldays, the buying of the Dawpool Estate

With the opening of the New Year, 1873, the *Atlantic* was scheduled to make a trip to South America in the new service, but this was cancelled, and she remained in her usual employment, Liverpool-New York via Queenstown instead, a voyage which she had already undertaken some 18 times.

Having once again been provisioned and coaled in the Bramley Moore Dock, and cleared by the various authorities as being completely sea worthy, on March 20th 1873, the *Atlantic* put out to sea. She had 28 saloon passengers and 499 adults, 69 children and 19 infants, 587 in all in the steerage, with a crew of 143, under the command of Captain James Agnew Williams. She had to wait for a suitable tide to cross the bar and left Liverpool at 2pm for Queenstown where she is said to have embarked 184 additional passengers, including four saloon passengers. This gave a grand total of 799 persons.

All four steamers of the *Oceanic* class Were designed to burn 58 tons of coal per day when going at an economical speed; the *Atlantic* sailed with 967 tons of mixed Welsh and Lancashire coals in her bunkers which was sufficient for just over 15 days steaming. Her longest passage on her previous 18 voyages was 13 days 10 hours and her shortest passage was 10 days 3 hours, the average coal used being 670 tons per voyage.

Unfortunately, however, the engineers were extremely extravagant in the way in which they used the coal and the vessel was burning 70 tons per day. To make matters worse, four days after leaving Queenstown, the *Atlantic* ran into the full force of an equinoxial gale, which slowed her down very much, although she was still going at the full power of her engines, burning 70 tons of coal per day, as it was not possible to set the sails. The gale lasted three days, during which time she ran 175 miles, instead of her usual nearly 300 in 24 hours.

At noon on March 31st, having been at sea 11 days, the chief engineer, Mr John Foxley, informed Captain Williams that there were only about 127 tons of coal left in the bunkers. The *Atlantic* was still 460 miles from Sandy Hook, and the Captain feared that if they met any more bad weather, they might run out of coal; so he decided, after holding a consultation with the chief engineer and the chief officer, John William Firth, to alter course for Halifax and obtain fresh supplies of coal, before proceeding to New York; Halifax being only 170 miles away.

At 1pm course was altered to North 24 East, and the vessel proceeded on her way, the weather having cleared very considerably. At midnight the Captain retired to the chart room, leaving strict orders to be wakened at 3am, but he failed to issue any instructions about casting the lead or keeping a specially strict look out; he thought that when he was roused he would be near the Sambro Light and would then heave to until daylight, before proceeding to Halifax, as he knew he would be in the vicinity of a dangerous coast. Unfortunately he was away out in his reckoning, as owing to the currents and the speed at which the ship was travelling, they had gone a greater distance than he thought. The boy who waited on him went into the wheelhouse at 2.40am with his cocoa and was going to call him, but the fourth officer, John Brown, stopped him. The second officer whose watch it was, and who was in charge of the vessel, said he would call him at 3am but this he failed to do.

At 3am those on the bridge were amazed to hear the cry from the look out "Breakers ahead", the engine room telegraphs were immediately rung over to full speed astern, but the vessel which was going full ahead at about 12 knots, struck a rock.

Capt James Williams gives the following account at the Court of Enquiry which opened April 5th 1873:-

Capt Williams' evidence. When he arrived in Halifax the day after the wreck, he prepared a statement of the particulars of the disaster to be sent by mail to England for the information of the owners; and he asked permission to read some portions of the letter as his statement, which were as follows:-

On the 28th day of March the Engineer's report showed the coal getting short, we having experienced then three very severe days weather. Coals on board, 319 tons; ship 1,130 miles from Sandy Hook; reducing the consumption the speed came down to 8 knots, and with moderate to strong breeze to 5 knots per hour, I kept on till the 31st when our coals were reduced to 127 tons, and the ship distant from Sandy Hook 460 miles. Lat. 41 deg. 39 min. N., Long. 63 deg. 54 min. W.

The ship at this time was making 7 knots per hour, the wind at South West. Glass falling, and a westerly swell, I thought the risk too great to keep on, as in the event of a westerly gale coming up, we might find ourselves shut from all sources of supply. At 1 o'clock p.m. after receiving the Engineer's report, I decided to come here, Sambro Island, bearing then North 5 deg. East, true distance 170 miles. We got both anchors over the bows, the leads ready and armed, the leadlines ready and overhauled during the afternoon. The wind was South South West, with rain. At 8 p.m. the wind veered to West, clear starlight; I took several azimuths by the sun during the afternoon, which gave 9 degrees easterly deviation. I also several times corrected the course by the Pole Star during the night, which gave the same deviation as above. The course steered by compass was North 24 deg. East with 9 deg. easterly deviation, which I considered ample allowance for the westerly set, and to lead 5 miles to the East of Sambro Island ledges.

I left my orders on the Bridge as to lookout, which word was passed to the Officers relieving at midnight, Second and Fourth. I corrected the course the last time at 12.20 a.m. when I repeated my caution and orders. I then went in to the Chart Room and sat down. My intention was to run on till 3 a.m. then heave the ship to and await day. At midnight the ship's run, by my estimate, was 122 miles, which would place her 48 miles South of Sambro.

The speed by log at 1.30 being 9 knots (Fourth Officer's report) per hour. The night at this time was cloudy and clear. At 2.40 my servant came up with, as ordered, my cocoa, when he was told not to wake me till 3 a.m., when the First Officer would call me. The first intimation I had of anything was the ship striking on Marr's Rock off Meaghar's Island, and remaining heeling slightly to port. The Officers were quickly at their stations, accompanied by the Quartermasters. The first sea swept away all the port boats, and the ship heeling over rapidly soon rendered the starboard boats useless. Every effort was made to send the people forward outside the ship, but the short time defeated all our efforts. The Second Officer was in the starboard lifeboat. I carried two ladies and placed them with him, and returned for more. Before I got as far as the Saloon entrance I found the ship going over still further. I managed to get hold of the weather rail, and get back to the lifeboat. I took the ladies and placed them in the main rigging, and went back. I called the Second Officer to come out, as the boat would roll over, which she did in a few minutes, carrying him with her, and 30 or 40 men. Finding I was of no use there, I returned to the main rigging, and found the ladies had gone.

The Chief Officer, Mr. Firth, got up into the mizzen rigging, where his retreat was soon cut off, and he had to remain there till 3 p.m. when the sea moderating with falling tide he was got off. Mr. Brady, Third Officer, finding the boats useless, went forward and with the assistance of Quartermasters Speakman and Owens, established communications by a rope to a small outlying rock, distant from our starboard bow about 40 yards. Owens swam first, but failed to get a footing. Speakman then tried and succeeded. A stout rope was hauled on the rock, along which Mr. Brady passed, followed by the boldest of the men. By this time it was 4 a.m. I was at this time in the main rigging, trying to get the passengers there collected to make an effort to get forward. Many went, but the larger number (several saloon passengers) lay there and died. The Purser was the first to succumb to the intense cold that prevailed. Finding myself of no use there, I got along outside the ship to the fore rigging, and got the fore sheets and tacks unrove and sent ashore. We now had five ropes to the rock, along which men to the number of 200 passed safely, though nearly exhausted on reaching the rock. Mr. Brady, accompanied by Quartermasters Owens and Speakman, now got a line across the inner channel, which was about 100 yards wide and shallow, though with a heavy surf running through. They then went up and gave the alarm, and sent a messenger to Halifax. About 50 got to the larger island by the line, though many were drowned in the attempt; amongst the number who were drowned was the Chief Steward by the passengers crowding him down. I, with the Fourth Officer, Mr. Brown, encouraged as much as we could the people about 450 in number, who remained on the ship's side to keep moving and from falling asleep. In many instances they gave entirely up, and died apparently without any pain. Twelve men clinging together laid down beside me, and despite of all efforts to rouse them died and slipped off into the sea.

At 5.30 a.m. the first boat came, but she was too small to be of any use; in about 20 minutes the first large boat was launched, and proceeded to take the passengers off the small rock; she was, in half an hour, followed by two other boats. I succeeded, fearing the ship would part and slide into deep water, in getting the boats to take on shore men from the ship first, and many were saved who, if left there till the last, would have perished from exhaustion. At this time I missed the Fourth Officer, and feared he had fallen in, when I saw him on the rocks encouraging and helping another boat along; when all had left but about 30 men, my hands being frozen and my legs stiff, they took me off, the rest following immediately. At 8.45 a.m. all the survivors were landed and lodged in a wooden hut belonging to a fisherman named Clancy, who with his daughter gave them all they had, made fires and warmed them all the day; they were drafted off to the various islands about and billeted amongst what houses there were. Mr. Ryan, the Resident Magistrate, filling his house and the others following his example.

At 1 p.m. I sent Mr. Brady to Halifax to give particulars, obtain food and assistance, also to get steamers down early and convey the crew and passengers to Halifax. At 5 p.m. the tide having fallen, she broke in two abaft the foremast, the ship falling over till the sea washed completely over; her cargo was now washed out. Having no other officer at hand I detached the boatswain and eight men to prevent the wreckers, who now swarmed around, from carrying away the saved goods, and left a watch of four men during the night to pick up the bodies of such as might wash ashore; they picked up but five during the night; at daylight the Customs Authorities came down and took charge. I gave Captain Sheridan provisional authority to employ what labour he required for salvage, with the understanding that the salvage should not be over 40 per cent of net value, and if this was objected to, to leave it to the arbitration of two Justices of the Peace. We embarked all our saved (amounting to about 429) in steamships *Lady Head* and *Delta,* and arrived in Halifax at 3 p.m.

where Mr. Morrow, the Cunard Agent (who had promptly afforded us every assistance) had places prepared for all. I have given the Company's carpenter orders to get about 200 shells to bury the dead, and an undertaker to attend to the saloon passengers' bodies, and Second Officer, as their friends might want them to be forwarded.

Examined by Mr Ritchie:

The Chart Room was 30 feet abaft the Bridge on the Upper Deck within easy call of the Bridge; I remained in the Chart Room from the time I left the Bridge until she struck.

At 12 o'clock at night the Third Officer reported we had made 122 miles since bearing up for Halifax. I supposed that at 3 o'clock we should be from 18 to 20 miles south of Sambro. After I left the Bridge I did not divest myself of my clothing. I had every confidence in the Second Officer.

Cross examined by Mr Blanchard:

We bore up for Halifax on account of shortness of coal. I have never been on this coast before. From the time I considered I was 48 miles from Sambro I did not use the lead. The charts used were Admiralty Charts. I do not recollect what soundings the charts showed. I knew I was within soundings. I did not sound because the night was clear, and the Sambro Light would be visible in clear weather 21 miles, and in moderate weather 15 miles. An Officer's eye would be 36 feet above the level of the sea while standing on the Bridge. I certainly supposed that because of the clearness of the night we could see the light at Sambro. From subsequent facts ascertained I now know that I must have been mistaken in the position of the ship at midnight.

Ismay, Imrie & Co in Liverpool heard the news by telegram the following morning. Text of telegram received 7.30am, April 2nd 1873, from J H Sparks, New York (words in capitals are code words):

Brady Third Officer arrived Halifax *Atlantic* ILLEGITIMATE (is a total wreck) Cape Prospect about CHESHIRE (700) CHAIN (passengers lost) BOULOGNE (250) people including Captain saved intended IMPRECATION (putting in short of coals) have despatched Pennell NAVAL (awaiting further particulars).

Text of telegram sent to Cunard, Halifax, Nova Scotia about 3pm, April 2nd 1873:

Anxiously awaiting particulars respecting *Atlantic* telegraph immediately.

As is always the case with a disaster of any magnitude, the wildest of rumours immediately started to circulate, the chief one being that the *Atlantic* had sailed short of coal. In order to try to allay the rumours Ismay sent the following letter to *The Times* for publication:-

April 3rd 1873
To the Editor of The Times,
London.
Sir,
Although much and painfully depressed by the grievous loss of life which has attended the shipwreck of the steamship *Atlantic,* and disinclined, therefore, to obtrude ourselves on public attention, we feel that it is our duty, as managers of the Oceanic Steam Navigation Company, to which she belongs, to take notice of a statement in your columns, to the effect that she was insufficiently supplied with coals.

We submit that the facts are quite otherwise, for we are in a position to prove that the quantity put on board this vessel before leaving Liverpool was 967 tons, and that her consumption for the outward passage to New York, upon an average taken from eighteen voyages which she had successfully accomplished, was only 744 tons, while the largest quantity ever consumed on the worst winter passage, say in December and January, never exceeded 896 tons. We have three distinct and independent checks upon these figures, recorded in writing at the time of the vessel's departure, all of which agree within a few tons; 967 being the minimum which they establish as having been taken on board.

We feel sure that you will consider that these figures are a complete answer to any charge of inadequate equipment, and we would add that, it has been throughout our object and most anxious desire, to provide all the vessels comprising this Company's fleet with every possible requirement, without regard to cost.

We have also endeavoured, and with much solicitude to provide for their careful and safe navigation, as you will see by extracts from general instruction and by special manuscript letter to the Commander, which for the satisfaction of the public we beg permission to subjoin. We feel confident that a judicial inquiry into the loss of this fine ship, for which we are most desirous, will establish beyond a doubt her excellent sea going qualities, and the completeness of her outfit in every department.

We are, Sir,
Your obedient servants,
Ismay, Imrie Co.

2 Enc: Extracts from book of instructions Rules 2 and 14. Copy of letter to Captain Williams given upon his appointment to the *Atlantic* February, 5th, 1873.

Rule 2
Responsibility of Commanders

The Commanders must distinctly understand that the issue of the following instructions does not in any way relieve them of any responsibility for the safe and efficient navigation of their respective vessels, and they are also enjoined to remember that whilst they are expected to use every diligence to secure a speedy voyage, *they must run no risk which might by any possibility result in an accident to their ship. It is to be hoped that they will ever bear in mind that the safety of the lives and the property entrusted to their care is the ruling principle that should govern them in the navigation of their ships, and no supposed gain of expedition, or saving of time on the voyage is to be purchased at the risk of accident.* The Company desires to establish and maintain for its vessels a reputation for safety, and only looks for such speed on the various voyages as is consistent with safe and prudent navigation.

Rule 14
Nearing the Land and Heaving the Lead

A wide berth to be given to all headlands, islands, shoals and the coast generally and the commanders are particularly enjoined on all occasions when nearing the land or in places of intricate navigation, to take frequent cross bearings of any well marked objects that may be visible and suitable for verifying the position of the ship.

At first it was decided to hold a Board of Trade inquiry at Liverpool but this was cancelled and it was held in Halifax. Ismay and his co-managers were very disappointed and the following letter was sent to the Board of Trade:-

April 15th 1873
To The Assistant Secretary,
Marine Department,
Board of Trade,
London.
Sir,
On the 9th instant we took leave to wait upon you in person, and also to present you with an urgent written request that you would be pleased to recommend that the present Canadian Board of Trade inquiry at Halifax regarding the loss of the s.s. *Atlantic* should be adjourned from that place to Liverpool so that every fact connected with the vessel should be laid before your Board, and made public and we are now much disappointed to learn from your favour of the 10th instant to hand this morning that this request cannot be granted.

We submit to you that this is a great hardship upon the Company which we represent, that it should be deprived of the opportunity of providing by the testimony of unimpeachable witnesses, and by facts which cannot be gainsaid, how complete and thorough in all respect was the equipment of the steamer *Atlantic* as regards coals, provisions, stores, and all necessary outfit, and how excellent were the vessel's seagoing qualities, both as regards model and strength of construction.

It is true that you suggest a tender of evidence before the Commission of Inquiry at Halifax, but we should urge upon your consideration that it is out of our power to furnish the testimony of witnesses at Halifax, nor yet to instruct any representative who is necessarily unacquainted with the innumerable details of such a business in a way that would enable him to correct in cross examination of witnesses there the errors and discrepancies which we could have corrected at any inquiry held in this country.

We remain, Sir,
Your obedient servants,
Ismay, Imrie & Co.

It was a most serious disaster for the company and it was very much criticised but Ismay, sorry as he was at what had happened took it as a challenge to be overcome, and answered the charges to the best of his ability.

April 28th 1873
To Sir William Fairbairn,
Manchester.
Sir,
We have not hitherto made any remarks upon your letter to 'The Times' newspaper on the subject of "The Strength of Iron Ships" because our attention has been much engrossed by other matters; but we now consider it necessary to address you in reference to your assertion that the *Atlantic* was "extremely weak for her length".

We can scarcely believe that anyone holding your prominent and authorative position, as an engineer, should have made so imperative a statement as this without having become acquainted, in the first instance, with the model of the vessel in question; the strength of her construction, the description and quality of the materials employed; and the mechanical adjustment of the various parts; and the general character of the workmanship; at the same time, we consider it due to her owners, as also to the public, that a clear answer should be given on these points.

If it should appear that you have merely expressed an abstract opinion, and without personal knowledge of the conditions to which we have referred, it will give us much pleasure to afford you the opportunity of inspecting any, or all of the steamers comprising the White Star fleet; either in the building yard, upon a voyage, or in graving dock after having made many voyages; taking care that all drawings and calculations shall be at your disposal, and we venture to think that, you will thenceforward change the opinions which you have somewhat prematurely expressed, and probably class these ships in future, in the list of those which you deem most reliable in point of strength and efficiency.

While making the foregoing remarks, and inviting your inspection of the vessel, we must not conceal from you the fact that we consider that this Company has been unfairly prejudiced by the remarks which have appeared under your signature, and we may feel ourselves compelled to seek some authorative position upon the point which you have raised.

We are, Sir,
Yours truly,
Ismay, Imrie & Co.

The findings of the court at Halifax were that Captain Williams had not exercised proper care and taken soundings, etc, when on a dangerous coast, and that the vessel sailed short of coal. But owing to the courage and heroism Captain Williams had displayed after the wreck, his certificate was suspended for two years instead of for life, as would otherwise have been the case. T H Ismay was exceedingly disappointed, both at the Court of Inquiry being held in Halifax instead of Liverpool, as was originally suggested, and also at the finding that the *Atlantic* had sailed short of coal.

Apart from Ismay, Imrie & Company pressing for a Board of Trade inquiry to be held in Liverpool, when the full facts could be made public, (they had nothing to hide), a question was asked in the House of Commons as to whether a public inquiry could not be held in Liverpool, as the public were not at all satisfied with the Halifax inquiry. Additionally there was a certain Mr James Brown of Lindridge near Teignmouth in Devonshire whose daughter had married a Mr Kruger and had three children by the marriage. On behalf of his daughter, who had lost her husband in the disaster, Mr Brown became extremely indignant and wrote some very forceful letters to the Board of Trade, urging that the inquiry in Halifax was most unsatisfactory, as he had heard that the *Atlantic* was both badly coaled and provisioned.

So indignant was Mr Brown, that when the inquiry in Liverpool was opened on May 10th 1873 under Admiral Schomberg, in the board room of the Sailors' Home, he wrote to the Board of Trade saying that he personally was going to Liverpool to cross examine the witnesses. He went, but when he arrived, he found to his anger that the court had adjourned temporarily while T H Ismay got additional evidence. But he managed to find Admiral Schomberg and Mr Ravenhill, the assessor, at the Adelphi Hotel. He presented a long letter to the Admiral, who after reading it, asked if it was all his own work or if he was a barrister.

In the meantime Ismay, Imrie & Company, who were absolutely determined to prove that the *Atlantic* had not sailed short of coal, were gathering their evidence together and on May 28th 1873, the inquiry was reopened. On June 11th the assessors reported their findings to the Board of Trade, which were that the *Atlantic* was properly provisioned in every way, apart from the amount of coal on board. It would have been more judicious to have had an additional 100 tons, which would have allowed for bad stoking, waste, and possibly the swift-burning character of the coal. They also drew attention to the fact that a proper check on how much coal had been consumed was not kept by the chief engineer. "No passenger ship of her class should be short of coal on the eleventh day of her voyage to New York, as the *Atlantic* in our opinion, undoubtedly was."

T H Ismay was astounded at the findings of the court on June 11th; he and his colleagues were still absolutely determined to prove that the *Atlantic* did not sail short of coal, so pressed the Board of Trade again and again; the matter was referred to the Chief Surveyor and London Surveyor (Messrs. Traill & MacFarlane Gray) to the Board of Trade. Their findings were "the *Atlantic* was lost while performing this voyage to Halifax; for that voyage she had an ample supply of fuel. Her loss was not through being driven on a lee shore, helpless, her fuel spent and the engines without power. She was run at full speed, engines and boilers all in perfect order, upon well known rocks, in fine weather. So efficiently were the engines and boilers working that the vessel had actually over run the distance intended at the time she struck. The question of fuel supply cannot therefore have had anything whatever to do with the loss of the *Atlantic* on her voyage to Halifax." But the legend is still alive to this day that the *Atlantic* sailed short of coal.

It was owing to this disaster, which could have wrecked the company, that the South American business was carried on again by the sailing vessels only; some of the capital lost by the *Atlantic* was recouped by the sale of the steamships *Asiatic* and *Tropic* which had been on this run.

After the loss of the *Atlantic* the company for the time being restricted itself to the North Atlantic trade. But this disaster did not deter Thomas Ismay. He was determined to prove that those who had confidence in him, and had given him their backing, should be justified. He never asked for more capital and to the end of his days no more was ever put into the company. Even when other North Atlantic companies did not pay a dividend, the Oceanic Steam Navigation Company never paid less than 7 per cent. No one outside the company knew what the earnings were until 1902 when they were published for the first time. Ismay knew exactly what other companies were doing; in fact he kept two special books, one for each of his great rivals, the Cunard and Inman Lines, and these are still in existence.

During the year prior to the loss of the *Atlantic,* Ismay, Imrie & Company had taken into service two ships built for the North Atlantic trade by Edward Harland's firm; these were the *Adriatic* and *Celtic,* almost identical ships to the original *Oceanic* class, but 17 feet longer.

At this time most ships were lit by candlelight. Thomas Ismay, always anxious to increase the passengers' comfort whenever possible, conceived in conjunction with his friend Edward Harland, the idea of lighting the ships with gas. This was accomplished with a plant made by Aveling Porter of Lincoln. Unfortunately it was not successful, owing to the fact that the movement of the ship caused the pipes to break; after a few voyages the gas plant was removed from the *Celtic* and she was lit in future by the usual method.

By the middle of 1875 the *Britannic* and *Germanic* were both in commission; these vessels were considerably larger than any of the previous steamers and faster. They were fitted with larger engines of the same type, built by Maudsley, Field & Company, which worked at 75lbs pressure, the steam being supplied from eight boilers heated by 32 furnaces, which burned 110 tons of coal per day.

For some time previously Edward Harland had been very much in favour of fitting an adjustable propeller to any new ships which his firm built, and the *Britannic* was so fitted, the idea being to lower the screw and so obtain deeper thrust. It was not considered successful and after a few voyages it was removed; the *Germanic* did not have the lowering screw but was orthodox from the start.

With these vessels the Atlantic fleet was complete and the White Star Line was able to maintain the fastest service on the Western Ocean for the next 12 years, but the services of the original steamer, the *Oceanic,* were no longer required. So, in the same year with Mr and Mrs Thomas Ismay on board she sailed for the Pacific, to be chartered for the next 20 years to the Occidental & Oriental Company. She was followed into this service by the *Belgic* and *Gaelic.*

During these last six years the Ismay family had suffered two sad losses. In 1869 Thomas's mother died at Lea in Kent where she was staying. She was sixty-three years old. As she died intestate all her property passed to Thomas, her elder son, including the two Maryport houses, Whillans Yard, and Ropery House. The former he sold to his brother, John, in December of the same year for £50 and later he also disposed of Ropery House.

Then at the beginning of 1871 they lost their eldest daughter, Mary, who contracted scarlet fever, and died in the home of her grandfather, Luke Bruce, 126 Faulkner Street, Liverpool. She was only 11 years old.

Although T H Ismay no longer owned any property in Maryport, his thoughts as ever, were still with his home town. In December, 1876 he started a fund for the old people of Maryport, £5 for coal, and £20 for blankets, to be distributed annually at Christmas; in the following year he added another £25 to take the form of a shilling's worth of groceries per person per week. These funds are still in existence today.

Then in November, 1878 he heard that the Church of Christchurch, down by the docks, needed a new clock for the spire, so he presented them with one which can still be seen there today.

In the meantime Bruce was growing up; he went to school at New Brighton, then on to Elstree, North London, and from there on to Harrow (1877-1878). He had taken after his mother and was very shy and extremely sensitive, consequently he was not happy during his schooldays. He began to put up a defensive facade of brusqueness to avoid appearing over-sensitive. This manner often caused people to dislike him, until they got to know him well. He

Bruce Ismay, aged 13

was devoted to both his parents, and his mother loved him too; but his father found him difficult. He was quick to learn and when asked his opinion would state it clearly and forthrightly; T H Ismay liked to consider a problem from all angles before reaching a decision, and so resented his quick-thinking son.

When Bruce left Harrow at only sixteen, he was sent to a tutor at Dinard in France. It was there he learnt to play tennis really well and he thoroughly enjoyed it for years to come. On September 13th, 1880 he entered the firm of Ismay, Imrie & Company to serve his apprenticeship.

During the summer holidays he had occasionally accompanied his father to his office; on these occasions he always hung his overcoat and hat with his father's in the office. When he reported for his first day's work he did this as usual, but after he had received his instructions and left the room, T H Ismay rang the bell for one of the clerks and said to him "Please inform the new office boy that he is not to leave his hat and coat lying about in my office". This snub in front of his father's staff so humiliated the boy that he rarely wore an overcoat again.

This is only one example of the lack of understanding with which T H Ismay treated his eldest son, and of the sense of inferiority he implanted in him.

On another occasion, when his father was detained in Liverpool at a meeting, Bruce arrived home first. Being a fine evening he decided he would like to have some exercise, riding in the fresh air. Unfortunately he took his father's favourite horse and as he galloped it on the sands in front of Beech Lawn, it stumbled and fell heavily, breaking its leg, and had to be destroyed. Mr Ismay was very angry indeed with Bruce for taking the animal without permission and for being, as he considered, so careless with it.

Poor Bruce was terribly upset about the whole incident, and as a result never rode again.

Some years previously, in 1877, the Ismays had bought an estate of 390 acres with magnificent views over the Dee and to the hills of Wales beyond. It was only 11 miles over the ferry from Liverpool. The house had been built in 1865 by James Regan who also erected some model farm buildings (which are still considered today to be some of the finest in Cheshire). When he died his daughters at first let the estate, but finally it was put up for sale and Mr Ismay then bought it.

Both he and his wife loved the quiet of a country life and in Dawpool they found what they wanted. The estate took its name from a tiny hamlet on the shore, from where ships had once sailed but, owing to the silting of the river, the little port had long been abandoned. They used the house for long weekends and holidays but, as Beech Lawn was nearer to Liverpool, it was still the principal family home.

CHAPTER 6

Growth of the White Star Line, the building of the new Dawpool House, presentation of the gilt dinner service

Over the years Mrs T H Ismay kept personal diaries of day-to-day events; those from 1881 to 1907 are still in existence and extracts from them are included in this and the following chapters. They throw a good deal of light on how a successful businessman and his family lived in the height of the Victorian era.

By 1880 the White Star Line had become one of the most prominent shipping companies, especially in the North Atlantic trade. Mr Ismay and his firm had become well known for the high standard they maintained in their ships. He had become a director of the London and North Western Railway, of the Royal Insurance Company and was serving on the board of governors of the Seamen's Orphanage and the Training Ship *Indefatigable*; the last he was particularly interested in. He and his family had a very large circle of friends; they had become highly respected and prosperous members of Liverpool society.

They let the farm at Dawpool, and used the house as they had done during the last three years but neither of them really cared for it - it was the position they loved. They felt it was now necessary to have a larger house as they entertained on a lavish scale; sometimes after a board meeting, as many as 20 people would stay the night at Beech Lawn. They were soon to celebrate their silver wedding, so they decided to mark the occasion by pulling down the old house at Dawpool, and building a splendid new one on the site.

Norman Shaw, who was later to become famous as the man who built the present Scotland Yard, in London, had already made a reputation for himself as an architect, so early in January the

Dawpool House

Ismays went to Shrewsbury to see a house which he had designed. They evidently liked it, as the following month they travelled to London to meet Mr Shaw and discuss plans for the new Dawpool. He drew up some rough plans which he took up to Liverpool in May, staying two days with them, and thoroughly discussing the new project. As with everything Thomas Ismay planned, he would only have the finest possible material used; in the finished house there was not a single nail in the whole structure, only the finest brass screws. It was to be a reproduction of an Elizabethan manor house, built of a red stone quarried locally. It took two years to complete. Mrs Ismay records:-

July 29th, Saturday, 1882. Thomas and I laid the foundation stone at the new house.

By the following year she writes:

May 19th, Saturday, 1883. Went to Dawpool, the house is progressing well, but the glass roof of the picture room will I think be an eyesore.

June 11th, Monday, 1883. Drove to Dawpool with Thomas, and Mr. Doyle (the builder), arranged the bells and gas on upper floor. Much fear no way of altering picture room roof as T.R.I. does not like Mr. Shaw's proposed alteration.

Early next year the work was nearing completion and Mrs Ismay records her visit to Dawpool as follows:-

February 26th, Tuesday, 1884. Breakfasted at 8 a.m. The gentlemen all went up to the house. Mr. Shaw seems well satisfied with the progress made. I asked them when they thought the house would be ready. They all said they saw no reason why it should not be finished by the end of May - I doubt it much myself.

But in spite of Mr Shaw's assurances Mrs Ismay's doubts were justified, as the house was not actually ready until December; in October Mrs Ismay was occupied with decorating and furnishing the house. She writes:-

October 8th, Wednesday. 1884. Thomas left Dawpool at 8 a.m Mr. Heaton and I after lunch. He's been most unsuccessful in many of his measurements, particularly in curtains, and puts to our mind much too heavy trimming.

After all these difficulties they still had to contend with the weather and Mrs Ismay recalls:-

December 4th, Thursday, 1884. The roads very heavy with snow. If the furniture had not been moved, almost think we should have deferred moving to Dawpool until the Spring. Not very inviting weather to begin a country life. We all slept in the house for the first time.

Tremendous care and thought had gone into the building of Dawpool; it was very large, the South front overlooking the Dee was over 250 feet long (the terrace is still there today.) It cost £53,000 to build, an immense sum in those days, and by today's standards the house was over ornate and oppressive, with all its elaborate interior decorations. It required twenty-two indoor servants and ten outdoor, to run it properly. When Mrs Ismay died in 1907, her three sons were each offered it in turn, but they all refused to live in it, so it was put up for sale. The house was looked upon as a 'fetter' on the selling aspect of the estate rather than an asset.

When the house was built the main road running round the estate was moved inland and for a long time was known as 'Ismay's cutting'.

In spite of all the care and money lavished on the house, when they moved in, they found that the chimneys smoked badly. Over the years they tried many times to cure this, but they were never successful and when the wind was in a certain direction, it was impossible to light a fire in the room affected.

The picture room at Dawpool

Whilst Thomas Ismay was engaged in building his new mansion, his partner, William Imrie, also decided on a new home so he bought the Homestead, a large stone built Victorian house, with a massive conservatory, standing in its own ground in Mossley Hill Road, Liverpool. (This house still survives as a convent.)

The White Star Line was now doing so well that the shareholders suggested, in 1881, that the articles of agreement should be altered so that Thomas Ismay and William Imrie would take a larger commission but neither of them would agree to do this. So the shareholders, wishing to show their appreciation, suggested that Thomas Ismay should sit to Mr Millais (later Sir John) for his portrait which they would present to him. They also commissioned the firm of Hunt & Roskell to make a dinner service of silver gilt which was designed by Mr G A Carter.

Owing to T H Ismay's various commitments, it was necessary for him and his wife to spend quite a lot of time in

London; they usually stayed at the Grand Hotel in Cumberland Avenue where they took a suite, accompanied by their personal valet and maid. Mr. Ismay's only surviving sister, Sarah, had married a Mr Robert Wood, who was a solicitor; they lived at Lee Terrace, Blackheath, and when John Ismay retired from the sea, he went to live next door to his sister, having married a Miss Kebbel.

They had always been a united family and whenever Mr and Mrs Thomas Ismay were in London, they frequently met his brother and sister either in London for theatre parties, etc, or in Blackheath. They were in London from the end of May until the end of June 1881, during which time Mr Ismay gave his first sitting to Mr Millais for his portrait; below are some extracts from Mrs Ismay's diaries showing the sort of life they led there:-

May 31st, Tuesday, 1881. T.H.I. and I went to the Italian Opera. Heard Albini in Mignon.

June 1st, Wednesday, 1881. At a Ball at Mr. Millais'. About 800 there. Saw a number of London Fashionables!

June 8th, Wednesday, 188r. Tried to get into the Albert Hall, but could not owing to the crowd.

By July they were back in Liverpool, and on July 4th they received the news that the *Britannic* had gone aground at Wexford in fog and the passengers and mail were being put ashore. T H Ismay remained the night at Faulkner Street (the home of his sister-in-law, Mary, who had married Captain Leslie). This was four days later according to the diaries:-

July 8th, Friday, 1881. At 12.20 *Britannic* a short time afterwards sprang a leak in the engine room, and was taken into Wexford Bay. T.H.I. and I remained at Mrs. Leslie's for the night.

July 9th, Saturday, 1881. T.H.I., Bruce and Captain Leslie left for Wexford with steam tug, pumps and diver.

July 11th, Monday, 1881. Received telegram from T.H.I. saying work progressing satisfactorily on *Britannic*.

July, 12th, Tuesday, 1881. Telegram from T.H.I. saying *Britannic* expected to leave Wexford in tow off our tugs.

July 13th, Wednesday, 1881. *Britannic* arrived at Bar at 5.0 p.m.

Thomas left her and got home about 7.30pm. Bruce and Captain Leslie remained on board the night. A number of people watched her coming up on New Brighton Pier, and Waterloo which she passed about 12pm.

Later in the year, for the first time Mr and Mrs Ismay were presented to Royalty and she writes:-

September 8th, Thursday, 1881. The North Docks opened by the Prince and Princess of Wales, the three Princesses also there, Mrs. Wood, T.H.I. and myself on board the *Claughton.* At the luncheon and presentation address at the Town Hall. The remainder of the party, children and servants on board *Celtic;* a beautiful day.

At the end of this year their son, James, who had been at school at Elstree, passed into Harrow. They were very pleased about this as 'Jimmy' had always been the favourite. He was happier here than his brother Bruce had been and a few years later his parents decided to send him on to a university. In 1884 Mrs Ismay writes:- "Thomas and I went to Cambridge to see the Colleges, the 'Backs' of which are very fine. We saw six, but on the whole prefer Oxford and would rather Jimmy went there."

When James came down from Oxford in 1889 he entered his father's office; two years later was made a partner, on the same day as Bruce, January 1st 1891.

Just after hearing the news that Jimmy had passed into Harrow Mr and Mrs Ismay went to visit a Mr Waterman to see his new house and she comments rather acidly: "It has fine grounds, the laundry is particularly good". Two days later Mrs Ismay again demonstrates her somewhat dry humour with the remark, "Thomas does not look at all well, possibly the effects of Dr. Gardiner's medicine".

By 1882 the Atlantic fleet was proving very satisfactory and the Pacific service was working well. The fleet of sailing ships, as

Doric

we have seen, had been running to Australia since 1867 (from 1870 under the direction of William Imrie) but Thomas Ismay now decided that it was time to start a new service of steam vessels to Australia and New Zealand.

Two companies with a great deal of experience in the New Zealand trade had amalgamated in this year to form the Shaw Savill & Albion Company. Thomas Ismay came to an arrangement with them by which the White Star Line was to supply ships and crew, but these would be managed by the Shaw Savill & Albion Company.

The *Ionic* and *Doric* were built specially for this trade and were the forerunners of a type which came to be regarded as practically standard for ships built by Harland & Wolff. They were a development of the original *Oceanic* series, having a single funnel and rigged as four-masted barques. They were the first White Star vessels to be built of steel and the engines were constructed by the builders. Each ship carried about 70 first class passengers. The *Ionic* was delivered to her owners in 1883 and was brought round to London, arriving on April 1st. Bruce Ismay had joined her at Belfast on March 26th and made the voyage to London aboard her.

The Prince of Wales (later King Edward VII), expressly asked to see over her and arrangements were made accordingly. T H Ismay travelled down from Liverpool by an early train on April 23rd to welcome His Royal Highness aboard the ship as she lay in the London Docks and then travelled home on the midnight train arriving back in Liverpool at 4am the following day.

Following on this event, T H Ismay went to Holyhead on July 6th to travel to London in the new *Doric,* and on this occasion he was accompanied by a large party, including the Duke of Sutherland and the Bishop of Newcastle.

When the two new ships were put into commission, they were chartered by the New Zealand Shipping Company until this company's own new ships were ready for service and until the Shaw Savill & Albion Company's ships *Arawa* and *Tainui* were available to join with the White Star Line's *Ionic, Doric, Arabic* and *Coptic* in a regular monthly service from London to New Zealand and Australia.

Thomas Ismay had previously been in London in May when he went to a private viewing at the Royal Academy to see the finished portrait of himself by Millais hanging on the line.

May 4th, Friday, 1883. At the Private View at the Academy. Sarah went with us. Quite a number of friends, Thomas's picture by Millais hung on the line. Many opinions respecting it, principally that it does not do him justice. I don't like the expression.

This year they decided to go for a yachting holiday to the Western Isles of Scotland and below are excerpts from Mrs Ismay's diary which give the story of this unfortunate episode:-

August 9th, Thursday, 1883. Ought to have started in *Vanadis,* but too strong a gale. Are not able to do so. Sent luggage on board.

August 11th, Saturday. Left Liverpool at noon accompanied by Mr. and Mrs. Wood and all the children for a yachting expedition on board the steam yacht *Vanadis,* arrived at Beaumaris 8 p.m. Everybody ill except Thomas and James.

August 12th, Sunday. At Beaumaris. Not well enough to go to Church.

August 13th, Monday. Stayed at Beaumaris as it is still blowing a gale. Thought not prudent to sail. We are all settling down and find Captain and crew most kind and attentive.

August 14th, Tuesday. Gale still continues. Captain and Thomas both think we must remain the day at Beaumaris. We all regret it as we are anxious to get to the Clyde.

August 15th, Wednesday. Started from Beaumaris at 5 a.m, Still blowing hard. After getting outside found a heavy sea and squalls. Therefore decided to return to Beaumaris, much to our disappointment, as Sarah and I quite thought we were entering Douglas Harbour. We steamed up to Caernarvon and had a pleasant afternoon.

August 16th, Thursday. Left Beaumaris at 6 a.m. Still blowing. Reached the Isle of Man about 11 a.m. Kept under the lea of the land and had lunch in quiet water. Started again at 2 p.m, and arrived at Lamlash a little after midnight.

August 17th, Friday. Left Lamlash at 6 a.m. and arrived Wemyss Bay at 9. Breakfasted on shore, called on Mr. John Burns then on board *Vanadis* and sailed for Holy Loch and landed at Kilman and drove to Ben More and called to see Mr. Duncan. Left at 6 p.m. for Rothesay where we arrived at 7 p.m.

August 18th, Saturday. Went on shore after breakfast and drove to Mount Stuart to see a new mansion being built by the Marquis of Bute. Did some marketing then on board to lunch. Left Rothesay at 1.30 p.m. and reached Campbelltown at 6.30 p.m. Lovely sail through Kyles of Bute.

August 19th, Sunday. Remained at Campbelltown. Went to Church, dined on shore then took a drive to the Pass, on board at 5 p.m. to tea.

August 20th, Monday. Left Campbelltown at 5.30 a.m. The

Vanadis rolled tremendously going round the Mull at Kintyre with a very nasty sea. Did not get up till 12 noon when we lunched and arrived Oban 4 p.m.

August 21st, Tuesday. Went on board Sir Donald Currie's yacht *Zingara,* also Sir Andrew Walker's yacht *Cuhona,* both very fine. Then on shore. Lunched at Station Hotel and sailed from Oban at 3 p.m. arrived at Tobermory at 6 p.m., a most beautiful sail from Oban. At Oban Bruce joined us.

August 22nd, Wednesday. Sir William Forwood breakfasted with us. He arrived in his yacht at Tobermory about 10 p.m. yesterday. We left Tobermory at 9 and steamed to Loch Scavaig. We attempted to land but after getting some distance from *Vanadis* thought it best to return there as there was such a high sea. We were sorry not to see Loch Coruish. After lunch we left and arrived at Loch Hounin at 5.30 and got splendid fishing and lovely scenery, occasional showers of rain.

August 23rd, Thursday. Had a good haul in the transet net. A nasty drizzling rain. Sailed for Loch Hawn at noon and had a most beautiful sail to Loch Torridon where we arrived at 5 p.m. I think the scenery to-day the finest yet. We went on shore and found the people very poor. Gathered some lovely flowers and remained the night.

August 24th, Friday. Left Loch Torridon at 9 a.m., raining heavily, for Stornaway where we arrived at 2 p.m. Had a nasty rough passage. After lunch we went on shore and walked through the Castle grounds, and house which belongs to Lady Matthews. Got on board about 6 p.m. and remained the night here.

August 25th, Saturday. Commenced coaling at 4 a.m. Left Stornaway at noon and had a very rough passage again as usual. Arrived at Gairloch at 5 p.m. anchorage very bad and *Vanadis* rolling very much, blowing hard. Sarah, Mr. Wood, Ethel and Bruce went on shore. James and Bower out in dinghy.

August 26th, Sunday. Went ashore. Some of us went to Church, service in Gaelic. Lunched at hotel then had a walk.

Blowing very hard. Got aboard again about 4 p.m.

August 27th, Monday. Rolled very much all night. Landed and took two carriages and drove to Loch Maree, a most beautiful drive and the finest scenery we have yet seen. Lunched at hotel then drove back. Sir A. Walker who was landing with a party invited us to dine aboard s.y, *Cuhona*. Left Gairloch at 6 a.m, and arrived Portree at 9 a.m, Very glad to have good anchorage.

August 28th, Tuesday. The others landed for a short time, pouring with rain. Started at 11 a.m, Saw a yacht ashore at Scalpa. Blowing pretty strong and were very pleased to come to anchor at Tobermory. It has been a continuous downpour all day. Arrived 7.15 p.m.

August 29th, Wednesday. Beautiful morning. Left Tobermory at 9 a.m, intend to go to Staffa and lana but found such a heavy sea the Captain said it would be impossible to land there being a very high wind and very rough sea. The *Vanadis* rolling so much Dora and I glad to lie on the floor, so decided to go to Oban arriving at 12.30 p.m. After lunch on shore had a pleasant walk.

August 30th, Thursday. Left Oban 6 a.m. through Sound of Mull for Staffa and lana hoping to land but found it impossible so only saw the caves from the yacht. We expected to reach Belfast but the wind was so high and right against us. The Captain and Thomas decided to run for shelter to Bonahaven Bay in the Sound of Islay. Landed and had a pleasant walk.

August 31st, Friday. Started at 6 a.m. and again had a very heavy sea but arrived at Belfast at 4 p.m. We landed and Mr. Harland met us and we drove to see Mrs. Harland at Ormiston. We had some tea then called on Mr. Wolff who was shooting. We however, met him and he gave us some grouse.

September 1st, Saturday. Mr. Wolff came on board to breakfast. Sarah and I went shopping. Left Belfast at 12.30 p.m. and encountered such bad weather decided to shelter under the Isle of Man this morning. It blew a gale all night and the *Vanadis* rolled terribly. Thomas remained on deck all night also the Captain.

September 2nd, Sunday. Left our anchorage for Peel but found we could not get in owing to the wind and decided to run to Holyhead for shelter and arrived about 8 p.m. very thankful. Blowing a gale and torrents of rain. Captain never experienced such weather during 24 years he has been yachting.

September 3rd, Monday. Went on shore after lunch in gig towed by steam launch, it was very stormy. We walked about Holyhead and went to the station where we saw Admiral Dent who said if we remained he would send his steam launch for us to-morrow.

September 4th, Tuesday. Landed after breakfast and had a walk on the breakwater. Admiral Dent sent his steam launch and we sailed about the harbour, lunched on board and then had tea with Mrs. Dent, aboard *Vanadis* for dinner.

September 5th, Wednesday. The wind and sea still high, have decided to remain till to-morrow. Admiral Dent came aboard, said he would send the steam launch. We landed at 2 p.m. and drove with the Dents to see Mr. Stanley and then drove to the Light House, returning on board 7 p.m.

September 6th, Thursday. Started from Holyhead at 6 a.m. raining hard and rough passage. Arrived in Mersey at 12.30 and had lunch then landed. Mr. Imrie met us and we drove out to Waterloo.

In the Autumn they brought the children to London and took lodgings at 102 Mount Street to show them the sights. They visited Westminster Abbey, the Crystal Palace, the Zoological Gardens in Regents Park, which they enjoyed very much, the Tower of London and St Paul's Cathedral. They also had seats for the Lord Mayor's show. They stayed nearly a month and then returned to Beech Lawn, in order to be at home for Bruce's 21st birthday on 12th December.

Whilst gathered there for Christmas they began to get worried as the *Celtic* was several days overdue in Liverpool, and on Boxing Day Mrs Ismay writes:-

December 26th, Wednesday, 1883. Very anxious about *Celtic* she being due Monday and not arrived, fear something must be wrong.

Four days later they had word of the *Celtic* as Mrs Ismay describes in her diary what had happened:-

December 30th, Sunday. Heard *Celtic* had broken her shaft 24 hours after leaving New York.

December 31st, *Monday.* Heard *Celtic* putting back to New York. Thomas very anxious about her.

January 7th, Monday, 1884. T.H.I. very anxious about *Celtic* as she is overdue. I wish we could hear something of her.

January 10th, Thursday. Aboard *Adriatic* for lunch, she is looking very spic and span, this being her first voyage after being overhauled.

January 11th, Friday. Heard news of *Celtic*. She had spoken to s.s. *Anglesey.*

January, 14th, Monday. Britannic signalled *Celtic* and took her in tow on Saturday morning.

January 15th, Tuesday, Britannic and *Celtic* arrived in Mersey. *Britannic* towed *Celtic* to Bar then came on. Two tugs towing *Celtic*. Large crowd assembled on shore to watch arrival of the steamers.

January 16th, Wednesday, Heard of *Germanic,* she being reported by *Westmorland* with shaft broken and returning to Liverpool under sail. This ship took *Celtic's* place. It is singular both ships should be disabled in the same way. We are very thankful to hear of her as Thomas has been exceedingly anxious.

January 24th, Thursday. Very thankful indeed to hear news of *Germanic* getting into Waterford to-day.

January 26th, Saturday. Germanic passing III tow of steam tugs 10 a.m. How very thankful I am to see her.

In April of this year was their silver wedding anniversary, "The 25th anniversary of our wedding year. Received a great number of presents and have great cause for thankfulness for all the mercies we have had bestowed upon us."

At Dawpool, which was nearing completion, they had an inscription put over the front door "This house was built by Thomas and Margaret Ismay in the 25th year of their Married Life." Soon after they moved into Dawpool, Bruce left for New Zealand aboard the *Doric* to see how the new service was working. He had less than a year to complete his apprenticeship in his father's office. As we have already seen, his father, when aged nineteen visited Chile; now he was sending his eldest son to see something of the world. He was away altogether eleven months.

Just before Bruce left he attended a memorable event. There had been great opposition to the opening of a railway on the Wirral, Thomas Ismay having in 1881 attended a meeting in London to oppose a railway to Heswall. But now three years later it was a reality and Mr Gladstone, as a Liverpool man, was asked to officiate at the opening ceremony. The whole of the Ismay family attended:-

October 16th, Thursday, 1884. Went to the cutting of the sod of the Wirral Railway by Mr. Gladstone, along with Bruce. We lunched afterwards and got splendid seats close to Mr. Gladstone and heard every word of his splendid speech. There were an immense number of people present.

The Prince and Princess of Wales visited Harland & Wolff in 1885 and Mr Wolff gave a ball in their honour. Mr and Mrs Ismay travelled over to Ireland to attend this event and were met by Mr and Mrs Pirrie. Mr Pirrie, who had been Harland & Wolff's first apprentice, eventually became Lord Pirrie.

In September a dinner was held aboard the *Adriatic* in the Mersey and the presentation took place of a silver gilt dinner service and his portrait by Millais to Thomas Ismay; at the same time Mr Imrie was presented with some pictures of his own choosing. These presentations were made by the shareholders of the White Star Line, in recognition of the work the two partners had done. This description is taken from the printed book, in which there are photographs of the plate given to T H Ismay at the time:-

An interesting and pleasant gathering took place on Wednesday evening September 16th, on board the R.M.S. *Adriatic* when about 70 shareholders in the Oceanic Steam Navigation Company, better known as the White Star Line, (of which Messrs. Ismay, Imrie Company are the Managing Owners) together with various heads of departments of the firm making in all about 100 guests, partook of dinner. Previous to the presentation to Mr. Ismay of a valuable service of plate designed and manufactured by Messrs. Hunt & Roskell of London, and his portrait, by Sir J. Millais, R.A. and to Mr. Imrie of two pictures selected by himself, one entitled, "Melittion" by Sir Frederick Leighton, P.R.A. and the other "The Feast of Pomona" by L. Alma-Tadema, R.A. The service of plate presented to Mr. Ismay is in silver gilt, and consists of a centre piece, four candelabra, two oval flower stands, four round and two oval fruit stands, two sugar vases and ladles, two claret or water jugs, four goblets, and twelve salt cellars, and spoons. The various pieces have been designed to illustrate the progress of the art of navigation from the earliest times to the present day, its means and objects. The centre piece is a magnificent illustration of the art of modelling in silver and the designer and modeller being Mr. G. A. Carter.

On this piece, and occupying the central position of the whole service, is a globe with the seas and continents marked upon it. Round it are seated figures of four of the chief navigators associated with Discovery; Jason, as leader of the earliest recorded expedition across the seas; Vasco da Gama, the discoverer of the route to India by doubling the Cape; Columbus; and Captain Cook. The base is ornamented with four small groups symbolical of the wind and of the sea and its attributes. At the angles of the plinth supporting the globe are four small groups typical of the four continents.

The lower moulding of this and of all the other pieces in the

*Part of the silver gilt dinner service
given to T H Ismay in 1885*

Service is enriched with the Greek Wave, a symbol of the sea, the base from which the subject – Navigation - springs. Other mouldings are formed of shells, cables, etc. Upon two of the four panels behind the figures of the great navigators are engraved the official seal of the Oceanic Steam Navigation Co. and Mr. Ismay's crest, and upon the other two appears the following inscription:

The Service of Plate, of which this is the centre, is presented to Thomas Henry Ismay, Esquire by the Shareholders of the White Star Line, in token of the esteem in which he is held by them, and in recognition of the fact that to the sound judgment, untiring energy, and singleness of purpose he has displayed in the management of their affairs for the past fifteen years, the prosperity of the Company is mainly due.

The dinner was served at 5 o'clock, and among those present were Mr Thomas HJackson, who occupied the Chair, Mr and Mrs. Ismay, Mr and Mrs Imrie, Mr and Mrs W S Graves, Sir E J Harland, Bart, Mr Wolff, Mrs. T H Jackson, Mr and Mrs Barrow, Mr. and Mrs. Haddock, Mr. and Mrs. Sealby, Mr and Mrs Pirrie, Mr and Mrs John Dugdale, Mr and Mrs. Philip Fletcher, Col. and Mrs McCorquodale, Mr James Jardine, Mr. and Mrs Louis Schwabe, Master C B Ismay, Mr and Mrs Robert Wood, Mr and Mrs G W Wood, Mr and Mrs J W H Lyne, Mrs H Eddowes, Captain and Mrs Spark, Mr William Leach, Mr John Hughes, Captain and Mrs. Leslie, Captain J S Ismay, Mr and Mrs. William Crosfield, Mr Robert Ritson, Mr and Mrs McKean, Mr and Mrs J B King, Mr and Mrs W H Davidson, Mr and Mrs Whiting, Captain and Miss Hewitt, Miss Ethel S Ismay, Miss Ada Ismay, Miss Imrie, Miss Amburger, Mrs Edward Jackson, Miss Crosfield, Mrs. H. A. Hankey, Mr Atherton, Miss M H Jackson, Miss E J Jackson, Mr. E. Hunsey, Mr W H Hughes and Mr G A Carter, (of Hunt and Roskell), Mr C Birchall, Mr R Holland, Mr Harold Lee, Captain Smith (Ship *Dawpool),* Mr S Gordon Horsburgh, Mr George Metcalf, Mr J W Thompson, Mr J E Rudkin, Mr J Marshall, Mr James C Farrie, Mr W Johnston, Mr J T Binning, Captain Hinds, Mr Graham, Mr Greagh, Mr Elliott, Mr John McPherson, Mr W H Wright, Mr Alexander Bruce, Mr. H. A. Pickthall, Mr T H Allen, and Mr J Livesey, Captain Parsell, Purser Russell, and Dr Kelley RJvLS. *Adriatic.*

After dinner was over the speeches followed and below are some of the extracts from them.

The Chairman - Some of our friends who have not had the opportunity of attending the Annual Meetings of the Company may desire to know what has led to our assembling to-day in special honour to our Managers. It may, therefore, be well if I refer to the Annual Meeting held on the 23rd February, 1881. The suggestion which has brought us together arose from the fact that circumstances had considerably changed from the time when the Company was formed and the original Articles of Association were framed. It was suggested and resolved unanimously, that the Articles should be so altered as to give the Managers a larger commission than they were then receiving; but when the proposal was made, Mr. Ismay, on behalf of his firm, at once refused to accept any further remuneration and added, that for better or worse, he was content with the existing arrangements. It was then proposed and adopted with the utmost cordiality, that some special acknowledgment, not only of the Manager's self denial in refusing that offer, but of the excellent way in which they had managed the Company's property, should be made. A Committee was accordingly formed to ask Mr. Ismay to sit for a portrait of himself by Sir J. E. Millais - which portrait I have no doubt a good many of you have seen at the Royal Academy in London- and to accept a Service of Plate, by Hunt & Roskell; and to present Mr. Imrie with two oil paintings to be selected by himself. Now, ladies and gentlemen, naturally some of you will ask how does it come about that so long a time as four years has elapsed between the appointment of the Committee and the completion of their duty? There are many reasons. Mr. Ismay has had to sit for his portrait, which took some time; and I think you will see that such a design as that before you in the Service of Plate could not be obtained in a day, and after it was obtained to have it carefully executed required a much longer time than some of us calculated on. Further, I think that Mr. Ismay himself has wished to delay this presentation, in the hope that the general shipping trade might improve, and we should then meet together under still more favourable auspices.

The Company has had to fight its way from the beginning against the keenest competition, and we have attained a position which I feel we may be all very justly proud of to-day. We have out of our original capital built 64,000 tons of shipping, which have cost over two million sterling; and we have now, in addition to our Atlantic Fleet, of which this noble ship we are in is a specimen, the *Coptic, Ionic, Doric, Belgic, Gaelic, Oceanic* and *Arabic*, in all 55,033 tons of shipping such as there is not to be found in any part of the world (Applause).

Now, I am sure it would not be Mr. Ismay's wish that I should enter upon any fulsome eulogy of his services, but I must take it upon myself to say, not only from my intimate knowledge of Mr. Ismay, but of business in Liverpool generally, that we owe the largest share of our prosperity to him. He has gone into every detail of our work. He has been approachable by everybody great and small, and he has shown a wonderful power of discrimination in finding out the right man for the right place. I may remark also, that we owe not a little to Mr. Ismay's coolness and good judgment into not being led into following in the wake of those who have rushed into large and costly steamers. I do not know what his views as to the future may be, for he has a knack of keeping them to himself, but this I may safely predict, that when he thinks the time has come to build larger and faster boats we, as Shareholders, shall be safe in his hands, for he will consider our interests before either the profit or the fame of the managers - (Applause). I would also mention this in regard to Mr. Ismay - that he has travelled far and wide in the interest of the Company. He has not been satisfied to let ships go abroad without knowing where and to whom they were going and the character of the trade in which they were employed. I now simply ask Mr. Ismay and Mr. Imrie to receive from the Shareholders these tokens of their affection and esteem, and with best wishes from us all - (Applause).

Mr Ismay:
Mr. Chairman, ladies and gentlemen I need not say that it is with difficulty I find words with which to express my thanks for this most generous gift - not because of its intrinsic value, although that is great, but because of the kindly thought which has prompted your spontaneous action in this matter - (Hear, hear). As a work of art your gift is unique. Each detail of the design is instructive, and for me has this special interest, that it recalls in pleasing and connecting form the growth of the Mercantile Marine, with which for over 30 years, I have been closely associated. More than sixteen years ago you entrusted me and those associated with me, with very full power - making us rather working and confidential partners than your Managers - and our pleasant gathering this evening is a sign and token most gratifying to my partners and myself that you believe that your confidence has not been misplaced ...

And now, before I sit down, I dare say you will expect me to say something about the general aspect of the trade in which we are engaged. Undoubtedly shipping is in a very depressed condition; and if we are to look for the cause of that depression, I think we shall find it, in the first place, in excessive tonnage. The sea is covered with ships, without a trade, seeking employment; and the difficulty that weighs most heavily upon the ship owners is, not so much an unlooked for want of cargo, as, that he has placed afloat more ships than there was ever any prospect of finding employment for. Now, in my opinion, what is wanted to meet this exceptional state of things is a reasonable agreement among owners - (Applause) - not to thrust upon overburdened markets more tonnage than it can support. (Hear, hear). But in the fall of last year we were informed, through the columns of "The Times", that my friend, Mr. John Burns, the Chairman of the oldest Company crossing the Atlantic – "Had resolved with his colleagues to preserve a distinct line of pre-eminence in speed and accommodation."

We were also informed that the result of this step would be that – "The area of competition would probably be restricted, and a relative increase in the supply of passengers give larger revenues to the foremost companies, from which the passenger may expect benefit as well as the shareholder."

But a well known Scottish poet has said "The best laid schemes of mice and men gang aft a'gley." (Laughter). And except for the accident of Government employment, the shareholders in the line referred to might by this time have felt that it is possible to grasp at the shadow of prestige, and lose the substance of profit. It is now fourteen years since the *Britannic* and *Germanic* were arranged for, and since then we have not added to the tonnage engaged in the American trade. Of course we have had many protests against what some were pleased to term our "rest and be thankful" policy. But, while I admit that most steamship Companies can maintain a front rank without adding to its fleet steamers embodying all the latest improvements in hull and machinery, still, in such addition, the interests of the Shareholders must be considered, and we, as Managers, must be prepared to satisfy them that the outlay has really been to their advantage. Your presence here to-day is a proof that I have not been altogether wrong in the views I have had (Applause) but, while great credit has been given to my partners and myself to what success may have been achieved, if we had not been ably assisted by a zealous, loyal, painstaking, and efficient staff both on shore and afloat the results might not have been so satisfactory to the shareholders, and, in receiving your congratulations, it is a great pleasure to me to know that I still have around me those who were with me in the early days of my business career (Hear, hear and applause). I do not think there is anything more I can say beyond expressing the hope and belief that, greatly as the shipping trade of this country has developed in the past, there are even greater developments in store for it in the future, and that Englishmen will still see with pride:-

"Instructed Ships sail forth to quick commerce
By which remotest regions are alive;
That make one city of the Universe,
That some may gain-and all may be supplied." - (Applause).

Mr Imrie:

Mr. Chairman, ladies and gentlemen, I can assure you that I greatly appreciate the cordial reception which the toast of my health has met with from you, and I have now to return to the Presentation Committee, and through them, to the Shareholders in the Oceanic Steam Navigation Company, my best thanks for the very handsome testimonial with which they have just presented me. The pictures will ever remind me of the very happy associations that have invariably surrounded your Managers in the discharge of their duties in connection with the business fraught with many cares and anxieties. If any efforts of mine have been of assistance to my partner, Mr. Ismay (who from his inception of the Company has devoted his best energies and concentrated his thoughts by night, as well as by day, to further the interests of the Shareholders, everything else having had to give way to the attainment of that end), I am more than satisfied, and as long as I live, I shall look back with pleasure upon this happy gathering on board of the *Adriatic* (Applause). I may take this opportunity of saying that this steamer, although she has completed her 125th round voyage, is still, as she has always been, one of the most favourite passenger ships in the New York trade. (Hear, hear). I am afraid I have failed to express what I feel towards our kind Shareholders, so I must claim their indulgence, and beg them to believe how greatly I shall always value their very fine gift, which will add such charm and beauty to our home. (Hear, hear).

Mr Ismay then proceeded to propose the next toast, which was that of "The Builders", Messrs. Harland & Wolff, and he said:

Mr. Chairman, ladies and gentlemen, you have given a great

deal of credit to your Managers to-day, but what could your Managers have done unless good ships had been placed in their hands? It is with much pleasure, therefore, that I rise to propose the toast of "The Builders" (Applause) and I am sure you will agree with me when I say that never did a toast deserve to meet with more cordial acceptance. To Sir Edward Harland, the designer and builder of the pioneer steamer of the White Star Line, the *Oceanic,* our thanks are more particularly due, for never was more beauty or greater strength and stability wrought in iron since the metal was introduced into shipbuilding than was put afloat when that steamer was launched (Hear, hear). Let me read to you what I saw, when I was in Japan, in a newspaper published at Yokohama. The writer is criticising a newly arrived steamer, of which he speaks in high terms, and says:- "We find it difficult to describe any vessel without taking as a standard of naval beauty that superbly graceful and perfect steamship the *Oceanic,* a masterpiece of naval architecture, for no vessel built approaches her in any way; if, therefore, fault is found with other vessels, they only suffer from comparison with the most perfect model with which we have knowledge."

Some of you will, no doubt, remember when the *Oceanic* made her first appearance, how public interest was excited by her great length, her admirable proportion and her novel, but stately rig. Great expectations were formed regarding her, both by her owners and builders, in which, however, all nautical critics at the time did not join. But the steamer more than fulfilled our most sanguine hopes, and on her second homeward trip logged 384 miles in one day, on a consumption of 70 tons of coal - a run at that time unprecedented (Hear, hear). What may be said of the *Oceanic* is to be said also of all the succeeding steamers; they have performed their work, summer and winter, with a speed and regularity which, taken as a whole, I venture to assert is unequalled. I say this, and say it emphatically, because, while others have paid our builders the high compliment of following their lead, they have not always had the grace to admit the skill they were endeavouring to imitate. (Hear, hear!) ...

In January, 1873 the *Baltic* crossed from New York to Queenstown in 7 days, 20 hours, 9 minutes. The *Britannic* nearly 12 years old, and with her original boilers on board made the passage from New York to Queenstown last October in 7 days, 11 hours on a consumption of 100 tons a day. And I may add that, since the White Star Line has carried the mails, the Post Office authorities have it on record that this Line can show shorter and more uniform time than any other Line on the Atlantic, if fleet be compared with fleet. (Applause) ...

Now Harland & Wolff gave us boats in which speed was obtained upon lines as profitable to the owners as creditable to the builders. They neither trebled consumption of coal nor reduced cargo capacity, and bearing these important points in mind, what they have done has yet to be beaten. (Hear, hear). I make these remarks because it is only fair that we should understand that the obligations we are under to our builders are of no ordinary character. (Hear, hear). We simply said "Give us the benefit of your experience and skill, and do your best to build steamers fitted for the most trying and exacting trade in the world." How well they performed their task is to be seen not only in the Atlantic trade. In the Pacific the *Arabic* has made the passage from Yokohama to San Francisco in 13 days, 21 hours, and the *Oceanic* in 14 days, 5 hours. The *Doric,* too, has made the passage from New Zealand to Plymouth in 37 days, 11 hours. All these passages were, at the time they were made, the fastest on record. (Hear, hear). Thus you see that, while we entrusted our builders, they threw heart and soul into their work. The result is that they have not only served us, I venture to say have served the interest of commerce all over the world. To Harland & Wolff belongs the honour of having placed upon the seas a type of steamer which was unknown until their genius created it, and which has since been accepted as the standard of the highest class of ocean going steamers, and they have thus conferred a benefit upon mankind; for as has been said by Lord Macaulay:- Projects which abridge distance have done most for the civilisation and happiness of our species.

(Applause).

Sir Edward Harland:
Mr. Chairman, Mr. Ismay, ladies and gentlemen permit me to take this, my first opportunity of conveying to you the most sincere thanks of Lady Harland for the most valuable present which, she says you could have given her, in the portrait of myself, which through your great kindness and consideration, you

were pleased to present to her last year. She says it has one charm, and that is that it is a vast improvement upon the original (Laughter) and another is, that the silver wedding marks in our experience the completion of 25 years of - in our instance, at least - happily married life (Hear, hear) and her desire sincerely is, that when this Company shall also have completed the 25th year of its existence you may have been able to know as much happiness and prosperity in your union of Managers and Shareholders, and that, in the meantime, you may have had many golden years of success. (Applause) ...

The result has been that for the last eight or nine years your Company has not added to its Atlantic fleet. I am told the period is much longer than that - 11 or 12 years. Time has completely outwitted me. I had no idea that so long a period had passed since the *Germanic,* your last vessel built for the Atlantic trade was sent out to do business for you. The result is even more interesting, for it shows that, during these long years of serious competition your old vessels have been able to compete successfully against newer, and faster, and larger vessels, with their splendid load of nothing in them and producing less than that as a dividend to their Shareholders. (Laughter). It was fortunate for us that we had such excellent supervision at our command. Mr. Ismay has travelled the world over, and, with a thorough knowledge of ship owning was at our call on points where a shipbuilder could be ready and anxious to consult the owners. On those occasions he was at our elbow to assure us when we had any doubt and to decide when it was beyond our particular duty to determine a question. (Hear, hear) We had only one idea, and that was to produce, not only the finest ships, but, commercially, the most successful that could be. It is, therefore, with immense pride that I am here to-day with my partners-all but one-to witness this interesting ceremony (Applause) and I doubt if there be such men to be found anywhere as your Managers. London may boast of many marvellous financial concerns, but when we come to docks and steamships there is no place like Liverpool; and I doubt whether anyone shows such perfect management as this; management conduces mainly to the success of an enterprise (Hear, hear) ... Whether you will find it prudent to remain contented with your present vessels is not for me to say. Your Managers we find to be very cautious indeed (Laughter) and although we may barely surmise that not far distant may be the day when they must launch again into something new, there is one thing I will undertake to say, and that is that when completed and floated on this mighty river, you will still have a vessel designed not merely to carry one class of traffic, though that may be the highest-the passenger trade ... Long may that success continue; if we should have the good fortune to be in any way called in and entrusted with your orders, our utmost efforts shall not be wanting to maintain and strengthen the reputation of the White Star Line (Applause).

Mr G W Wolff:
Mr. Chairman, ladies and gentlemen when I came here this afternoon, Mr. Ismay told me, to my surprise - I may almost say, my disagreeable surprise - that I should be called upon to propose a toast. The toast is the health of "The Shareholders' Committee" who have selected this testimonial to Mr. Ismay and Mr. Imrie. It does not often fall to my lot to take the ornamental part of speech making. That is generally done by my partner, Sir Edward, while I attend to the more serious part of the business. (Hear, hear and laughter). But the toast which I have now to propose does nor require any special effort on my part. I am sure nothing could be more gratifying, not only to the recipients, but to the Shareholders who make the presentation than the ceremony of this evening. I do not understand why other and older companies have not had similar presentations (Laughter). It may be that I am so much from home, and do not study the news of the day as I ought to; but I don't recollect seeing that the Shareholders of the oldest Company presented their Managers or Directors with services of plate though, after the example we have set this evening it may be imitated. The only fault I have to find with the Committee is the long time they have taken before giving us this opportunity of meeting. I don't know the reason but it does not seem to have been lack of funds, for there is enough, not only to pay for what there is here, but to present Mrs. Ismay with another portrait. All I can say on behalf of the Shareholders is that we feel exceedingly obliged and indebted to those gentlemen for the trouble they have taken, and for the very beautiful results of their labours ... I was very glad to hear what was said about my uncle, Mr. Schwabe, for no man could take a greater interest in this Company. I do not think that without his assistance from the very beginning, this

Company would have taken the position it holds at present . . . I am sure that there is no man who has done more than Mr. Haddock. He travelled with us the first trip the *Oceanic* made, and Mr. Barrow has since gone round the world - there could be no better advertisement for your ships than that. Therefore, ladies and gentlemen I ask you to join in drinking the health of the members of the Committee, who have shown so much taste in selecting this testimonial, and have laboured so much in connections therewith. (Applause).

After speeches had been made by several more of the company the proceedings closed. Three days later the Press had the following to report:-

LIVERPOOL REVIEW, SEPTEMBER 19th, 1885.
Whilst other steam ship companies have been groaning under the pressure of the times, no sign of distress has been heard to proceed from the Office in Water Street, where the White Star Shareholders find their destinies guarded and their interests "taken in and done for" by Mr. T. H. Ismay and his partner, Mr. W. Imrie. Rumours have from time to time found their way around the mercantile community as to the happy fate of the Shareholders in this Line. Now the cat is out of the bag with a vengeance; and it appears that during all the time of the depression from which others have suffered, the White Star has come out not only scatheless, but actually the better off. They have had, as it were, a mark placed on their portals, and the demon of ill luck has passed them over in the course of his devastating flight. Now this good fortune, of course, is not without cause, and that cause is not difficult to find. Shrewd and far seeing caution, together with enterprise, judiciously set forth at the right moment and in the right direction - and that is the talisman which has secured the brilliant result; and the Shareholders by their magnificent presentation to Messrs. Ismay and Imrie on Wednesday have shown a worthy appreciation of those gentlemen's earnest and self denying labours. The service of plate, which has been three years in the manufacturer's hands - thanks to its complex and ornate character - cost over four thousand guineas, and the portrait of Mr. Ismay, by Sir J. E. Millais, represents one thousand guineas more. The pictures, by Sir F. Leighton and Mr. Alma-Tadema, which

were presented to Mr. Imrie, also represented a large expenditure, and yet the presentation fund is not exhausted, and it is just a little bit of a problem to find a use for the balance. In such princely fashion do the lucky Shareholders in the White Star Line reward the labours of their Managers.

CHAPTER 7

Bruce Ismay's New Zealand tour, the collision between the 'Britannic' and 'Celtic', founding of the Liverpool Seamen's Pension Fund, T H Ismay's Indian tour

At this time competition between the various North Atlantic shipping companies, White Star, Cunard, Inman and Guion Lines, was intense. Some years previously in 1878 the head of the Cunard Line, John Burns, had sought to eliminate one whom he knew to be a formidable opponent by suggesting to T H Ismay that their two companies should be amalgamated. But Ismay refused as he did not consider it in the interests of his shareholders; correspondence between the two men continued for some years and below are some extracts which indicate the different policies of the two companies:-

10, Water Street, Liverpool.
February 3rd, 1885.
To John Burns Esq.,
Wemyss Castle.
Dear Mr. Burns,
Since I had the pleasure of seeing you here last month, I have given considerable thought to the subject of our conversation as to how the existing condition of the New York trade can be dealt with, in order to bring about a more satisfactory state of things, and perhaps it may be well if I now lay before you the views I have formed, in the hope that we may yet be able to come to some understanding which would benefit the trade generally.

This appears to me to be all the more desirable at the present juncture, when, in face of the fact that the volume of business with the United States has for some time past been showing a serious and continuous shrinkage, large additions of tonnage are still being made to the trade-already overburdened with it - the bulk of those additions emanating from the Company of which you are the Chairman.

At the outset then, as the Cunard and White Star Lines, associated with the Inman Line hold the Mail Contract from this side, it appears to me that we should first consider how we can make the Tuesday, Thursday, and Saturday sailings from Liverpool as efficient as possible to the Postal Authorities, Passengers and Shippers, those days giving a good workable division of the week. In order to effect this advantageously, something should be done to improve the Inman sailing on the Tuesday in which my Company will be glad to assist, or we would willingly fall in with any arrangement you might make with the Inman Company to that end. For example the *Gallia* and *Oregon,* instead of being despatched as extra boats on alternate Wednesdays, might possibly be arranged to sail on the Tuesdays in place of two of the Inman steamers.

It is to my mind a question whether the introduction of your additional tonnage into the New York trade (bringing up your total tonnage in 1885 to nearly double that of 1880), the bulk of which is added at a time of greatly reduced passenger and freight business, is likely to benefit your Company, for I find that, in some weeks during which your rearranged sailings are advertised, your steamers alone would accommodate twice the number of saloon passengers that are likely to be crossing, and, as the other Lines in the trade may reasonably hope to secure, at least, a share of the passenger traffic, it follows that such numbers as the Cunard Company may be able to obtain will be totally inadequate to remunerate them for the extra steamers employed. As bearing upon this I refer you to the figures given in your first and last published statement of accounts:-

1880:
Tonnage: 61, 379
Profit: £161,016
Earnings per ton: £2 12s 6d

1883:
Tonnage: 82, 945

Profit: £91, 343
Earnings per ton: £1 2s 0d.

The change which you propose to make in your sailing day from New York, from Wednesday to Saturday, is one which I view with much concern seeing that it will cause the Cunard and White Star sailings to clash, with the inevitable result of aggravating the present intense competition and further reducing rates, already low enough.

So far as the White Star Line is concerned I may remind you that it is 11 years since the *Britannic* and *Germanic,* the last additions to our New York fleet, were launched, and, although I can assure you we have every desire to avoid aggravating the difficulties of the situation by adding to our tonnage and would much prefer to adopt the motto of "Live and let live", your action, if persisted in, will necessarily compel my company to build more powerful steamers for the trade, in self defence.

I hope it is needless for me to say that in thus addressing you I have been actuated by the most friendly motives, and it only remains for me to add that, as so great a responsibility attaches to the management of enterprises such as those with which we are both intimately connected, it will be a source of much gratification to me if any good result should be the outcome of this letter.

I remain, dear Mr. Burns,
Yours faithfully,
Thomas H. Ismay.

The following day Mr Burns replied to Mr Ismay:

30, Jamaica Street, Glasgow.
February 4th, 1885.
Dear Mr. Ismay,

I have received your letter of yesterday, and will be glad to see you when I go to Liverpool next week for my Board Meeting; but in the meantime, let me say, that I do not share the views which you expressed in regard to the probability of the Cunard Company being inadequately remunerated by the policy which has been inaugurated by the Directors.

The experience of the past can bear no affinity to the

prospects of the future, and I am strong in the belief that with the fleet which we now possess we are bound to utilise the capital to the best advantage in the interests of our Shareholders - and that can only be done by the rotation of our ships in a shorter period of time than we have hitherto been able to accomplish.

The scheme of sailings, therefore, to which you allude, has been considered and decided upon, purely from a mechanical point of view, without the primary intention of following the example of others in impinging upon days of sailing which have been appropriated by different lines of steamships. In the case of the Cunard Company, their day of sailing has been attacked by many marauders, and, let me remind you, good naturedly, by yourself when it suited your purpose.

As to the White Star Line building more powerful steamers, I have not a word to say-simply because it does not concern me nor would it weigh with me in the conduct of affairs relating to the Cunard Company.

I thoroughly appreciate the motives which have influenced you in writing to me as you have done, and I cannot too strongly endorse the feeling which you express, of the responsibility inseparable from the management of maritime enterprise at all times, but especially so as affecting the interests which you and I have at present to guide and protect.

I fully reciprocate your desire that good results may follow from any intercourse which may take place between us.

Believe me,
Yours sincerely,
John Burns.

Two days later Mr Ismay followed up with:-

10, Water Street, Liverpool.
February 6th, 1885.
Dear Mr. Burns,

I have your letter of the 4th instant, upon which I refrain from passing any comment further than this.

I cannot admit that the occasional sailing of the *Baltic* as an extra ship, to relieve the pressure of our saloon and steerage business during the season only, (when the Cunard Company were also despatching extra sailings), and to which I presume you specially refer, bears any comparison to the organised weekly opposition to the White Star Line which the Cunard Company are about to inaugurate.

I remain, dear Mr. Burns,
Yours faithfully,
Thomas H. Ismay.

In addition to these differences of opinion, discussions were also going on with the Post Office as to the subsidy that the shipping lines would receive for carrying their mail. Below is an extract from the personal file kept by Ismay, Imrie & Company on their dealings with the Cunard Steam-Ship Company.

MEMO Re: *Cunard Steam Ship Company.*
November 19th, 1885.
T. H. Ismay met John Burns in London, when latter proposed to give notice to the General Post Office to terminate contract, in order that the Cunard Company might be in a position to treat for a larger share of Mail Money, Inman & Company being no longer capable of efficient service, and Cunard Company possessing expensive fleet.

November 27th, 1885.
John Burns wrote Thomas Ismay that failing a satisfactory adjustment with Inmans, re Mail Money the Cunard Company must give six months' notice to terminate contract, informing Post Office that upon its expiry, the Cunard Company would be prepared to offer a postal service twice a week on terms to be arranged.

December 22nd, 1885.
Agreement concluded between Cunard, White Star and Inman Companies whereby the two latter companies agreed to pay to Cunard Company one-third of their mail earnings, notice given the 1st June, 1886 to terminate contracts with Cunard, White Star and Inman Companies, on 1st December, 1886.
From March 1st, 1887 when new mail contract with Cunard and White Star commenced to December 31st, 1889 White Star paid Cunard one-fifth of their half share of Mail Money, in consideration of superiority of Cunard service, the payment thus

being continued four months after the *Teutonic* began running.

Just before Christmas in 1885 Bruce Ismay came home. He was nearly twenty-three years old and had developed into a fine looking young man. He was 6 ft 4 in tall, slim and athletic, always immaculately turned out. While on his tour of New Zealand and Australia he had played a lot of tennis and had umpired some of the matches in Australia. He had greatly enjoyed the trip and benefited from the experience of meeting so many different people.

His father met him at Liverpool and was pleased to see him again. They did not always see eye to eye and there was a feeling of constraint between them owing to Thomas Ismay's unconscious jealousy of his son. However, Bruce had affection and respect for his father, although he was frequently hurt by his rather harsh manner. His mother was delighted to have him home for Christmas. This year there was a large party at Dawpool and nineteen sat down for Christmas dinner.

But Bruce was not to be home for very long; he soon departed to New York where he was to gain experience in the White Star office, with the idea of later becoming White Star agent there which he did in May 1887, thus becoming the youngest agent to represent a leading shipping company.

In some ways he was unfortunate. It is a curious fact that whenever a major change took place in his life, a disaster, completely outside his control also occurred, culminating in the worst disaster of all, the sinking of the *Titanic* in 1912. Three weeks after he took over the agency, the *Britannic* which was bound for New York collided with the *Celtic* which was on passage for Liverpool. This occurred in dense fog, about 300 miles east of Sandy Hook at 6am. The *Britannic* was immediately stopped when she was struck by the *Celtic* and the boats were lowered. Panic broke out amongst the steerage passengers, mostly emigrants, and the captain was forced to use his revolver to maintain order. Both vessels were badly damaged and their masters decided to return to New York in company with each other, showing electric lights and firing guns at one-minute intervals.

T H Ismay was most concerned about this accident, about which sensational articles appeared in the New York papers; as

Mrs Ismay records these "were most distressing to read".

An inquiry was held at New York on June 7th and 8th before Mr W R Hoare, Her Majesty's Acting Consul General. The evidence given was that the *Britannic* was going at 15.5 knots and the *Celtic* dead slow. Both vessels had heard each other's signals, but only came in sight of one another at a distance of 300 or 400 yards. Their position was then at right angles to one another, *Celtic* heading for *Britannic*'s port side. In the hope of clearing the *Celtic,* Captain Perry, of the *Britannic,* put his vessel full speed ahead but too late; the *Celtic* struck her abaft the engines, in No 4 compartment which immediately filled.

Celtic's bows were severely damaged just before the bulkhead.

Both vessels returned to New York safely, but three of the *Britannic*'s steerage passengers were killed and nine injured. At the inquiry both captains were censured for going at an excessive speed during fog. The captain of the *Britannic* was further reprimanded for not sounding his whistle and not reducing speed on hearing the *Celtic*'s whistle.

Soon after Bruce left for America the new church at Thurstaston was dedicated. It had been built by the two daughters of James Hegan, the previous owner of Dawpool, in memory of their father. Mr and Mrs Ismay had presented a window in memory of their eldest daughter Mary and their son Henry who had both died many years previously. The local residents were delighted with the appearance of their new church, but it presented certain problems. Mrs Ismay commented, "The church looks very nice, but it is bitterly cold and very damp, the heating does not seem to work properly". It was in fact closed for some months whilst various improvements were made; later she records "In our new church again, at last the new furnace seems to answer".

Several interesting developments were taking place in the district about this time. The railways were expanding and communications generally were greatly improved. For some time previously, work had been going on to connect Birkenhead with Liverpool by an underground railway tunnel. Previously it had only been possible to cross the Mersey by ferry-boat.

February 1st, Monday, 1886. We crossed to Liverpool in the new Mersey railway getting in the train at Borough Road and were exactly 10 minutes in reaching James Street Station.

This was a great convenience for those living on the Birkenhead side. In addition to this they were extending the railway up the Wirral to West Kirby, and in May Mrs Ismay writes:

May 8th, Saturday, 1886. Mrs. Haddock and I left London at 1.30 p.m. Changed at Hooton and came to Thurstaston, it is a great convenience being able to come direct.

T H Ismay was by now an important figure in Liverpool and when he moved to Dawpool he also became involved in local affairs in the County of Cheshire. He was made a magistrate and travelled to Chester to be sworn in. He was also interested in the management of the West Kirby Infirmary of which he eventually became a governor.

This year saw the Ismays entertaining royalty. The Prince of Siam called at Dawpool on January 5th 1886, and later in the year when the Queen came to the Exhibition in Liverpool, the Mayor asked Mr Ismay to "entertain the Queen on board the ferry boat *Claughton* for tea and accompany her on the river", which he did.

Their children were growing up fast. Ada and Dora were 14, Lottie and Bower 12, so it was decided to send the girls away to boarding school. Mr and Mrs Ismay went to look at various establishments.

February 13th, Saturday, 1886. Went to Rickmansworth to see Miss Forbes. It is lovely country, but we think the Miss Forbes too old. I fear they have passed their best.

Finally they decided on a school at New Southgate, North London. In October Mr and Mrs Ismay wished to travel to London to see the girls; they decided to make the journey into a short holiday and to drive there in the American carriage. It must have been a delightful drive right across rural England and below are Mrs Ismay's impressions of the trip:

October 2nd, Saturday, 1886. Left Dawpool at 9 a.m, Starting on a driving tour, intending to drive to London. Thomas, myself and Taylor in the American carriage, a most lovely bright day. Drive to Hawkstone 45 miles.

October 3rd, Sunday. Went to Hawkstone Church. Bruce joined us at 12.30 p.m. After lunch walked though Lords Hill Park.

October 4th, Monday. Left Hawkstone Hotel at 10.30 a.m., Bruce going home by rail. Called at Mr. James Bibby's where we had lunch, then drove on to Bridgnorth where we spent the night. 35 miles.

October 5th, Tuesday. Left Bridgnorth at 10.15 a.m, Drove through lovely country to Stonebridge where we lunched and rested the horses, then drove on to Birmingham. 30 miles.

October 6th, Wednesday. Started from Birmingham at 1 p.m. Reached Coventry at 3.30 p.m. Had tea then drove to Combe Abbey to call on Mrs. Lloyd. She was in Scotland, but the housekeeper took us over the house, which belonged to Earl Craven and is full of interesting pictures. Afterwards called on Mrs. Moon.

October 7th, Thursday. Left Coventry at 10.30 a.m. for Kenilworth and saw there the lovely rooms. Drove on to Wroxhall Abbey, where we lunched with Mr. and Mrs. Broughton Dugdale. Then on to Leamington 18 miles. The cobs look quite fresh.

October 8th, Friday, Left Leamington 9.45 a.m. for Warwick, saw over Warwick Castle, which is very grand then on to Stratford-on-Avon. Went through Shakespeare's house and the Church where his tomb is, then on to Banbury. 35 miles.

October 9th, Saturday. Bought a little furniture for the Lodge, then left Banbury at 10.30 a.m. for Buckingham where we lunched starting again at 3 p.m. for Aylesbury. 35 miles.

October 10th, Sunday. Left Aylesbury at 9.15 a.m, The hotel so dirty we really could not stay, so went to Bentley Priory. 30 miles.

October 11th, Monday. Left Bentley Priory for Hatfield and went over the Marquis of Salisbury's, drove to New Southgate to see Ada and Dora, reached Euston at 4.20 p.m. where we left the cobs after an enjoyable drive of 280 miles.

In the year 1887 Queen Victoria had been on the throne for 50 years and the whole Empire was making preparations to celebrate her Golden Jubilee. As it was also T H Ismay's fiftieth year, he decided he would like to mark the event by something permanent, and below is a letter he wrote to the Mayor of Liverpool in this connection:-

Dawpool,
Thurstaston, Birkenhead.
June 4th, 1887.
Dear Mr. Mayor,
The forthcoming celebration of the 50th Anniversary of Her Majesty Queen Victoria's accession to the throne of England is an event of the widest significance, in-as-much as it not only serves to remind us of the many blessings which have been bestowed upon the nation during her long and prosperous reign, but it also affords exceptional opportunity to those who may have been favoured to testify their thankfulness by giving help to projects for the promotion of the welfare and happiness of their less favoured fellow countrymen.

Liverpool, as the greatest seaport in the world, has a numerous sea-faring population, amongst whom, much distress exists, frequently from circumstances beyond their control, and whilst considerable assistance has been rendered to the sailor's widows and orphans, beyond the building and partial endowment of the excellent home at Egremont, comparatively little has been done for the sailor himself. Provident Societies are not available for him, as in the case of other labouring classes employed in less hazardous trades and occupations ashore, and the old or distressed sailor who has failed to make provision for his declining years, has too often to rely upon the uncertain assistance of his relatives and friends, or - dread necessity - seek admission to the Work House.

With the object of relieving such cases I would suggest the establishment of a fund on the outlines of the enclosed memorandum, to be called "The Liverpool Seamen's Pension Fund", towards which I should be pleased in acknowledgment of the completion of my fiftieth year to contribute £20,000, and from the interest of which pensions of £20 per annum may be granted to old and worn out Liverpool sailors. I do not propose that this fund shall be numbered amongst the already long list of charities seeking subscriptions as their principle means of support, but donations or bequests would naturally extend its sphere of usefulness, and it will be managed without expense of any kind, and the whole of the income derived from it will be applied to the object which I have in view.

Believe me, dear Mr. Mayor,
Yours very truly,
Thomas H. Ismay.

MEMORANDUM

The object of the fund is to provide pensions for British sailors who have sailed out of Liverpool, or in Liverpool owned ships, and who have been unable to make adequate provision for their declining years.

The pension, which it is proposed shall be fixed at £20 per year will not be granted to any person other than a British sailor and will be continued at the absolute discretion of the Committee.

No person should be eligible for the pension who is able to serve at sea, or who has not attained the age of 50 years. Those persons only will be admitted as candidates who can prove 25 years of service at sea in the Mercantile Marine as Captain, Deck Officer or Seaman. The fund may be vested in the name of the Mercantile Marine Service Association, who will have the power of selecting suitable candidates for the pension.

T H Ismay's wife as usual, approved her husband's action, and she records June 4th Saturday, 1887, in her diary:- "Thomas sent a letter to the Mayor announcing his intention of giving £20,000 to found the Liverpool Seamen's Pension Fund. May God's blessing rest on this work."

And on June 6th, Monday, 1887 she writes:- "Thomas's gift appeared in the papers to-day, it seems to have given universal satisfaction and I am very pleased he has done it during his lifetime, and, trust it may be acceptable in the sight of Him who has given all."

Below is a quotation from a report given by the Mercantile Marine Service Association.

"Mr Ismay is regarded as a friend in thousands of homes, where his name is associated with the comfort, happiness, and prosperity of those who have found pleasure in his service."

A fortnight after the founding of this new fund Mr and Mrs Ismay went to London to see the jubilee procession: "We had splendid seats in the L.N.W.R. offices. We had a grand view of the Abbey. We saw part of the procession after lunch at the L.N.W.R. offices."

The following month there was a review of the Fleet at Spithead and they travelled from Dawpool to attend. Here is Mrs Ismay's description:-

July 22nd, Friday, 1887. Left Euston at 10.30 a.m. joining a large party at Waterloo for Southampton where we went on board the *Banshees,* after lunch steamed through the lines of warships. There are a great number, a lovely day.

July 23rd, Saturday. There is a great crowd aboard the *Banshee.* Mrs. Fletcher shared my cabin. Left Southampton 12 noon to take up our position. The Royal Yacht steamed up about 5.30 p.m. The illuminations were magnificent, I never saw anything so grand. Anchored off Spithead for the night.

July 24th, Sunday. At service on board the *Agincourt,* left Southampton at 8.30 a.m. for London. Got to Euston at 11.30 a.m.

In August they attended another naval occasion when the Channel Squadron came to the Mersey:

August 31st, Wednesday, 1887. Admiral Hewitt distributed the prizes on board the *Indefatigable,* Bruce, Jimmy, Ethel, Dora and myself were there. Mr. and Mrs. John Laird were At Home at the Town Hall. We declined not expecting to land in time. Thomas dined at the Town Hall and met the officers of the Fleet.

As part of the jubilee celebrations, the previous week T H Ismay had opened a new wing of the Bootie Borough Hospital. "A large number of people present. Thomas spoke well, and to the point in all he said. All the children except Bruce and Bower went with me."

Some nine years after the founding of the Oceanic Steam Navigation Co Ltd, in 1878 a Liverpool family named Turner founded a new company known as the Asiatic Steam Navigation Company; its business was principally coastal trading between the ports of India and Ceylon, conveying general cargo and passengers in small steam vessels, which had been given Indian names. The head offices were in Liverpool and years later in 1907, Bruce Ismay became chairman of the company, until 1934 when he retired.

The company, which is still in existence, moved its head office to the present address in London after the 1914 war. Mr Imrie and Mr Ismay had both taken a large interest in the formation of this company and, partly to see its workings and to meet the agents, and partly for a holiday, Thomas and Margaret Ismay set out on a journey to India, taking Mr Wolff with them Mr and Mrs Ismay left Dawpool on October 26th 1887 and did not return home until March the following year.

They travelled over land by train across Europe, doing as much sightseeing as time would allow, whilst passing through France, Switzerland and Italy. At Venice they boarded the s.s. *Niram* and crossed the Mediterranean landing at Alexandria; they visited Cairo, the Pyramids and the River Nile, etc. later they boarded the s.s. *Peshawur* bound for Bombay.

They travelled all over India by train, elephant, pony, carriage and horse and steam launch, and had many adventures; on one occasion the railway lines had been washed away in a landslide so they had to abandon the train and walk some miles before another train could take them to their destination.

On another occasion they were travelling by night sleeper from Lucknow to Allahabad (the City of God). Mr Wolff had a disagreement over the railway fare at Cawnpore station, whereupon the station master cut Mr Wolff's carriage off the train. The following morning on reaching Allahabad Mr and Mrs Ismay were surprised to find no Mr Wolff and Mr Wolff was amazed and very angry to find himself still in Cawnpore station on a siding. T H Ismay after describing the incident records "A most discreditable thing to do."

Wherever they travelled in India, T H Ismay was continually asked the same question, "When are you going to start a White Star service to India?" His reply was "The freights are much too low, but if you care to start a company of your own, my friend Mr Wolff will build you some very fine steamers."

Like most Victorians, one of the most important things in the life of the Ismays was their religion; they always attended church on Sundays and were regular Communicants. T H Ismay was always grateful for all his good fortune and never forgot to thank God for it. He ends the year 1887 in his diary:-

"A most beautiful moonlight night to close the old year, with a feeling of great thankfulness to our Heavenly Father for all His tender mercies;"

and on New Year's Day, 1888 he wrote "May God's Blessing rest on the work of the Year, and grant that I may be useful to others not for my own glory, but in acknowledgement of God's great goodness to me."

CHAPTER 8

Bruce Ismay's marriage. The 'Teutonic' - first armed merchant cruise, Bruce Ismay made a partner and comes to live in England

From March 24th 1888, Mrs Ismay resumed writing her diary, and on this day we read:-

"Arrived home after a delightful, interesting journey to Egypt, India, Burma and Ceylon to find all well."

Whilst they had been away, their son, Bruce, in New York had met and become unofficially engaged to Miss Florence Schieffelin; when he had first arrived in America, disquieting reports were received at home of his behaviour there. He had at last escaped from his father's strict discipline, and the somewhat oppressive atmosphere of restraint that pervaded his home and life at Dawpool. With other young men of his own age, amongst whom was Harold Sanderson, (who was later to become head of the White Star Line), he proceeded to "paint New York very red indeed".

His parents were very worried about all this, and were wondering just what they could do about it, when suddenly the whole matter was resolved. Bruce met Florence Schieffelin, and from then on his whole life was changed, he gave up his former life and thought only of her. She was the eldest daughter of Mr and Mrs George Schieffelin, who were members of one of the oldest and most respected families in New York society. Bruce Ismay was taken to spend a weekend with an English friend on Long Island, which was near the house of a Mrs Hude Beekman, and here he met her favourite niece, a gay and beautiful girl, who was known as the 'Belle of New York', and the young Englishman was enchanted with her; however, at this first meeting she was not particularly impressed with him. After this meeting he watched every afternoon, from the window of a house on Fifth Avenue where he was living, for her to drive past with her aunt with whom she spent a great deal of time.

They met on several occasions and on Thanksgiving Day Mrs Hude Beekman gave a party at the Tuxedo Club, New Jersey, to which he was invited, and, of course, Miss Schieffelin was there too. As soon as he arrived he managed to persuade her to accompany him for a walk by the lake. When they returned, she had agreed to marry him.

Her father was not very pleased with this engagement. It was not that he had any fault to find personally with Bruce Ismay as a husband for his daughter, but he was devoted to her and foresaw that she would be taken to live miles away in England; also he considered that she was rather too young. So he told them that they must wait awhile, until they were absolutely sure of themselves. As Bruce received the same advice from his parents by a letter from India, they agreed to wait one year.

By April the following year it was obvious to Mr Schieffelin that the young couple were very much in love and determined to marry. So he agreed to the announcement of their engagement but he made one condition, which was that Bruce should promise that he and Florence would always live in America. Bruce readily agreed to this, as he liked the United States, and being a popular young man, had many friends there. The engagement was duly announced in the Press on April 7th 1888, his parents' 28th wedding anniversary; below is an extract from one of the newpapers showing typical contemporary American journalism :-

New York 'Truth' April 12th, 1888. "Miss Florence Schieffelin, whose engagement with Mr. J. Bruce Ismay has just been announced, is a charming girl with real brown hair, beautiful eyes and a singularly winsome manner. She has been an undisputed belle during her two seasons and a number of swells, who grow on our native heath feel desolated that an Englishman, be he never so desirable, should have won such a genuine prize. Miss Schieffelin is the daughter of Mr. George R. Schieffelin. Her mother was a Miss Delaplaine, a name that is a guarantee for beauty, brains, birth and worth. She is a niece of that gracious and graceful woman, Mrs. James Hude Beekman."

On December 4th, 1888, at the Church of the Heavenly Rest they were married, and below is a description of this event:-

New York 'Ocean', December, 1888. The marriage of the young and popular agent of the noted White Star Line, Mr. J. Bruce Ismay, to Miss Florence Schieffelin, the handsome daughter of Mr. and Mrs. George R. Schieffelin of 8, East 45th Street, took place December 4th. Miss Florence made one of the handsomest brides of the season; and, as she walked up the aisle of the Church leaning on her father's arm, she did indeed look beautiful, arrayed as she was in a dress of white satin brocade, with long round train, and front of silver embroidered mull, her ornaments were diamonds and pearls; her bouquet, white roses and lilies of the valley. Her two young sisters acted as maids of honour, there were no bridesmaids. As is usual on such an occasion, the bride attracted special attention, although the bridegroom was not neglected on this score, which he stood with great fortitude, showing no signs of nervousness, whatever he may have felt. Mr. Ernest Bliss, of England, was best man. Mr. J. Bruce Ismay is a fine specimen of young manhood, being about twenty-six years of age, tall and graceful. He has, at this early age, achieved, what might be deemed an enviable position in the marine world, where he is widely known, popular and a great favourite, as he also is in the social world of New York. His many friends on both sides of the 'streak' are unanimous in their happy congratulations for the future welfare and happiness of this favourite and his bride.

Bruce Ismay's mother was staying in London at the Grand Hotel and she records:-

December 4th, Tuesday, 1888. Bruce and Florence Schieffelin are married to-day at the Church of the Heavenly Rest, New York; may God's best blessing rest upon them.

Meanwhile back in Liverpool quite a lot was happening in the shipping world. The last of the Atlantic mail fleet, the *Germanic,* was now 12 years old and the time had come to start thinking of replacements. During the war scare with Russia three years before, T H Ismay had offered to put the whole of the White Star fleet at the disposal of the Admiralty. Now he put forward another scheme - that vessels should be built under Admiralty supervision and subsidised by the Government, these ships to be readily converted into armed merchant cruisers in the event of an emergency. This was agreed by the Government so the White Star Line promptly asked Sir Edward Harland to draw up plans for two such ships.

These were submitted to the Government and judged to be the best ever put forward; in March 1887, the keel of the first one was laid. This was followed by the second shortly afterwards; there were named *Teutonic* and *Majestic*. They were magnificently fitted, twin-screw vessels of approximately 10,000 tons each and capable of 20 knots. They were the first Atlantic liners to have truly modern silhouettes, as at last, owing to the introduction of twin screws, steamers were able to depend upon their engines alone, and consequently no sails were necessary.

Mrs T H Ismay took a keen interest in the building of these ships and we see from her diary that on July 16th 1888 she went to London and stayed at the Grand Hotel, and went; "To Trollopes and saw a panel for new steamer's saloon. Then went and met Mr. and Mrs. Pirrie at Heatons, to see proposed decorations for Smoking Room on new steamer."

Two months later, they went to Ireland to inspect the new ship, and Mrs Ismay writes:-

September 27th, Thursday, 1888. Arrived at Belfast at 7.30 a.m, having had a beautiful crossing. Mrs. Pirrie's brougham met us, and we went direct to Ormiston. Mr. Wolff and Sir Edward Harland dined with us.

September 29th, Saturday. Mr. Pirrie took us over the Works, and we saw the new boats, their size is enormous. We have had a most pleasant visit to Ormiston.

Just two months previous to this visit to Harland & Wolff to see how work was progressing on the new vessels, the Inman Line took delivery of their two new ships, the *City of Paris* and the *City of New York*. Mrs Ismay went on board the latter:

July 26th, Thursday, 1888. Met Thomas at Liverpool, and we went aboard the *City of New York,* her saloon is important looking with a large dome, but the other part is very low. Library and Ladies' Dressing Room pretty, but the State Rooms very complicated, and dark, and I was not favourably impressed.

It was during this year that T H Ismay was appointed a member of Lord Hartington's Royal Commission on the Administration of the Army and Navy; owing to this he was unable to attend the marriage of his eldest son in New York.

This was not the only Royal Commission T H Ismay served on; four years before he had been a member of Lord Ravensworth's Admiralty Committee, to enquire into the contract system as compared with the dockyard system of building and repairing Her Majesty's ships. In 1889 he was elected chairman of the Board of Trade Lifesaving Appliances Committee, and two years later he served on Admiral Sir George Tryon's Admiralty Committee on the Royal Naval Reserves (Sir George Tryon is chiefly remembered owing to the unfortunate collision between HMS *Victoria* and HMS *Camperdown* when he lost his life).

In 1891 Ismay was appointed to serve as a member of the Royal Commission on Labour; he was frequently asked to stand for Parliament but this he would never do.

But to return to 1888, as the year progressed Mr and Mrs Ismay continued to live the full social life of the time, and amongst other events they attended the Glasgow Exhibition:-

September 6th, Thursday, 1888. In Glasgow for the Exhibition. Breakfasted at 8.30 a.m. and we started for the Exhibition at 10.30 a.m. Spent six hours in it. I think it's one of the best we have seen. A very fine show of steamship models. The man in charge said the White Star Line was an eminent and enterprising firm.

When in London they went to the new Gilbert and Sullivan opera:-

October 16th, Tuesday, 1888. Went to the Army and Navy Stores. In the evening to the Savoy Theatre to see 'Yeoman of the Guard' . It is very pretty, and the music good.

Mrs Ismay at this time offered to furnish a girls' ward at the Convalescent Home:-

August 20th, Monday, 1888. Very wet day. Went to the Committee Meeting at the Convalescent Home, and told the Secretary that if agreeable to them, I would furnish the girls' ward, which they accepted.

October 27th, Saturday, 1888. Drove over to Convalescent Home, and was much disappointed to find the ward all wrong, beds not what were ordered, pictures badly hung. It must all be altered.

In December preparations were going on for the reception of their son Bruce and his bride, but unfortunately Mrs Imrie contracted typhoid; she became very ill and after over a fortnight's anxiety, she died on December 10th. Mr and Mrs Imrie had no children of their own, but an adopted daughter, Amy, to whom Mr Imrie left the bulk of his fortune in trust. She entered a convent when her father died, and on her death the money went towards the building of the new Liverpool Cathedral. Meanwhile, prior to embarking in the *Adriatic* on December 11th to return home to England, Mr and Mrs Bruce Ismay had travelled to Philadelphia where they stayed at the Hotel Lafayette for a few days.

They arrived in England three days before Christmas and Mrs Ismay writes:-

December 22nd, Saturday, 1888. T. H. Ismay went in early and went aboard the *Adriatic* to meet Bruce and Florence, after which they drove out. Bells ringing. Supper at night to over a hundred got up by Jimmy, fireworks and a large bonfire. They met with a hearty welcome from all.

An extract from the *New York Home Journal*, 23rd January 1889 described this happy occasion:-

Mr. Bruce Ismay, son of T. H. Ismay, the respected head of the White Star Line, arrived with his bride a few weeks since, at his father's country place, Dawpool, in Cheshire. The newly married couple received a right royal welcome. A Liverpool paper says; "On the carriage arriving at the entrance lodge at Dawpool, the horses were taken out and the vehicle containing Mr. and Mrs. Bruce Ismay was drawn to the house. In the evening about a thousand of the residents at Thurstaston and Irby were in celebration of the event entertained at supper at Dawpool Farm. Mr. James Ismay, brother of Mr. Bruce Ismay, occupied the Chair. At night a large bonfire was lighted on the Cricket Ground, and there was a display of fireworks, dancing on the green, and a selection of music given by the Hoylake Band. Altogether the homecoming of Mr. Bruce Ismay and his fair bride was made the occasion of a very hearty demonstration and happy reunion among his many friends and neighbours."

The Ismay family were naturally very eager and curious to meet Bruce's wife, and from the first moment they loved her. Her sisters-in-law in particular were delighted with her. With her elegant New York clothes, her American accent and her lack of formality, she brought a new and exciting influence into their lives. This was Victorian England, where young ladies were not even allowed to read the newspapers; and where, unless papa spoke first, a whole meal was conducted in silence. The Ismay girls were accustomed to this heavy sombre atmosphere, but Mrs Bruce Ismay, brought up in a completely different and less inhibited society, chattered gaily throughout luncheon on her first day, much to the surprise of her father-in-law and to the secret admiration of her husband's sisters. The latter were fascinated with everything about her, and when it was time to retire for the night, they all made for the Oak Room (Florence's bedroom), where they persuaded her to show them her lovely trousseau.

She remembers her visits to Dawpool most vividly. It was intensely cold, as the house had no central heating, and fires were not lighted in the bedrooms until teatime. Every night before going to bed she heaped coal on the fire, hoping it would last until morning, but it never did. In spite of the size of the house it was ill-equipped with bathrooms, and it was necessary to have a bath brought into the bedroom, complete with vast copper jugs of hot water with which to fill it. These were so heavy that it was almost impossible for her to lift them.

Family prayers, which included all the staff, were conducted by T H Ismay every morning at 7.30. In order to be ready for these, Florence rose in her freezing bedroom at 6.30. Promptly at 8 o'clock T H Ismay departed for Liverpool. He usually walked to the station at Thurstaston, where he took a train to James Street Station; if as he walked down the drive, he saw a fallen leaf he placed a stone upon it, and if when he came home in the evening it was still there, he would send for all ten gardeners and demand to know what they had been doing all day.

The balls and dances which had been arranged for the homecoming of the Bruce Ismays were cancelled owing to the death of Mrs Imrie. But Mr and Mrs Graves (another of T H Ismay's partners), Were very anxious to meet the bride and asked them to dinner at their home Dowsefield, Allerton, with a special request that Florence should wear her wedding gown. Owing to the intense cold she had severe chilblains on her feet and the only footwear she could get on was an outsize pair of bedroom slippers. So in these, and her beautiful bride's dress, she went to dine.

Soon after Christmas they went to Belfast to stay with Sir Edward Harland, where Bruce spent a lot of time shooting. This was one of his hobbies, and he was an extremely good shot; years later he rented a shoot near Shap, and another in Scotland. His wife accompanied him on one of these expeditions. Being her first experience of an English shooting party, when it started to rain she put up her umbrella, with the result that there was not a bird to be seen for miles. It took her a long time to live this down. When they returned from Ireland, they went to London for a few days with Mrs T H Ismay; on February 20th they returned on board the *Germanic,* to New York where they rented a house, No 444 Madison Avenue.

In the meantime another review of the Fleet was to be held at Spithead in August. Work was progressing on the *Teutonic* at Belfast, so that she could take her place at this review as the first armed merchant cruiser. Below we have Mrs T H Ismay's description of the Prince of Wales' visit to Harland & Wolff to open the new dock:-

May 18th, Saturday, 1889. T.H.I., Ethel, and myself left for Belfast by way of Fleetwood.

May 19th, Sunday. Had a very calm crossing. Mr. Wolff met us at the boat, Sir Edward Harland and Mr. Pirrie lunched with us.

May 20th, Monday. The gentlemen went aboard the *Teutonic,* Mrs. Pirrie had a large garden party. Mr. Wolff had a dinner party.

May 21st, Tuesday. Left Mr. Wolff at 11 a.m. for the *Teutonic.* The Prince of Wales named the new dock, then came on board; Sir Edward Harland, and Thomas received him. He went on the bridge, and we sailed into the dock, and he declared it open. In the evening a ball was given to which we all went.

May 22nd, Wednesday. We lunched at the Town Hall to meet His Royal Highness. I was introduced to him, and he again shook hands. After lunch drove to the Park where the Prince presented new flags to the Black Watch, which was a beautiful sight, we were quite close to him - a beautiful day.

May 23rd, Thursday. The gentlemen on board *Teutonic,* she is a beautiful ship, and I trust she will be as successful as we all wish. We left for home by way of Fleetwood.

May 24th, Friday. Had a delightfully smooth crossing and arrived at Dawpool at 11 a.m. after a most pleasant visit to Mr. Wolff, who has been exceedingly kind.

A month later T H Ismay and W S Graves went over to Belfast for the launching of the *Majestic,* on June 29th.

By the end of July the *Teutonic* was out on her trials; this time Mrs Ismay remained at home but she records in her diary:-

July 27th, Saturday, 1889. A large party of gentlemen went in a special train to Holyhead for *Teutonic* trial trip.

July 29th, Monday. Thomas got home at 6 o'clock, the guests all having enjoyed the trip. Unfortunately they had it very foggy which made Thomas so anxious, he was up all night.

Thomas Ismay loved his ships and whenever he was on board he spent most of his time on the bridge with the captain. In this he differed from his son Bruce, who, after his father died, became head of the firm. When Bruce went on the maiden voyage of most of the vessels, as he felt it was his duty, he spent most of the time in his cabin, away from the captain, the bridge and the passengers, receiving written reports on the ship's progress and behaviour.

William Imrie, who was also very retiring, did not cross the Atlantic often, but on the few occasions when he did so, hardly anyone knew his identity.

While in the Mersey the *Teutonic* was converted into an armed merchant cruiser in 24 hours. She was fitted with eight 4.7 in. quick firing guns, positioned on the hurricane deck, amidships, at the break of the forecastle and on the poop which were specially strengthened to carry this armament. On August 1st she set out thus equipped for Spithead, and as usual, Mrs Ismay attended the event.

August 1st, Thursday, 1889. Seventeen of us left by the 8.45 a.m. train for Liverpool to go aboard the *Teutonic.* Got on board the tender, and found about 180 guests. The day fine, and we had a beautiful sail.

August 2nd, Friday. A lovely morning, and had a quiet night, no one suffering from seasickness. Got to Spithead about 12 noon and had a splendid view of the Fleet, they all dipped as we passed. The German Fleet arrived about 4 p.m. and about ten guests came aboard about 8.30 p.m.

August 3rd, Saturday. A wet rather windy morning. Heard about 2 o'clock that the Review was put off till Monday owing to the weather, which is a great disappointment. A dance was got up after dinner, which the young people enjoyed.

August 4th, Sunday. Had a beautiful little Service on board. At 4 o'clock the Prince of Wales, and German Emperor came on board and went over the ship. We got under way about 5.30 p.m. About 100 guests left the ship.

August 5th, Monday. A lovely morning, the ship quite steady, arrived in the Mersey 6 a.m, Everyone delighted with the cruise, it

Mr and Mrs J Bruce Ismay onboard Teutonic *in 1889*

certainly has gone well. Everyone on board singing the praises of the *Teutonic,* and Thomas for a treat took the *Indefatigable* boys who have contributed much to the pleasure. We landed at 7 a.m.

Everyone was most impressed with the White Star Line's new vessel, especially the German Emperor, who was heard to say to his uncle, the Prince of Wales (later King Edward VII), "We must have some of these."

Two days later having landed her armaments, she sailed for New York on her maiden voyage with the whole Ismay family on board, also the Pirries, and the Carlisles (the Hon Alexander Montgomery Carlisle was Harland & Wolff's chief designer and was later to be responsible for building the *Olympic* and *Titanic*).

August 7th, Wednesday, 1889. Left Dawpool at 2.30 p.m. to go on board the *Teutonic* at 4 p.m. rather a windy day. Mr. Imrie and Mr. Graves came to see us off with several friends.

August 8th, Thursday. Found some nice people on board, Sir Henry and Lady Lock and family, Lady Shrewsbury, Lady Selkirk, Sir Lyon and Lady Playfair. Arrived at Queenstown at 10.30 a.m. and left at 2 p.m. after taking mails aboard. Heard Mrs. Maybrick had been found guilty of poisoning her husband.

August 9th, Friday, 1889. Rather a bad night, also stormy this morning, although we all went into the Saloon for breakfast. It got worse during the afternoon, and one after another succumbed. A high wind, and a nasty sea, which made the *Teutonic* pitch.

August 10th, Saturday. The wind and sea very high, none of us got up for breakfast. But during the day some of us got up on deck. About 10 o'clock the sea came right on board, and took Sir Henry Lock right off his feet. Fortunately he was not hurt.

August 11th, Sunday. None of us able to go to Service except Thomas, but got up and went on deck in the afternoon.

August 12th, Monday. The sea and wind have gone down, but now we have a dense fog.

August 13th, Tuesday. Still very foggy, but had a concert, which would have been a failure, but for Mr. York. Thomas was in the Chair, and made some remarks which amused the audience. A collection was made, and £28 got for the Seamen's Orphanage.

August 14th, Wednesday, It appears that Thomas's remarks have given offence to some people on board, although unintended by him. In fact what they say is both unfair and untrue. Made the land late at night, reaching Sandy Hook just after midnight. Passage 6 days, 14 hours, 20 minutes.

August 15th, Thursday. Bruce came on board about 5 a.m. looking very ill and thin. Florence was on the wharf when we arrived and we landed about 11 a.m. Thomas, Dora, Lottie and myself went to the Windsor Hotel, Ethel, Ada and Bower to Bruces. We all dined with Bruce and Florence.

While in New York they met Mr and Mrs Schieffelin for the first time who entertained them in their home. Bower Ismay met their daughter, Constance, who was later to become his wife. Mr and Mrs Ismay also saw a good deal of their son, Bruce, and his wife. On August 21st they embarked in the *Teutonic* for the return trip to England:-

"We are all very sorry to part from Bruce and Florence, who have certainly made our visit most pleasant. Got under way at 2 p.m."

August 22nd, Thursday, 1889. We have about 110 passengers in the first class. Weather beautiful with a calm sea.

August 23rd, Friday. Another calm fine day, no movement at all, which makes it difficult to realise one is on the Atlantic, everything works so well.

August 24th, Saturday. Very foggy, but clear at times, we saw numbers of fishing boats. At 1.45 p.m. a poor fireman jumped overboard, a boat was lowered and he was saved; a wonderful thing in mid-Atlantic, it occupied 17 minutes before he was on board again.

August 25th, Sundry. Had a very nice Service. It was very foggy all day.

August 26th, Monday. Very foggy indeed, the foghorn going perpetually.

August 27th, Tuesday. A nasty beam sea, which made the *Teutonic* roll very much, but she rode it gracefully so that only the worst sailors noticed it. I managed to go down to dinner, Mrs. Pirrie sang to us afterwards.

August 28th, Wednesday. During the night the rolling ceased, and when we got up the sea had quite gone down. We sighted land at 10.30 a.m., arrived at Queenstown 2 p.m. Jimmy came to meet us.

August 29th, Thursday. Breakfasted at 7 a.m. having arrived in the Mersey at 3 a.m, Making our passage 6 days, 16 hours, 34 minutes. Landed from the *Teutonic* at 7.30 a.m. All very sorry to leave the noble ship. Drove in a cab home, and thought Dawpool looking its best.

In September they paid a visit to T H Ismay's home town of Maryport, where they stayed with the Squire, Mr Senhouse.

September 24th, Tuesday, 1889. Left Liverpool with Thomas by 11.35 a.m. train for Maryport to open a Bazaar there tomorrow. We are staying with Mr. Senhouse at Netherhall.

September 25th, Wednesday, Thomas and I walked up some of the old streets, and then called at Mr. Cockton's and went to see the lifeboat launched, then walked back to Netherhall. Lunched at 1 p.m. and started for the Bazaar at 2 p.m. Large number at the opening. Thomas delivered his remarks nicely, bought a few things, had tea at Netherhall and left for Liverpool by 6 p.m. train.

They were only home for a few weeks, and then they were off on their travels again, this time to Paris where they intended to visit the Great Exhibition. They spent several days in Paris, seeing their daughters, Ada and Dora, who were at school there; amongst other adventures they all climbed to the top of the Eiffel Tower, specially erected by Gustavus Eiffel for the exhibition.

They were back at Dawpool for Christmas, when they missed their eldest son and his wife very much, but were delighted to receive a telegram on December 30th informing them of the birth of their first grandchild, later to be christened Margaret

Bruce Ismay. To celebrate the New Year, they held a dance at Dawpool:-

January 8th, Wednesday, 1890. About 240 here, 40 to 50 falling off at the last, principally from cold. It passed off most successfully. 24 guests were staying in the house.

Later in the year they had a short holiday in Bournemouth and Mrs Ismay writes in her diary:-

March 10th to 17th, 1890. Had a walk on the pier, Sarah and Mrs. Wood are with us. A great number of invalids about, the air balmy and mild. Bournemouth is a pretty place, and delightful for a short time, but very distressing to me to see so many young people evidently suffering from consumption. Drove to Branksome Chine. Drove over to see Christchurch Priory.

For the next two or three months they were in London several times. T H Ismay attended a banquet given by Lord Hartington at the Crystal Palace. He accompanied his wife to the latest Gilbert and Sullivan opera, this time the 'Gondoliers' at the Savoy Theatre. They attended the confirmation of their younger pair of twins, Lottie at her school at Anerley and Bower at Harrow.

Back in Liverpool Thomas Ismay attended the annual general meeting of the Oceanic Steam Navigation Company, and 22 of the shareholders dined at Dawpool.

In July Bruce Ismay and his family came home for a visit on board the *Majestic*. During their stay T H Ismay proposed to Bruce that he and his brother James should be made partners in the firm of Ismay, Imrie & Co. He also told Bruce that if he wished to follow him as head of the firm, he must return to live permanently in England, otherwise James would assume control. It was a difficult decision for Bruce to make, as he and Florence were very happy in New York, and he liked his position as White Star agent. Also on his marriage he had given a promise to his father-in-law that they would always live in America.

At first he decided to continue in the United States, much to his father's displeasure. However, on their return to New York on September 17th, 1890 he discussed the matter thoroughly with his wife and with his father-in-law. Mr Schieffelin advised his daughter that they should agree to let Bruce withdraw the promise, as he felt that he was an ambitious man, and although happy now, would eventually resent his younger brother being head of the firm, and might subconsciously hold it against the Schieffelin family. So they finally returned in September 1891 to find a permanent home in England.

Whilst they were home on holiday in 1890, it was a glorious summer and a garden party was held at Dawpool which over 300 people attended; later the Dawpool cricket club held their annual sports day, when over 2,000 people were present, and "Florence presented the prizes".

In August Bruce Ismay and his wife went to Paris for a few days taking with them his sister Ethel; his parents took the opportunity of a few days' holiday in Wales and they decided to drive with the cobs and the American carriage to Llangollen. On the return journey Mrs Ismay writes:-

September 1st, Monday, 1890. Thomas left for Liverpool by train, I drove back to Dawpool, halting the cobs at Mold for meat and water, and on to Queensferry where we halted again. Arrived at Dawpool 4.30 p.m. having had a very pleasant visit.

On September 17th Bruce and Florence, with their baby and her nanny, embarked in the *Majestic* for America:- "We are all very grieved to part with them."

Later in the month Mrs Ismay went with her husband on a short visit to Ripon and Harrogate, and whilst there they went to see Harewood House which was open on Thursdays: "Did not think much of the building, but it has some beautiful portraits and Chippendale furniture. Visited York and the Minster, which is grand. Drove through beautiful scenery to Bolton Abbey."

At the beginning of the New Year Mrs Ismay records:-

January 1st, Thursday, 1891. Bruce and Jimmy admitted as partners to the Firm. I pray that they may be guided to do what is right, and have the integrity of their father.

January 3rd, Saturday, 1891. A very disagreeable day, thawing. Thomas did my housekeeping up to December. I was sorry to find it considerably in excess of former years. T.H.I. thought it very satisfactory.

In the middle of the following month, they decided to go to Teneriffe and Santa Cruz whilst major alterations and repairs were taking place at Dawpool which would occupy some time. Taking Ethel and Dora with them, they travelled down to Plymouth to await the arrival of the *Ionic* from Gravesend, and stayed at the Grand Hotel. Unfortunately owing to fog the *Ionic* could not leave Gravesend, and the Ismay family were forced to remain in the hotel. Mrs Ismay comments:-

February 26th, Thursday, 1891. After lunch had a wire saying *Ionic* had left Gravesend, so we hoped to get away tomorrow. We shall not be sorry to leave, as this hotel is far from comfortable.

They had a fairly smooth passage out and enjoyed Teneriffe; then went on to Santa Cruz, where again they had an uncomfortable hotel. They were very glad when the *Doric* appeared to take them home. The passage was extremely rough with March winds and Mrs Ismay records:-

March 16th, Monday, 1891. A stormy day, rolling heavily. We all felt very unsocial except Thomas who enjoyed it, and said it was a fine bit of sailing. I only got on to the sofa, and the others not up at all.

The *Doric* arrived at Plymouth and the Ismay family disembarked and Mrs Ismay records:-

March 18th, Wednesday, 1891. Arrived at Plymouth 5 a.m. Landed at 8.30 a.m., got luggage passed and walked to the station, buying fruit, cream, bread and butter on the way. We travelled as far as Templecombe, where Thomas left us going to London. We went to the Imperial Hotel, Bournemouth, where Sarah had taken up excellent rooms.

Returning to Dawpool in April, they found the house still full of workpeople, but were delighted to hear that they had a grandson, who was to be christened Thomas Henry, but was known as Henry. Later Bruce and Florence Ismay had another son, who was christened Thomas Bruce, and who was known as Tom.

By August preparations were in hand for the homecoming of Bruce and his family. Thomas Ismay was appalled at the thought of having his eldest son and his family to live at Dawpool for any length of time, so he decided to rent a house for them. He found Wiston House, Mossley Hill, and Mrs Ismay sent Ellen, one of the Dawpool staff "to go and cook for Florence, wages £30 a year".

Meanwhile in New York they were enduring a heat wave and the baby Henry, who was only six months' old, was suffering from chronic diarrhoea. The doctor, knowing that they were returning to live in England, thought that the sea trip would help the baby to get well. But unfortunately this was not the case. Mrs Bruce Ismay was always an exceedingly bad traveller on the sea, and during this whole voyage was confined to her bunk. The baby was in the care of a young Irish nursemaid who did not give him the attention he required. On arrival at Liverpool, T H Ismay met them off the *Teutonic;* he was shocked at the appearance of the baby and said "That baby is going to die, he must see a doctor instantly". Mrs Ismay describes this day and those that followed in her diary:-

September 30th, Wednesday, 1891. Thomas and Jimmy drove in to meet Bruce and telephoned us to say that the baby was very poorly, and that he had telephoned for Dr. Russell. They got home

Sandheys, Mossley Hill, Liverpool, home of J Bruce Ismay, 1893 - 1920

at 10.30 a.m., and I was shocked to see the little thing looking so ill. Dr. Russell thought badly of him. In the evening the baby got so much worse that we sent for Dr. Russell again, and he remained the night.

October 1st, Thursday. The baby no better. Seems weaker to me. Dr. Russell left at 8 a.m. and returned at 11.30 a.m. Gave him brandy and beef tea, at 3 p.m. he became much worse and at 4 p.m. he passed away. We are sadly grieved about it.

October 2nd, Friday. Thomas in the house all day-in great distress, and very sorry that Bruce and Florence should have such a sad homecoming.

October 3rd, Saturday. Mr. Jackson's carriage with our own with the body, Thomas, Bruce and Jimmy left here at 9.45 a.m. for Anfield Cemetery, where the little baby was laid, they got back here about 3 p.m.

Yet again Bruce Ismay's ill fortune had pursued him, as it seemed to do whenever he reached a milestone in his life.
After the tragic loss of his eldest son, whose death he never forgot, Bruce Ismay rather avoided children; when the other children arrived Thomas, Evelyn and George, he had a large wing built on at Sandheys specially to accommodate them separately, with the exception of Margaret, his elder daughter, to whom he was always devoted.
The remaining weeks of the year were filled for Mr and Mrs Thomas Ismay with their usual round of activities.

November 28th, Saturday, 1891. Thomas and I went to Port Sunlight to the opening of Messrs. Lever's Dining and Recreation Hall by Mr. and Mrs. Gladstone. Mr. Gladstone spoke splendidly, it was a great treat to hear him. Thomas introduced me to him.

Then in December T H Ismay was on the Grand Jury, which necessitated spending a whole day in Chester.

December 21st, Monday, 1891. Thomas told Bruce and Jimmy of his intention to retire from the firm January 1st.

December 25th, Friday. Fourteen of us went to Church, we are 18 at every meal.

On December 29th Mr and Mrs Bruce Ismay moved to their new home taking Ellen with them.

Mrs Ismay ends the year 1891 with the comment "T.H.I. has decided to resign from the firm, but remaining as chairman and retaining full power."

CHAPTER 9

*Disappearance of the 'Naronic', T H Ismay refusing a baronetcy,
T H Ismay's last illness and death at Dawpool*

In 1892 although T H Ismay had 'retired' from the firm of Ismay, Imrie & Company, he remained as chairman, still taking a great interest in its affairs and his decisions on most things was final. He now had more time to devote to the various boards on which he served and to the charities in which he was so interested. Amongst these was a school for deaf and dumb children and in September he took 200 of them for a day's cruise in the *Teutonic*. About this time he became president of the Royal Infirmary and gave £1,000 to start an endowment fund.

There was a lot of unemployment at this time and T H Ismay had some unemployed men from Liverpool transported to Dawpool, where he gave them the task of weeding the heather. He took the view that it was much better for their self-respect to be given a job to do, rather than to live on charity. The story of this episode is still told today in the village of Thurstaston.

He was made High Sheriff of Cheshire and one of his duties was to attend the County Assizes. The whole family went to see T H Ismay in his Sheriff's robes with his Sheriff's carriage; Mrs Ismay recalls she was very sorry when his term of office came to an end.

His son Bruce and his wife went to live in the rented house, Wiston House, in the Mossley Hill Road, and Mrs Bruce Ismay says it was a "horrid house". Her first years in England were not happy. She had just lost her eldest son and was very lonely. Having left all her friends in New York where she was very well-known, she came to settle in the middle of winter in a rented house in a Liverpool suburb where she did not know a soul, and her husband was out all day. Fortunately her younger sister, Constance, to whom she was devoted, came to stay with her for a long period.

At the end of this year T H Ismay's favourite son, James, was married to Lady Margaret Seymour, the eldest daughter of the Marquis of Hertford. T H Ismay did not entirely approve of this marriage, as he felt that he and his family were business people and should not be marrying into the aristocracy. However, he became very fond of his daughter-in-law, and as James had always been his favourite son, he was soon reconciled to the idea.

After he was married James lived at Caldy Manor, about two miles from Dawpool, and every Saturday during the summer he organised a cricket match on the playing field at Dawpool. The Dawpool cricket club played matches against West Kirby, Heswall, etc, and against the Training Ship, HMS *Conway*. T H Ismay was interested in the *Conway*, and he and members of his family attended the prize givings on board. However, he did not feel quite the same about the *Comoay* officer cadets as he did about the boys of the *Indefatigable* (the training ship he had helped to found for poor boys, to assist them to get a start in life).

Shortly after the beginning of 1893, the company met with yet another disaster. Two new ships had been built in the previous year by Harland & Wolff, as cargo and cattle ships, on the usual cost plus basis, to trade between Liverpool and New York. These were the *Naronic*, and her sister-ship the *Bovic*.

On February 11th the *Naronic* left the Alexandra Dock for New York; she put off her pilot, William Davis, at Port Lynas and thereafter completely disappeared; she was never seen or heard of again. On March 4th about three weeks later, the steamer *Coventry*, on voyage to England from Virginia, USA, reported that in latitude 40 N and longitude 47.37 W, at 2am they saw a ship's lifeboat floating keel uppermost with ss *Naronic* painted on the keel. Later, at 2pm the same day a second lifeboat was seen in latitude 44.34 N and longitude 46.25 W.

The Board of Trade ordered an inquiry into the disappearance of the *Naronic;* this was held in St. George's Hall, Liverpool, in July, Mr Paxton appearing for the Board of Trade and Mr Dickinson of Hill Dickinson for the owners.

Mr Paxton said the *Naronic* left the Alexandra Dock on February 11th at 6am with 74 crew, including 14 cattlemen. She carried a general cargo of 3,572 tons and 1,017 tons of Welsh coal. She was a twin screw vessel of 6,594 tons and her total displacement was 10,290 tons. From the stowage plans it appeared she was drawing 20ft 3 ins of water forward and 20ft 9 ins aft. She was on her seventh voyage. Her pilot, Davis, could not leave her at the Bar owing to the high seas, but was put off at Port Lynas, when he reported her as behaving very well; he was the last person to see her afloat.

W S Graves (of Ismay, Imrie & Company) said the *Naronic* was launched on May 26th 1892. She had cost £121,685, there was no contract, and the company were their own insurers. Captain Roberts, her master (lost with her), had sailed in command on her three previous voyages and Captain Thompson (master of the *Bovic)* had been in command on the first three voyages.

Her chief officer, White, had been with the White Star Line since 1874, and held a master's certificate. She was specially built for transporting cattle and had a Board of Trade certificate for 150 passengers. She was 470ft long with a 53ft beam which was divided into ten water-tight compartments and would still float with four open to the sea; she had two triple expansion engines of 3,000 horse-power, which burned 50 tons of coal per day.

There was nothing dangerous in the cargo and no ice within 100 miles. Mr Graves told the Court that her sister ship, the *Bovic*, was in the Alexandra Dock and was open to their inspection.

After very carefully considering the matter from all points of view the Court published its findings, which were that they were at a complete loss as to what had caused the *Naronic* to disappear. She had joined the number of ships which disappeared without trace.

Mr Graves was so upset and worried about the whole affair that be became very seriously ill and Mrs Ismay comments in her diary: "We were very grieved to see Mr. Graves, I sincerely hope the trip to New Zealand will cure him." Apparently it did so, as he eventually quite recovered.

In May of the following year Mr and Mrs Ismay taking their daughters, Ethel and Ada, sailed aboard the *Majestic* for America, to visit the Chicago Exhibition.

Through the kindness of a Mr Webb, the family had a private railway coach attached to the train which took them from New

York to Chicago. They thoroughly enjoyed the Exhibition and returned to New York by way of Washington, again in a private railway carriage. While in Washington T H Ismay went to the White House and had an interview with the President of the United States. After staying in New York for a few days where they were entertained by the Schieffelins (Mrs Bruce Ismay's family) they sailed on May 29th on board the *Teutonic* for Liverpool.

When they reached home they found their son Bruce and his wife had seen a new house which they proposed to purchase. It was Sandheys in the Mossley Hill Road, a large Georgian style house standing in ten acres of ground.

In 1895 the *Germanic* came back into service from Belfast after a complete overhaul, having been re-engined with triple expansions. When she came back to Liverpool T H Ismay and his eldest son were on board to see how she behaved; also in the dock in Liverpool at the same time was the pioneer vessel, *Oceanic*, returned from the Pacific. Mrs Ismay writes:-

May 13th, Monday, 1895. Ethel and I went in by the 10 a.m. train to see the *Germanic*. She has been beautifully done up. New engines, boilers, etc., and looks well. She sails for New York Wednesday next. Then on board *Oceanic* to lunch. It is 15 years since we went out to Japan in her, and she has not been in England since, I looked upon her as my favourite ship but she disappointed me.

One of the great disadvantages experienced by people travelling to and from Liverpool and New York was that the railway station was nowhere near the docks, but in July a new station was opened. Mrs Ismay who was present wrote in her diary:-

July 10th, Wednesday, 1895. The Riverside Station for Atlantic passengers formally opened, Thomas responded to the toast, "Success to the Atlantic trade" and made to my thinking a most excellent speech. The Mersey Docks & Harbour Board gave a large luncheon, Lord Stalbridge and several of the L.N.W.R. Directors came down by special train. The *Majestic* came alongside the stage. Captain Smith in charge for the first time.

This year the family as usual gathered at Dawpool for Christmas and it was here on Christmas Eve that they were shocked to hear of the sudden death of Sir Edward Harland. Thomas Ismay crossed to Belfast to attend his funeral on December 28th. He was very upset at his friend's death. They had been intimately connected for twenty-five years in building up the great enterprise, and the White Star Line owed a great deal to Sir Edward Harland for the magnificent ships that he had built for them. So T H Ismay felt that he would like to make a permanent memorial to him; on the occasion of the Engineers' Dinner on January 29th, 1896, he asked the Lord Mayor to announce that the White Star Line intended to give £2,000 to the trustees of the Liverpool University College, in memory of Sir Edward Harland, for a scholarship to be called 'The Edward Harland Memorial Scholarship'.

The White Star Line had commissioned a new vessel to replace the *Naronic*. It was an enlarged and improved design, and known as the *Georgic*. Both Thomas and Bruce Ismay came round in her to Liverpool from Belfast, "having had a most pleasant trip".

A month later Mr and Mrs Ismay decided to cross to Southern Ireland for the Killarney races. The only convenient vessel available in which to travel to Queenstown was the Cunard *Campania*. Mrs Ismay describes the trip on the rival company's vessel:-

August 29th, Saturday, 1896. I drove to Birkenhead to go on *Campania* for Queenstown. Thomas and Mrs. Fletcher were on board, we sailed at 5 p.m. had a nasty passage and a very small cabin.

They arrived at Queenstown at 5.40am having had "a nasty passage, the *Campania* rolling a good deal". On September 1st they returned home in their own *Majestic* and Mrs Ismay comments "The ship looked beautifully bright and clean".

Forty years after these comments in Mrs Ismay's diary the White Star Line and the Cunard Steam Ship Company were amalgamated. An old White Star captain tells the following story:

When the *Adriatic,* which was then 28 years old, lay alongside the Princes Landing Stage in Liverpool, two Cunard

Thomas Henry Ismay

Officers went aboard her. They were absolutely amazed at her condition, and remarked that she looked exactly as if she had just come from the builder's yard. Then one turned to the other and commented "Oh, well, she'll look just the same as the others when we've had her for a little while!"

Good as the Cunard standards were, there were probably no ships in the world which were kept as meticulously as the ships of the White Star Line.

In April of this year Mr and Mrs Ismay's second daughter, married Geoffrey Drage; the Bishop of Chichester, a friend of the family, took the service in Thurstaston Church. About 400 people were at the reception.

Then in the following year in January, Gustavus Schwabe

died. He had been the original instigator of the founding of the Oceanic Steam Navigation Company. He had retired some years before and died in his home, 19 Kensington Palace Gardens, London, at the age of 84.

In June Mr Ismay joined his wife in London. She had been staying with her daughter Ethel, when he received a letter from a Mr Schomberg-MacDonnell "With reference to an important matter". Mrs Ismay writes:-

June 16th, Wednesday, 1897. Thomas went to the Foreign Office, and found that the Queen wishes to confer a baronetcy on him, which is a great honour particularly as it comes from no political reason, but as a recognition of good work done, and this being the 60th year of Her Majesty's reign. Causes him to waver as to whether he ought to accept. Mrs. Wilberforce - lunched here and strongly urged him to accept.

June 17, Thursday, 1897. Thomas wired for Bruce to come up. He got here at 9 a.m. and we discussed this proposed honour. He was quite agreeable for Thomas to do what he thought best, but from the first Thomas felt that he would rather decline. I am proud he has been offered a Baronetcy, but think he will be happier to remain as he began.

After some hours anxious thought and discussion with his family, and despite various friends and colleagues urging him to accept the offer, he finally decided:-

June 18th, Friday, 1897. Thomas went to Euston and sent his letter to Mr. Schomberg-MacDonnell declining the honour the Queen wished to confer on him. I think he will feel the happier for it and be better satisfied at remaining Mr. Ismay than if he had been Sir Thomas.

Below is the letter to which she refers:-

The Board Room, Euston Station.
June 18th, 1897.
To the Hon. Schomberg-MacDonnell, C.B.
Foreign Office.

Dear Mr. MacDonnell,

With regard to our conversation of yesterday, after giving the matter referred to my most careful and anxious consideration, I have come to the conclusion, that while deeply grateful to Her Majesty for thinking of conferring such an honour upon me, I feel it will be better most respectfully to decline the very flattering proposal. Will you please convey to the Prime Minister my appreciation of the terms on which he conveyed to you the Queen's gracious message, and my regret that I am unable to fall in with his wishes. May I add that I hope Lord Salisbury will understand the spirit in which this letter is written, and thank you personally for your kind expressions.

Believe me,
Yours sincerely,
Thomas H. Ismay.

As well as being the Queen's 60th year on the throne, it was also the year of Thomas Ismay's 60th birthday and to mark the occasion he gave each of his four daughters and his two daughters-in-law £250 each.

Just after this, there was a Review of Her Majesty's ships at Spithead, and again the *Teutonic* was transformed into an armed merchant cruiser, and with a large party aboard she sailed for Spithead. The 170 guests included some of the most prominent people in the land. Mrs Ismay writes:-

June 26th, Saturday, 1897. A lovely day for the Review. The *Teutonic* sailed down the line of ships so that we saw all. After dinner we had some speeches. Thomas spoke very well. It has been a magnificent sight. The illuminations were very grand. The *Magnetic* sailed through the lines to see them.

June 27th, Sunday, 1897. About 160 guests left us at Spithead, Sarah and Robert Wood, Ethel and Geoff amongst them. All delighted with the trip. The Bishop of Chichester read the Prayers and a collection was made for the *Indefatigable*. £55 was collected. Ethel and Geoff at the Queen's Garden Party.

June 28th, Monday, 1897. The *Teutonic* arrived in Liverpool at 11 a.m. Everyone on board highly pleased with the trip. The

Lord Mayor of Liverpool made a nice speech after breakfast, and Thomas returned thanks and made a few very nice remarks. I should think there never was such a successful trip. Everything having gone without the slightest hitch.

The sensation of this review was undoubtedly the appearance of a weird looking craft named *Turbinia*. This extraordinary vessel caused such a sensation that 60 years later her activities are still discussed. As is well known, the Admiralty have always been cautious over adopting anything new, but the Hon Charles Parsons was quite determined to cause such a stir with the new type of turbine engine which he had invented that they could not overlook it. So he brought his little vessel down to Spithead and darted in and out of the line of warships at speeds reaching 32 knots - a speed far greater than any before attained. Admiralty pinnaces etc, set off in pursuit but were left far behind.

The *Turbinia* tied up alongside the *Teutonic* and T H Ismay, his son Bruce, and one of their guests, Sir George Baden Powell, went aboard her and were given a demonstration run.

One of the newspapers of the time reporting the incident says:

They were very daring to go aboard the new scorcher. The vessel steamed quietly enough away, and was lost in the maze of hulls which the perspective afforded. Presently, however, she was described emerging therefrom, and at a rate of speed which it is no exaggeration to describe as terrific, with flames belching from her funnel, with a good third of her keel fairly forced out of the water, and leaving a high curling wake behind, she tore through the seas like a thing bewitched. Those on her deck were seen holding on to the rails and the like, and bending almost double to withstand the wind she created. It was a sight positively staggering while it lasted, and there was almost an uncanny element about it. Presently she slackened speed, and in due time T. H. Ismay and his colleagues returned to the *Teutonic,* where they were questioned about their remarkable experience. Both T. H. Ismay and J. Bruce Ismay admitted that their experience had been unique, not altogether devoid of an element of nervousness. For the inventor of the *Turbinia,* in view of the personality of his guests, had been placed on his mettle, and caused his vessel to put forth every ounce of speed she possessed, with the result that she broke her own speed record, and when observed from the *Teutonic* in the height of her mad career, displaying something over 40 miles per hour.

Although father and son were undoubtedly impressed with this performance, they did not adopt turbines as motive power for their vessels. High speed is very expensive so they decided to leave turbines alone; it was the Allan Line who first adopted them on the Atlantic. As a matter of fact, the first and only White Star liner built with geared turbines was the *Doric,* twenty-six years later, when T H Ismay had been dead for nearly a quarter of a century, and his son had severed all connection with the White Star Line for some ten years.

For some time past Harland & Wolff had been working on the plans of two new ships to sail in the Liverpool-New York service. They were to be called *Oceanic* (after the pioneer vessel of the line) and *Olympic,* and were to be the largest and most elaborately and luxuriously furnished vessels in the world.

On July 24th Mr and Mrs Ismay went over to Belfast to see the interior decorations for the first of the proposed new ships; although they liked the library and some of the decorations they were not entirely satisfied, so T H Ismay decided to call in Trollope & Company, and also to enlist the advice of Mr Norman Shaw. Mr Shaw had designed, and was busy superintending the building of the new White Star offices, 30 James Street, Liverpool. The exterior of the building closely resembles New Scotland Yard which he had also designed. The company moved into the new offices on the last day of the old year and in the first month of the New Year Mrs Ismay went to inspect the new offices and she recorded her impressions which were:-

January 29th, Saturday, 1898. The carriage came for me at 10.30. I called at the Office and went all over them with Jimmy. They look very businesslike, but I miss the cosiness of the old ones, and don't quite like where Mr. Imrie is.

Mr Imrie did not have an office to himself, but was in an alcove in the corner of one of the main offices, which was curtained off.

Several consultations between Mr Shaw, Trollope & Company with Mr and Mrs Ismay were necessary during the year, to decide on the interior decorations for the *Oceanic.*

And so we come to 1899, the year in which T H Ismay died, and the whole destiny of the White Star Line was changed.

At the beginning of this year Mr and Mrs Ismay crossed to Queenstown in the *Teutonic,* and from there travelled up to Belfast for the launching of the *Oceanic,* which Mrs Ismay describes:-

January 14th, Saturday, 1899. Mr. Pirrie left for the yard at 6 o'clock, Thomas at 9 and Mrs. Pirrie and I at 10. The *Oceanic* was safely launched at about 11.20 a.m. A most beautiful sight it was to see the noble ship, glide so gracefully into the water. May she be all that we could wish.

The following month when they were staying at Brighton they were horrified to read in the evening papers that the *Germanic* had sunk at her berth in New York. It transpired that she was being coaled in the height of a blizzard and, owing to the fact that all her coaling doors were open on the port side exposed to the blizzard, also that ice formed on her superstructure, together with the uneven distribution of the coal, she listed to port; the water entered the bunkers and she sank at her moorings. However, salvage did not present much difficulty and she returned to Belfast for repairs; in June she was back in service.

Apart from an occasional cold, or an attack of lumbago, T H Ismay had enjoyed good health for most of his life and had been very active. There were few countries in the world he had not visited with his beloved 'Maggie'. But shortly after the launching of his fine new ship (which he planned to follow with a consort to be called *Olympic),* he began to complain of pains in his chest. His own doctor and several others were called in to give their opinion, but he became so ill that everyone in the firm of Ismay, Imrie and Company was very concerned about the health of the founder. The plans for a consort to the *Oceanic* were shelved and forgotten, and the name was not given to a vessel until twelve years later.

Poor Mrs Ismay had a lot to bear at this time as the children's devoted nurse Mardie, who had been with them for 30 years and who, although she could neither read nor write, had looked after all the children from infancy, also became ill and died suddenly. It was a tremendous shock; the children and indeed Mr and Mrs Ismay themselves were very upset as "she was a faithful nurse and friend".

At the end of March Mr Ismay was well enough to go away for a short holiday. They went to Windermere, where they had stayed some forty years before, and it was while staying here that T H Ismay suffered the first really bad attack of his liver complaint. Mrs Ismay writes:-

April 3rd, Monday, 1899. Thomas was seized with a violent pain at the bottom of the bowel, I got him to bed, applied a hot fomentation, and sent for the doctor, who gave him a dose of morphia.

This attack was diagnosed as being appendicitis and the doctor said it would be unwise for him to travel for a few days. So they did not return home until April 6th, by which time T H Ismay was feeling much better; but after the journey he was still far from well. It was their 40th wedding anniversary and their children presented them with a "beautiful silver tankard". He suffered several attacks during the next few weeks, but was able to travel to London on April 26th where they all stayed at Brown's Hotel and from where Mr Ismay attended the dinner of the Royal Academy.

After they returned to Liverpool the attacks continued again and the doctors now thought that he had gall stones, as "the gall duct was considerably enlarged". He was, however, able to attend a meeting of the Oceanic Steam Navigation Company in May and in June he travelled to London again to attend meetings of the LNWR. In July he and his family crossed to Belfast to see the *Oceanic* nearly completed and for Mr Ismay to receive the Freedom of the City of Belfast. But in August he collapsed again, just as the *Oceanic* was due to appear in the Mersey. So from his wife's diaries we have the picture of the founder of the White Star Line lying desperately ill at Dawpool as his latest magnificent vessel sets out on her maiden voyage, on which he had so much wanted to go.

It was decided he was not well enough to go to America in

T H Ismay receiving the Freedom of the City of Belfast, 1899. J Bruce Ismay is standing behind his father

the *Oceanic*, but on August 26th he insisted on going aboard her; he stayed three quarters of an hour and was very pleased with her, but the effort took its toll as by August 28th he was obviously much worse. His wife was so worried that she asked for a specialist of the liver, as this appeared to be the main trouble. They sent for Mr Mayo Robson of Leeds. He arrived at midnight and after examining the patient said that an operation would be necessary, but that it could only be done with cocaine. Mr Ismay agreed to this and the operation was performed on August 31st at his own home. The surgeon found that a large abscess had formed in the gall-duct, but the operation was considered to be a success. His two elder sons came and stayed in the house until it was all over.

But he did not pick up and by September 4th it was apparent to Mr Robson that a further operation was necessary, this time to be performed under a general anaesthetic. This was done the same night at 9pm. The next day, although he was so weak and ill that his daughters did not wish to leave him, he insisted that they should go aboard the new *Oceanic* for tea. He suffered great pain and seemed to realise he was dying, as he asked his wife to arrange that prayers should be offered for him in church.

As he lay so seriously ill the Emperor of Germany who was staying at Windsor Castle sent Mrs Ismay the following telegram:-

"Am most distressed at the news of the illness of your husband. I hope and trust that he may be spared to you, for he is one of the most prominent figures in the shipping world, and well known to me from the visit lance paid the *Teutonic* some years ago. Have just heard from a German gentleman who was a passenger on board the *Oceanic,* that she is a marvel of perfection in building and fittings, and well worthy of the celebrated line and the illustrious owner she belongs to."

On September 13th he had the first of a series of heart attacks which occurred at intervals until the middle of November. Mrs Ismay writes:-

November 23rd, Thursday, 1899. A very quiet night having had a draught from which he is very drowsy. Moved into my bed, but was only awake at intervals, and took little nourishment. At 5.45 p.m. he had a severe tightness in the chest and my beloved one passed peacefully away at 5 minutes past six. I had his hand until they removed me.

November 24th, Friday, 1899. A terrible awakening. My loved one has gone. Mr. Imrie and Mr. Graves came round, also Mary, Captain Leslie and Mrs. Haddock.

November 27th, Monday, 1899. My beloved one laid to rest in Thurstaston Churchyard. The Bishop of Chichester assisted. I was given strength to attend. I wanted to follow them to the end. All seems now gone for me. A very large representative gathering present. Boys from the *Indefatigable,* Seamen's Orphanage, and H.M.S. *Cotuoay,* A sad day for me.

November 28th, Tuesday, 1899. There is a terrible, terrible blank in the house. Shall we ever be able to live without him. All my life was centred in him, and as the time goes on it can only get worse for me.

All the time that her husband had been ill, Mrs Ismay had only left his side for brief periods, and had nursed him with utter devotion. She received many letters of condolence including the following telegram from the German Emperor:-

"I grieve to hear that your husband has departed this life. The shipping world has lost one of its most illustrious members, and the country mourns a life of work crowned with unparallelled success."

The people of Liverpool were shocked to hear the news, as very little had been published in the newspapers by the special request of the family. T H Ismay liked to read the newspapers every day and news of his illness had therefore been kept out. At his funeral, which had a very large attendance indeed, the Duke of Westminster insisted on being present but caught cold and five weeks to the day, he was buried himself. After T H Ismay's will was published he was then known to be a millionaire.

He gave many bequests to charity, those in which he had always been so interested:-

    The Liverpool Seamen's Orphan Institution.
    The Liverpool Bluecoat Hospital.
    The Bootle Borough Hospital.
    Birkenhead Children's Infirmary.
    The West Kirby Convalescent Home for Children.
    The Railway Benevolent Institution.
    The Training Ship *Indefatigable.*
    The Incumbent of St Mary's Church, Maryport.
    The Parish Church of Thurstaston.
    The Liverpool Seamen's Pension Fund

and £10,000 to Mrs Ismay to found a Fund to be called The Margaret Ismay Fund, which will supplement the benefits conferred by the Liverpool Seamen's Pension Fund.

His friend, James Barrow, gave £1,000 to the Liverpool Seamen's Pension Fund, in memory of a friendship which had lasted for over forty years. In the churchyard at Thurstaston where he is buried, there are numerous monuments erected to his memory by the various people and organisations who had known him and wished to try and keep his memory alive.

Mrs Ismay spent Christmas with her family at Dawpool, but it was the last Christmas she was to spend in their home. All future Christmasses she spent either with her son Bruce at Sandheys or with her daughter Ethel in London. She made the following entry in her diary for this Christmas Day:-

December 25th, Monday, 1899. The very saddest Christmas Day I have ever spent in my life. Fortunately I was in bed with influenza, but we had spent every Christmas Day together for over 40 years, and the feeling of loneliness is too dreadful.

On top of this great loss, on December 27th she heard that her son Bower had passed his medical examination and been accepted for service in the Army in South Africa. She ends the year:-

December 31st, Sunday, 1899. The end of the very saddest day of my life. Also very poorly and in bed. May 1900 be more peaceful and blessed.

CHAPTER 10

Sale of the White Star Line to the International Mercantile Marine

From the day of his father's death, Bruce Ismay controlled the destinies of the White Star Line, supported by his brother, James, and his father's two old friends, W Imrie and W S Graves. The policy of the company remained exactly the same. Thomas Ismay had always insisted that as it was the shareholders' capital which had launched the Oceanic Steam Navigation Company they were, therefore, to be the first consideration. Although his son had considerable financial skill and a quick clear-thinking brain, he would not have been capable of building up the firm as his father had done. Bruce Ismay's talents lay in excellent administration of the already thriving concern.

He was much misunderstood by those who did not know him intimately. He was shy and sensitive, which gave him an unfortunate manner, brusque and arrogant. This had developed over the years, owing to the constant humiliations to which his father had subjected him. He was full of destructive criticism and some of his office staff were frightened of his biting sarcasm. He was dogmatic when asked for advice, which he gave readily, but having given it, he dismissed the subject and brooked no argument. His insistence on punctuality was almost fanatical. Members of the staff at 30 James Street, Liverpool were well aware of this, and if they had an appointment with him, would arrive three or four minutes before time, waiting to knock on his door on the tick of the appointed hour.

He was unpopular with the Press, as he hated publicity and refused either to see them or to talk to them; if he was approached personally, he usually informed the reporter that the White Star Line had a publicity department to answer questions. He never made a speech in his life as he was incapable of speaking in public. This lack of the power of self-expression, and unpopularity with the Press was later to be his undoing. However, to those who knew him well and to whom he gave his confidence, he showed a completely different side of his character. They knew him as kind and considerate, full of integrity, and generous in an unobtrusive way.

He liked to think over his problems in solitude and sometimes walked the four miles from his home to the office; he would also take rides on the top of a tram to the terminus and back, and on his return would have the solution.

On one of these occasions he saw some children playing on the roof of a building. On reaching the office he sent for Mr. Shelley (one of the staff and later publicity manager), described the building with its flat roof and asked what it was. Mr Shelley made some inquiries and discovered it was an orphanage. Whereupon Bruce Ismay instructed him to make out a cheque for £500 and send it to them immediately.

Eighteen months after Bruce Ismay became chairman of the White Star Line, the *Celtic,* the last ship ordered by his father was launched at Belfast. His mother made the following entry in her diary:

April 4th, Thursday, 1901. The *Celtic* successfully launched. This is the last order my dearest one gave to Messrs. Harland & Wolff. She is the largest ship in the world.

With the building of this vessel the White Star Line embarked a stage further on their policy of building big ships capable of carrying a very large cargo, and at the same time a great number of passengers, over 2,800. The company were already pioneers in the big ocean-going freighter, carrying a limited number of passengers, and had enjoyed great success.

Now with the *Celtic* came a new departure; she was principally a passenger liner of moderate speed with 17,000 tons of cargo, which made her exceptionally steady in bad weather. Coal consumption was reduced from the 400 tons daily used in the *Oceanic* to 260 tons by accepting a maximum speed of three knots less. The *Celtic* was an immediate success, many passengers preferring the great steadiness of the slower vessel. She was such a success, in fact, that the White Star Line quickly ordered a sister, the *Cedric,* a similar vessel which came into service on February 11th 1903, they followed her up with the *Baltic.*

Ismay, Imrie & Company wanted the *Baltic* to be the largest vessel in the world. As the hull had been laid down sometime previously and was in an advanced stage of construction, it was necessary to cut her amidships, and insert an additional twenty-seven feet, which increased her tonnage by 2,840 gross.

When she entered service on June 29th 1904, it was found that with similar engines as the two previous ships she was always behind schedule, so alterations had to be made in the valve settings in the engines, to enable her to keep pace with the *Celtic* and *Cedric.*

The last of the 'Big Four', the *Adriatic* (which was even larger than the *Baltic),* was therefore given more powerful machinery, as her gross tonnage was 24,540 as compared with that of the *Celtic,* which was 20,904. To provide extra steam for the more powerful engines, four additional single-ended boilers were fitted. She sailed on her maiden voyage on May 8th 1907.

These four ships worked the Liverpool service almost continuously from 1907 until 1928 and were always the 'Pride of the Mersey'.

But to return to 1901; in this year the shipping world was again in a state of depression, the number of emigrants to America had decreased considerably, and the 'Rate War' between the various shipping companies was as bitter as ever.

A new figure now appeared on the scene, J Pierpont Morgan, an extremely wealthy American financier. He had a scheme to buy up certain companies and form a common pool, which would eliminate the 'Rate War' and make the tonnage interchangeable.

The Americans regretted that they had no ships of their own in the Atlantic trade. True, they had the old Inman Line, now known as the American Line, but under United States law no ship could fly the US flag unless built in their own country. Pierpont Morgan had had a good deal to do with the merging of the railroads, and now decided to do likewise with the steamship companies. He bought up the Red Star Line, the Dominion, the Atlantic Transport and the Leyland Lines, which together with the American Line made the combine which was known as the International Mercantile Marine.

In 1902 he approached the White Star Line. His proposition was to pay the 75 shareholders ten times the value of the line's earnings for the year 1900. This offer was made completely in the dark, as the earnings of the White Star Line were always kept a closely guarded secret, although the management of the company knew exactly the financial position of their rivals. In fact 1900 was a particularly profitable year for shipping, as the British Government had chartered numerous merchant vessels for use as transports during the Boer War.

The sale would mean that the shareholders would make a considerable profit on their original holdings. It was also proposed that J Bruce Ismay should continue as managing director and chairman of the White Star Line and that the other partners, William Imrie, James Ismay and W S Graves would retire. Later both James Ismay and W S Graves went to live in the South of England, James going to Iwerne Minster, Dorset, in the house which is now the small public school for boys, Claysmore. Here he devoted himself wholeheartedly to life in the country, doing a tremendous amount of good for the village and at the same time farming his several thousand acres with tremendous drive and efficiency. He practised high production methods, founded a pedigree herd, and several times the Ministry of Agriculture gave reports of what was happening at Iwerne as an example of a well run estate.

W S Graves bought a small estate near Horsham in Sussex, where he lived till his death. William Imrie retired to the 'Homestead', Mossley Hill, where he died in 1907. His real interest in the firm had terminated in 1895, when the North Western Shipping Company came to an end, with the sale of the last of the sailing vessels.

Only Harold Sanderson would remain. He and Bruce Ismay had been friends since 1886, when they met in New York. H A Sanderson had been invited to join the firm of Ismay, Imrie & Company in 1895 by his friend; he was made a partner in 1900.

The preceding sales of the other lines had had very little effect on the ordinary British citizen, but the proposed sale of the White Star Line, aroused a great deal of criticism. The Englishman was very proud of this line; after all it owned the largest passenger ships in the world, and it had attained international supremacy. The thought of selling the flag to the

'Yankees' appalled them, as well as "what was to happen in the event of war?" However, owing to the ties with the British Government and the United States Law already mentioned, the ships would remain British and sail under the British flag.

Mr Pirrie, head of Harland & Wolff, and also a shareholder of the White Star Line, was very much in favour of the sale as he foresaw that Harland & Wolff would now build, not only for the White Star Line as previously, but for the whole of the International Mercantile Marine combine.

It was a difficult decision for Bruce Ismay, the Ismay family and the shareholders; for whereas Thomas Ismay had been a millionaire, when he died his estate had been divided amongst three sons and four daughters. Bruce's share was only £100,000 in an unbreakable trust and he, therefore, had not the same resources on which to rely; but he felt that by retaining his position as managing director, he would still be able to mould the future of the company.

Another difficulty was that not all the members of the Ismay family wished to sever their connection with the White Star Line. In his will T H Ismay had instructed that none of his daughters should invest capital in any other shipping company, so if the Oceanic Steam Navigation Company were to be sold, they would be forced to relinquish their shares. However, as 75 per cent of the shareholders wished to accept Pierpont Morgan's offer, all parties were forced to accept, and in December 1902 the sale was completed.

As the arrangements for the sale of the White Star Line reached a conclusion, T H Ismay's widow made the following entries in her diary, which show quite clearly what she thought of it all:-

May 1st, Thursday, 1902. We ought to have dined at Sandheys and remained the night, but I could not go. The White Star was a conception of my dearest one and his life's work that I feel this change, although I have no doubt that Bruce has done the best for all concerned.

May 17th, Saturday. The Annual Meeting of the Oceanic Steam Navigation Company, and the last one I fear, as it has passed into the hands of others. It is a great wrench being 'His' life's work. I trust with God's blessing that it may all be for the best. Bruce came out to see me. He feels the change greatly.

May 22nd, Thursday. I signed the Agreement between the White Star and Mr. Pierpont Morgan.

The whole transaction so upset Mrs Ismay that seven days later she records:-

May 29th, Thursday. Some friends arrived, I hope they will be comfortable, but somehow now I don't feel equal to making arrangements, my life seems quite altered.

It was arranged that the White Star Line would become part of the International Mercantile Marine Company in December, and Mrs Ismay recorded for that day:-

December 1st, Monday. Messrs. Morgan have paid all the Shareholders of the Oceanic Steam Navigation Company for their shares. This ends the White Star Line in which so much interest, thought and care was bestowed and which was my dearest one's life's work. Bruce continues with the firm as Manager.

Undoubtedly, if Thomas Ismay had been alive this sale would never have taken place; he had founded the firm and devoted his life to making it the foremost steamship company in the world. The new shipping trust or Morgan Combine, as it was known, also entered into agreements with the Holland-America, Norddeutscher Lloyd, and Hamburg-American Lines. Only the Cunard and the French Line remained independent.

Lord Inverclyde, chairman of the Cunard Company, realised that they could not carryon against such powerful competition, so he decided to ask the British Government of the day if they would assist with the cost of building two new vessels capable of travelling at 24.5 knots, a speed never before attained, and to give a subsidy for running these vessels. If the Government would agree to do this, the Cunard Company would remain wholely British, the fleet would be at the disposal of the British Government in the event of war, and the company could not sell their interest for 25 years. This, finally, was agreed and they decided to experiment with the two new ships, the *Caronia* and *Carmania* (the 'Pretty Sisters' as they became known) which were then being built by John Brown & Company at Clydebank. The *Caronia* was fitted with reciprocating engines and the *Carmania* with turbines, in order to decide which was the superior. The latter, with turbines driving three screws proved the faster vessel, so it was decided that the famous pair which were to follow, the *Lusitania* and the *Mauretania* should be similarly fitted. These vessels were over 30,000 tons and were the world's largest by a generous margin.

CHAPTER 11

Bruce Ismay president of the IMM Company, the death of Mrs T H Ismay

To go back to 1903. One year after the formation of the International Mercantile Marine, the whole combine was in an unstable financial position. Clement A Griscom, the former chief of the American Line, was president. He was getting on in years and was in poor health.

Bruce Ismay, at forty-one, was chairman and managing director of the White Star Line; he was a director of the London and North Western Railway, the Liverpool London & Globe Insurance Company, the Sea Insurance Company, the Pacific Loan & Investment Company, the Asiatic Steamship Company and the Liverpool and London Steamship Protection Association. Late in the year he was approached by Pierpont Morgan and his associates and asked to take over the presidency of the International Mercantile Marine. This idea did not at first appeal to him at all, as he disliked the thought of the entertaining and publicity this post would entail. Also it would mean giving up his railway work and he had always thought that this would be a pleasant occupation for him in his later years, on retirement from the White Star Line.

However, the directors of the International Mercantile Marine amongst whom were Sir Clinton Dawkins (head of the British committee), Mr Charles Steele of New York, and Mr Pirrie of Harland & Wolff, all brought great pressure to bear on him. So on January 24th 1904 he sailed with his wife for New York aboard the *Oceanic,* to discuss the matter further. While in New York he sent the following letters to H A Sanderson in England giving the position of the International Mercantile Marine and Pierpont Morgan's views on the subject.

EXTRACTS FROM LETTERS WRITTEN BY J BRUCE ISMAY TO HAROLD SANDERSON FROM HOLLAND HOUSE, NEW YORK, FEBRUARY 7th, 1904:

I was met on arrival by Griscom, his son and Jim Wright.

Griscom came on board, and told me he wished to have a talk with me before I saw anyone else, so went up to his rooms at 10 o'clock on Friday morning, and had two hours talk with him.

He was very friendly and cordial, and I am extremely sorry to say I find him much altered for the worse since I was last here, and fear he is in a most indifferent state of health.

He told me his object in seeing me was to ask me to take the position of president, as he felt strongly the power and control should be in Liverpool, and that I was the proper and only person fit to undertake and carryon the business in a satisfactory manner, and he assured me I could count on the loyal co-operation and hearty assistance of himself, his son, and Wilding, in fact, of all the people on this side. I told him I was sorry he had decided to resign from the presidency, and fully appreciated his kind references to myself, and also his wish that I should assume the office of president; but that before I could arrive at any decision in regard thereto, I would require to have the fullest information in reference to the financial position of the company, as I felt it would be absolutely impossible to hope to achieve any measure of success if we were to be constantly hampered by lack of funds. In this he quite agreed, and was in accord with my views that unless money was forthcoming, it would be foolish of me to undertake the responsibility of managing the I.M.M. Company, and promised to support me to get the situation cleared up when we have the meeting with Steele and Morgan.

I asked him whether, in his opinion, it was possible to make the I.M.M. Company a commercial success, and to this question he replied in the affirmative, adding that if he was younger and in a better state of health, there is nothing he would like more than to undertake the work, but that it would be essential that money should be at his command, for he well knew from his own experience during the last twenty years what it meant to be hampered for lack of funds. He also agreed that it is necessary the Leyland Line position should be defined, as at present the situation was an impossible one. We also touched on a great many matters of detail, but nothing transpired which affected the main point.

I came down town with him, and went to the office, where I found a telephone message from Steele, advising me he was laid up at home with a cold, and would not be down town.

Morgan is off on a jaunt in Canada, but fancy he returns to the city to-day, so hope to arrange a meeting of Morgan, Steele, Griscom and myself early this week when I hope the whole matter may be frankly and fully discussed.

February 9th, 1904:

I saw Steele yesterday for about an hour. He is better, but still far from well. After a little general conversation, I asked him what was the position of affairs here, and he told me "Bad, and most unsatisfactory". I asked what he proposed doing about it, and he replied by saying I was the one to deal with the situation, and that they wanted me to undertake the presidency and assume full and absolute control. I replied that before I could even seriously consider the suggestion, I must know what was the financial position of the company. He told me it was bad. I then said, "I suppose J. P. Morgan & Company are prepared to put their hands in their pocket, and help the I.M.M. Company?" He said he did not know about that "Then," I said, "if you cannot see your way to stand behind the I.M.M. Company, you might as well put up the shutters at once", to which he answered, "Well, I suppose we must see it through; at the same time, we have already between $2,000,000 and $3,000,000 invested in it."

He then gave me a lot of figures, which I glanced through last night, but have not mastered, showing how the $50,000,000 has been disposed of, and sundry other information, which I intend going through to-day with Swartz, if possible.

We got on to the position of the Leyland Line, which is one that must be dealt with. I cannot do better, or explain the position to you more fully, than by asking you to request Wilding to show you the copies of *all* cables that have passed between him and the people here. The position is a ludicrous and impossible one, and must be straightened out. Steele is most annoyed about it.

I am writing you at the hotel and am just off to meet Morgan, Steele and Griscom at the former's house, so shall doubtless be in a position to cable you this afternoon the result of my interview. It is a difficult proposition, and I intend going slow, and giving the matter the most earnest and careful consideration. It is easy to jump in, but it would be difficult, if not impossible, to climb out.
Yours sincerely,
J. Bruce Ismay.

Holland House, New York,
Tuesday evening, February 9th, 1904.
To Harold A. Sanderson, Esq., 30, James Street, Liverpool.
Oceanic.
My dear Harold,
I sent you the following cable this afternoon, viz:-
"Had meeting Morgan, Steele, Griscom present, offered me presidency and unlimited control. Morgan thinks my residing here portion each year absolutely necessary. This entirely new proposition. He does not consider my nationality any drawback, but possibly advantageous. Accepting proposal would involve dividing my time between England and America, and giving up all outside interests. Expect in time my stay in America would be comparatively short. He expressed his views most strongly, and very anxious I should accept. Have told him will give proposal consideration. Most difficult know what to do; please cable your views and mother's fully. Am very anxious and curious to receive your reply," and also to have my mother's views thereon, and hope you have been able to go over to Dawpool and discuss the matter with her.
As arranged, I went to Morgan's house this morning, and there met Morgan, Steele and Griscom, and we had a discussion on the whole situation.
Morgan was extremely cordial and pleasant, and opened out by saying he was extremely dissatisfied with the present position of affairs, and felt the whole organisation was on wrong lines. He stated he did not mind losing money, but he did object to doing so owing to poor organisation. He felt things were on a wrong basis, and that, in his opinion, I was the only man he knew that could straighten matters out. He was prepared to make me president and give me unlimited control, and anything I decided was to be final,

and he was tired of all the cabling that was going on between America and England, and wanted to feel there was some individual who was absolutely responsible for the working of the I.M.M.

He further stated in his opinion it was essential that if I accepted the proposal he made that I should take a house in New York, and spend a certain portion of the year here, it might be four or six months, but of that I would be the best judge.

In regard to finances he stated his feeling was that the earnings of the subsidiary companies should be allocated to paying the fixed charges, any surplus over and above this should go to pay Pirrie, and was willing this, (Pirrie's indebtedness) should be a prior charge on the company to any indebtedness to his firm. In the event of the company not earning sufficient to pay the fixed charges he was himself prepared to make any deficiency good for three years. I told him I considered nothing could be fairer than this, and he replied, "Could any man say more", to which I said "No".

After he had got through I said that no one was more anxious to make the I.M.M. a success than I was, but referred to a conversation I had had with him seven months ago, when the question of an Englishman being the president of the company was discussed, and that he then stated he felt it was not possible. To this he replied that he had no recollection of the incident, but now felt strongly that instead of this being a drawback, it would be an advantage, as it would let the public see that they intended to do all they knew to make the I.M.M. a commercial success.

I next stated the proposition in regard to my living in New York was an entirely new one, and that I did not like the idea. He replied that in view of the company, being an American one, it was necessary I should, as president, have a domicile here, and that it was for me to decide how much of my time it was necessary to spend here, recognising the fact that the business must be controlled and emanate in England.

We had a good deal of general conversation, the interview lasting the best part of two hours, and ending by my saying I would carefully consider the matter.

There is no doubt Morgan, Steele and Griscom are really anxious I should take the position, but I do not like the idea of living here, even for a period of each year; it would mean my giving up all my outside interests, the L. & N.W., Globe, Sea and other companies in which I take an interest. On the other hand, it is an opportunity of pulling together a concern that at present is as low in the public opinion as it can well get, and there is a good deal to be said, both for and against. I would like to put it on its feet but it means giving up a great deal to do so. I believe I would get the loyal support of all interested in the concern, and this is a great deal, but it would mean a great deal of hard and worrying work, to say nothing of having to do many unpleasant things; still, it is a great opportunity.

Ned Bewind called this afternoon, and said he hoped I would accept Morgan's proposition. I told him it was so entirely different to what I contemplated that it would need careful consideration. He said he hoped I would give it favourable consideration.

It is a most difficult situation, and I hope you will assist me in coming to a decision, as all I want to do is for the best of all concerned ... My feeling is to tell Morgan I propose returning home on the 24th inst., and that with the understanding I shall not be expected to spend more than three to four months here, say from middle January to middle of May, and that if he is prepared to give me £20,000 a year to begin with, that I will favourably consider his proposition; but before coming to a decision I wish to talk the matter over with you, and that within a week of my arrival home will cable him definitely, and that if my answer is in the affirmative, I will return to America within two weeks, and undertake the responsibility of re-organising the I.M.M. This will give me ample time to think over the matter, hear my mother's and your views, and do not think this delay will in any way be to the detriment of the I.M.M.

I feel the matter is of so serious a nature that it is not one in which a hurried decision can be expected, and I am anxious in both our interests to have the opportunity of talking over the matter with you, and possibly Pirrie. I may say that Morgan is much down on Pirrie and stated that if the combine had not gone through he would have been bankrupt six months ago, as he could not have carried the load he had on his shoulders.

I think I have written you fully, and explained the position and do not know I can add anything more.

Yours very sincerely,
J. Bruce Ismay.

The day following the writing of this letter, Mr Sanderson having received a cable went to Dawpool to see Mrs Ismay, and she wrote the following to her son:-

February 10th, 1904.
Dawpool,
My dearest Bruce,
Mr. Sanderson telephoned this morning saying he had received an important cable from you, and that he thought he had better come out and see me. Mr. Imrie and Amy were coming out to lunch, so I asked Mr. Sanderson to come with them, which he did, and after lunch, he read your cable to me. It was much as I expected except in one thing, which of course is a great blow to me that you must be in America half your time, but while deeply regretting this, I must put personal feelings on one side for I know it is a proud and important position you are offered, and you naturally wish to see the great undertaking in a prosperous condition, and for this to be so, I feel that you are the only one whose management can achieve this.

I think your own inclination is to accept, and I do not wonder at it, for it is well known what exceptional power you have. I am sure you will have given the subject deep and anxious consideration, and we can only trust that whatever decision you arrive at, that it will be the right one. I have every confidence that it will be, in the natural course of events, you have a large part of your life before you, and I hope you may be spared to bring the great concern with which you are so deeply interested to a successful issue. We must not forget that you are asked to give up many important interests on this side, for I suppose you will not be able to retain the North Western, or your other directorships. I am sorry at this, for I had it in my mind that railway work was what you would take up as your interest later on, for I should like to think that you will have some leisure in your lifetime.

Mr. Sanderson cabled you early this evening, so I expect before you receive this your decision is made.

I don't think there is anything more to say, I shall look anxiously for further news, trusting that you and Florence are well and with much love,
Ever dearest Bruce,
Your loving Mother

February 11th, 1904.
9, Broadway, New York.
To Harold A. Sanderson, Esq., 30, James Street, Liverpool.
My dear Harold,

I yesterday received the following cable from you, viz.:- "Have been Dawpool consult Mrs. Ismay. We both are disappointed that should be required divide your time between England and States, but feel you should not regard this condition as insuperable, if otherwise your inclination is to accept. Hope can be arranged residence in States reduced to minimum and seasonable periods," and am glad to see therefrom that you have been to Dawpool to talk over the matter with my mother.

It is most difficult to arrive at a conclusion as to what is the best course to pursue, and I am hopeful of being able to arrange to postpone giving any answer until I have had an opportunity of discussing the matter with you. Steele is, I know, anxious for a reply, as he telephoned me yesterday, asking if I had anything to say to him.

The idea of spending much of my time in America is not congenial to me, but if I could arrange to limit it to say, three months, it would not be so bad.

I hoped your cable could have given me some indication as to what are your views, but you do not do so, merely telling me I should not consider the proviso of living in New York insuperable if my *"inclination"* is to accept. I think you know that if I had considered my own inclination and feelings absolutely, I should, in all probability, have resigned ere this, but I am trying to look at the matter from a general point of view, and whether by taking the position, even for a limited period, would be to the benefit of all concerned. If I should accept, it means my having to give up a good deal personally, and sever my connection with the L. & N.W. Rly., and all outside companies in which I am interested. The railway I always considered would give me occupation for my old age. If I give it up now, I could not expect to get on the board at some future time, say five years hence.

However, there is really nothing I can add to what I have already written you, and nothing has developed since. I saw Morgan on Tuesday; in fact, I did not see any of them yesterday.

I am going to Boston to-morrow with Lee, and hope to get back on Saturday evening.

Assuming I can get Steele to agree to my not coming to any decision until I have had a talk with you at home, I shall in all probability get away by the *Celtic;* failing this I will return by the *Cedric,* as I have quite given up all idea of visiting the Mediterrean this time.

Trusting all is working smoothly, and that you are all well,
Yours very sincerely,
J. Bruce Ismay.

While still considering the matter of the presidency, Ismay went to Boston to visit the *Republic* and see the general workings of the port. Below are his views in a letter to his friend Harold Sanderson:-

Extract from letter dated February 15th 1904:
I went over to Boston with Lee on Friday morning, reaching there at 3 p.m., and at once went to the *Republic.*

The wharf is not an ideal one from which to work a first-class passenger business, but there is room for much improvement in their present practise.

The new officers are, I think, good, and there should be no difficulty in the organisation thereof, but at present they are "all sixes and sevens". I cannot say I was favourably impressed by Mr. Britton, and time will show if he is the right man.

We dined on board the *Republic,* and I was much surprised to find that Captain McAuley had three friends to dinner and the doctor two; surely they know this is strictly against our rules!

I saw the ship away at 8 a.m. on Saturday; she was somewhat late owing to some of the firemen being absent.

She was in a dreadful state of dirt, largely owing to the use of the ash ejector, which had smothered her with ashes, and owing to the severe weather it was not possible to clean her.

On leaving the wharf she had no one in the look-out bridge, no fog horn was sounded to warn visitors of her departure, no United States mail flag was flying from the mizzen, and a canvas save-all was hanging over her side. The screens on the promenade deck were half up and half down. They should have all been down and stowed away.

Her departure was most unsatisfactory, and most discreditable to all concerned. There was no one from the office to see her away; in fact, the whole thing was as bad as it could well be.

Please write Captain McAuley for an explanation on the several points mentioned. If he cannot maintain the discipline we must have, he is not the man we want.

Steele called at the hotel yesterday afternoon, and I had three hours with him, going over the same ground. We are, generally speaking, in accord as to what should be done. He is anxious I should come to some decision with reference to the presidency, but, appreciating the seriousness of the step does not wish to unduly press me. He repeated how very anxious Mr. Morgan and himself were I should accept his offer.

This morning I sent you the following cable:-

"Steele unwilling unduly press for reply, but anxious for decision. Assuming I do not consider American residence insuperable, is it mother's and your opinion I should accept. Very difficult decide; Steele, Morgan and others most anxious should accept. I hesitate taking such important step. Would much like you cable definite advice after receiving letter *Oceanic*." and hope to receive some definite advice on receipt of my letter per *Oceanic* and am writing Steele to the effect that I will give him a decided answer on Thursday.

It is most difficult to know what is the best thing to do, there is so much to be said on both sides; but if I only considered *myself*, I would decline the responsibility. Of course, should I accept, it means you would have a deal more on your shoulders, as I could not possibly give the same close attention to White Star business in the future as in the past, and we must always bear in mind that the White Star is the *most important* part of the business, and must be kept up to its present efficiency.

Although the Leyland Line was part of the IMM, Mr Wilding, the manager, instead of operating it in the best interests of the combine, was still carrying on as though it was an independent company, thus causing a great deal of annoyance to the heads of the combine. With the persuasion of his American colleagues, and on the advice of his mother and Harold Sanderson, Ismay decided to accept the presidency, and so on February 19th 1904 he sent the following letter to Harold Sanderson:-

9, Broadway, New York,
February 19th, 1904.
To Harold Sanderson, Esq., 30, James Street, Liverpool.
My dear Harold,

Your cable of the 17th inst., duly reached me, reading as follows:- "Been Dawpool. We feel that provided financial position offers no bar, you would do well to accept; but would suggest, as matter is of great importance you should endeavour if practicable carry out your idea of giving decision after arrival home and discussion here," and after thinking the matter over, I sent you on the same day this message, viz.:- "My letter *Oceanic* fully explained position, nothing new transpired since. Under these circumstances, hardly think a further discussion Liverpool would throw fresh light on situation, or assist in reaching decision. Having regarded your views, propose accepting before sailing Wednesday. Cable if you agree," and on the 18th the following cable came to hand:- "Quite agree, only mentioned delaying actual acceptance thinking that your own wish."

I do not really think that any good purpose would be served by deferring coming to a decision until my return home, and hardly think further discussion would throw any fresh light on the subject.

I have sent a note to Steele advising him that when he has expressed his willingness to agree to the terms and conditions of which I am prepared to fall in with his wishes, and can give me some absolute and definite assurance that the Leyland Line is under the control of the I.M.M. Company, I will give him my answer.

The position assumed by the Leyland Line is extraordinary, and it is necessary to know if they were controlled by the I.M.M. Company or not, and a cable has been sent by Steele to Dawkins, telling him to see Wilding and clear up this position. Their action fully bears out a statement made by Roper to you and myself viz.: that the Leyland Line was quite prepared to work in harmony with the I.M.M. Company so long as it suited him to do so, but if the interests of the I.M.M. Company were contrary to the interests of the Leyland Line, then it was his business to protect the interests of the Leyland Line, even if in so doing he was injuring the I.M.M. Company. Their action with reference to the freight agreement, and now their refusal to withdraw tonnage from the

Boston-Liverpool berth, is quite in accord with, and fully bears out Roper's contention, and Bray has been the means of rendering the I.M.M. Company ridiculous in the eyes of the steamship world generally.

I told Steele yesterday that unless the situation was cleared up, and the position of the Leyland Line towards the I.M.M. clearly defined, neither I nor anyone else would, I should think, be prepared to accept the position of president of the I.M.M. Company.

I am now waiting to hear from Steele; in the meantime my sailing is getting very close, and nothing done, so far. It is the same old plan of leaving things until the last moment, and then trying to rush them through.

Griscom still away, but I understand he is progressing, and now out of bed.

I think the Continental lines should have consulted the British lines before putting out an 18 dollar pre-paid Scandinavian rate, and so cabled you. While we agree to their putting on this line as a tentative measure, I certainly had in mind that they would concur with us before taking any step.

The Italian business is in a state of absolute demoralisation and the outlook of passenger business generally most gloomy. We have decided this morning to quote an East bound Italian rate of 22 dollars less 2 dollars commission. I suggested to Boas it would be well to reduce at once to 10 dollars and he agreed, and so cabled Ballin, who replied he feared if we did this, the Italian Government might claim that if we could carry Italians one way for 10 dollars we could do so both ways. I am of opinion the only way to bring matters to a head is to make things as bad as possible, and then people will be more willing to come to some agreement.

We hope to receive a cable from you to-day advising us as to the decision arrived at by the Cunard directors.

I had a talk with Vernon on Wednesday. He was very friendly, but we did not discuss matters in any detail. He strongly urged me to take up the I.M.M. Company and says he believes it can be made a financial and commercial success.

Trusting all goes on smoothly, and that you are all well.

Yours sincerely,

J. Bruce Ismay.

Holland House,
New York. February 21st, 1904.
To Chas. Steele, Esq.,
34, West 49th Street, New York City.
Dear Steele,

Referring to the interview we had at Mr. Morgan's house on Tuesday, the 10th inst., when Mr. Morgan, Mr. Griscom and yourself were present, at which I was offered and requested to accept the presidency of the International Mercantile Marine Company; having given the matter my earnest and most careful consideration, have decided to fall in with the wishes of Mr. Morgan and yourself, and am prepared (subject to the understanding contained in the memorandum agreed with you yesterday, and subsequently approved by Mr. Morgan, being executed, and the letter written with reference to the Leyland Line), to assume the duties and responsibilities of the position.

There is no doubt the I.M.M. Company is at present in an extremely unsatisfactory condition, both in regard to finance and organisation, and you will appreciate it will require a great deal of hard and anxious work to put it on a proper working basis; but this I am prepared to undertake, feeling, as I do, that I have the goodwill and confidence of Mr. Morgan and yourself, and that I can count on you both to assist me in every way that lies in your power to attain the end we all have in view.

I would like to say, had I consulted my own feelings in this matter I should, without the slightest hesitation, have declined the offer; and have been very largely influenced in my decision by a desire to render any assistance I can to Mr. Morgan and yourself to place the I.M.M. Company in a satisfactory position, and although it may be a long and hard road to travel, I believe if we all work heartily and loyally together, that ultimately we shall meet with some measure of success.

Thanking you for all your kindness and courtesy, and hoping we have many years of pleasant co-operation before us.

Yours sincerely,
J. Bruce Ismay.

MEMORANDUM OF THE UNDERSTANDING UNDER WHICH J. BRUCE ISMAY IS WILLING TO CONSIDER UNDERTAKING THE DUTIES OF PRESIDENT AND

MANAGING DIRECTOR OF THE INTERNATIONAL MERCANTILE MARINE COMPANY.

It is understood:-

1. That J. Bruce Ismay shall have the title of president and managing director.

2. That his management of the business of the I.M.M. Company shall be unlimited and uncontrolled, and his decision on all points other than financial matters must be final.

3. That the entire control of all the subsidiary Companies of the I.M.M. Company shall be vested in him, and that his decision on all matters of policy and management of these Companies shall be final so far as the I.M.M. Company can control the same.

4. That he shall have the absolute power of appointing and dismissing, without any appeal, any persons in the employ of the I.M.M. Company, or any of the subsidiary companies so far as the I.M.M. Company can control the same.

5. That all the companies in which the I.M.M. Company has an interest shall be subject to and conform to his instructions, and that such instructions shall be final so far as the I.M.M. Company can control the same.

6. That he will receive the hearty and loyal support and cooperation of those most largely interested in the welfare of the I.M.M. Company.

7. That he shall arrange to have a residence in New York, the time it may be necessary he should reside in America being left absolutely to his judgment and discretion.

8. That the business in America and Canada, and the West Indies shall be conducted in such manner as he may think best.

9. That he shall be at liberty to resign the position at any time; by giving six months notice, and conversely the board shall have the right to call for his resignation on like notice.

10. That he shall receive as a remuneration for filling this position the sum of $50,000 per annum, in addition to the compensation now received by him from the White Star Line, and as a member of the British committee and voting trustee.

11. That Mr. Morgan is prepared, in the event of the earnings of the I.M.M. Company and subsidiary companies not being sufficient to meet the fixed charges of the I.M.M. Company and subsidiary companies, to advance the monies necessary to make

good any deficiencies for a term of three years after January 1st, 1904.

12. That Mr. Morgan undertakes the above liability on the understanding that the net earnings of the I.M.M. Company and subsidiary companies will be allocated first to pay such charges.

13. Mr. Morgan is willing, in the event of the earnings of the I.M.M. Company and subsidiary companies being in excess of the amount necessary to meet the fixed charges of the I.M.M. Company and subsidiary companies, that any surplus is to be allocated to meet the indebtedness of the I.M.M. Company and subsidiary companies to Harland and Wolff, before being obliged to any indebtedness that may be owing to his firm.

14. That the finance committee shall in no way control or interfere with the perogatives of the president and managing director, as set forth in this memorandum.

15. Finally, it is distinctly understood that the board of directors, the finance committee, and those who may control the destiny of the I.M.M. Company and the subsidiary companies are prepared to give unlimited control in all matters to J. Bruce Ismay, and are willing to place absolute and entire confidence in him in every respect, subject only to the powers of the finance committee regarding financial matters, and the power of the board to call for Mr. Ismay's resignation as hereinbefore stated.

(Signed) J. Pierpont Morgan, P. A. B. Widener, Charles Steele.

On February 24th, 1904 Mr and Mrs Bruce Ismay embarked in the *Cedric* bound for Liverpool. Bruce Ismay had finally accepted the position of president of the International Mercantile Marine Company and while on the voyage home he wrote and received the following letters:-

Dawpool,
Thurstaston, Birkenhead.
My dearest Bruce,
All well; you are nearing home, and very welcome you will be. I hope you have had a good passage, and that it has been a rest to you for I am sure you must have needed it, after all the anxiety you have had in deciding such a difficult question, for there was so much for and against it. It is gratifying to find the high opinion

Mr. Morgan has of you, and from the bottom of my heart I congratulate you, and wish every success will be with you, it is a proud position they have conferred on you, and it will be through no fault of yours if you do not make the Company a success.

I do hope that you will be able to tell me that the time you will have to spend in New York will not have to be very long, for that indeed would be a great wrench to me to be divided from you all; for I have looked on Florence as part of us, for she has always been so loving and affectionate. I am glad on her account that she will be more with her parents, which will be a great joy to them.

Very many thanks, dear Bruce, for sending me the correspondence with Mr. Sanderson, which has kept me fully informed of all that has taken place, and in which I have been deeply interested, and many friends whom I have heard speak about it have all been in favour of your accepting it, Mr. Graves particularly so.

Now I am waiting anxiously for details of your plans. I wonder when you will come to Dawpool. I hope if convenient to you over Sunday, your room is quite ready. Shall I ask Margaret and Tom to come on Sunday? They don't miss their work, for they go in by the early train, I should like them to come if you don't mind; perhaps you will telephone after you get to Sandheys.

Lottie went to Jimmy's yesterday for some races to-day and to-morrow, but there is such a hard frost, I doubt if there will be any, Bower and Connie are also going.

I hear Jimmy is very busy furnishing his new house, also with political work. I had a long letter from Ada from Khartoum, she seems to be having a very good time, she leaves there on the 8th for Cairo, where she will probably stay about a month with Edith Gibson, then make her way home.

Your Auntie Wood is still here, and will I hope stay a little longer, for Lottie has an invitation from Mrs. Burns, Lord Inverclyde's sister-in-law for two dances in Glasgow. I think from the loth till the 14th.

As I hope so soon to see you, I will not write more, so with very much love and hoping you are quite well and all good wishes,

Ever your loving Mother.
March 1st, 1904.

Just heard from Sandheys that they are all well, don't forget to telephone if Margaret and Tom may come if you are able to.

On board R.M.S. *Cedric,* March 2nd, 1904.
(Off Queenstown).
To Sir Clinton E. Dawkins, K.C.B., 22, Old Broad Street, London, E.C.
Dear Sir Clinton,

It was extremely pleasing to receive your very welcome message, reading as follows:- "Our most sincere congratulations. We all look forward to many years pleasant work with you, and assure you of our hearty and full co-operation," and it is unnecessary to say how much I appreciate the kind thought that prompted you to so cable.

I was in a very difficult position in New York, and the decision arrived at was largely influenced by the strong personal pressure brought to bear on me by Mr. Morgan, Mr. Steele and several others of our American friends. Had it not been for this and had I purely consulted my own feelings, nothing would have induced me to accept the position of president of the I.M.M. Company, as I had looked forward in the near future to a life of ease and enjoyment.

However, having accepted the very onerous and responsible post, it is my intention to do all in my power to place the I.M.M. Company in a different position to the extremely unenviable one in which it now stands, and it is most satisfactory to feel I can rely on having the hearty and full co-operation of Pirrie, Wilding and your goodself.

It would be idle on my part to hope to accomplish anything unless I felt I had the sympathy of all interested in the I.M.M. Company, and my recent visit to America assured me such was the case there, and you will readily understand how gratifying it was to receive similar assurance from you here.

I cannot say I am at all sanguine as to the future of the I.M.M. Company, but if we all work loyally together for its welfare, we may, in years to come, attain some measure of success, but we have a long and difficult road to travel.

At the present time there seems to be a state of war in every trade in which we are engaged, and, in both the passenger and freight branches of the business the outlook being most discouraging. However, we must "put our backs into it", and try to rectify matters as soon and as much as possible.

It is my present intention to return to the States as soon as possible, as I am anxious to see the carrying out of the organisation already decided upon, but hope, before doing so, to have an opportunity of discussing matters with you.

Steele talked of coming over for a week, sailing from New York on the 9th inst., and returning in time to allow Mr. Morgan to leave on April 6th, and my movements will, to a certain extent, be influenced by what he decides to do.

Messrs. Morgan and Steele were extremely kind to me during my stay in America, and I much appreciate the full and absolute control they have placed in my hands, and it will be my endeavour to prove to them that their confidence is not misplaced.

Mr. Morgan seems determined, so far as lies in his power to do everything possible to put the I.M.M. Company on its feet, and make it a commercial success, and we, on our part, must lend him every assistance to attain this end.

Trusting you are all very well, and with renewed thanks for your kind message, believe me,

Yours sincerely,
J. Bruce Ismay.

2, Dale Street, Liverpool.
March 3rd, 1904
My dear Bruce,

I notice the s.s. *Cedric* is reported at Ireland, and I presume you will reach home to-night.

I received from your office a portrait of your late father; this I take it for granted comes from you, and I now write to thank you very much for giving me so striking a likeness, which will certainly keep him in remembrance.

I suppose I ought to congratulate you on being appointed president of the great company, although it will probably greatly increase your labours; perhaps I should use the words that Mr. Griscom once wrote to me and say that "my congratulations should rather be for the company".

Yours very truly,
David Jardine.

Queens Island, Belfast.
March 5th, 1904.
My dear Bruce,

I have yours of the 2nd inst., written on board the *Cedric* off Queenstown, and am sure your decision to accept the position of president of the I.M.M. Company must have been as great a relief to Mr. Morgan and our other American friends, as it was to your colleagues on this side. I quite understand with what mixed feelings you must have approached the consideration of the proposition, and how gladly you would, had you seen a way out, have evaded the distinction that has been thrust upon you, but what would have been your gain would undoubtedly have been our loss, and I do not mind confessing that it was with something very like a sigh of relief that I heard that all had been satisfactorily settled. I am convinced that this feeling is shared by all concerned, and that you may confidently rely upon receiving that hearty, loyal and active co-operation from everyone connected with the company, upon which, as you say, depends the success or failure of our enterprise.

Personally I have not the slightest misgiving as to the ultimate result of our exertions, any tremors that I may have had having passed away with your assumption of the reins. Nevertheless I fully recognise, and have all along, that our great stumbling block is, and will be for some time to come, want of capital, and you may rely upon my continuing to do everything that lies in my power to assist you in this respect. It must, however, be borne in mind that neither my own resources nor those of my firm are inexhaustible, and, as a matter of fact, they are exhausted at the present moment.

This is not a pleasant confession for one who has so long been accustomed to conduct his legitimate business on a ready cash basis to have to make, but it is none the the less true, and it was the consciousness that such a state of affairs was rapidly approaching and not any uneasiness as to the ultimate repayment of the money I have advanced that compelled me to protest when Mr. Steele suggested, as I thought, that I should find the money to complete the *Baltic,* such being an utter impossibility-nevertheless I am glad to hear that both he and Mr. Morgan consent to my firm's claims on the company ranking in priority to those of their own firm, as also of the willingness and anxiety of Mr. Morgan to do everything in his power to make the Company a success.

No doubt there is much demanding your personal attention in America at once, but all the same I hope you will be able to prolong your stay on this side sufficiently to enable us to avail ourselves of Mr. Steele's offer to come over and discuss the financial position, as I think that such a discussion prior to your return to America would be of the very greatest advantage to all concerned. I wired Sir Clinton to this effect last night, and now await your and his advices when you have decided what you will do, meantime remaining,

Yours sincerely,
Pirrie.

After her husband's death Mrs T H Ismay had continued to live at Dawpool with one or other of her children and their families staying with her. She made frequent trips to Harrogate to take the waters and enjoyed holidays on the Continent, but as far as she was concerned her love for her husband was the most important thing in her life, and now he had gone she had no real interest in living.

As the year 1900 opened, Mrs Ismay was staying with her daughter, Ethel and her husband Geoffrey Drage, at their London home.

The Boer War was still in progress, and Bower Ismay, her youngest son, having volunteered for the Army, was due to leave for South Africa shortly. He came to see his mother and told her he wished to marry Constance Schieffelin (Mrs Bruce Ismay's younger sister). He had known her since 1889, when the whole Ismay family had visited New York on the maiden voyage of the *Teutonic;* she had stayed in England with her sister on many occasions since.

His mother was not pleased with this idea as she felt that they were both too young, and it was too soon after his father's death. However, Bower had his way and they were married at St Paul's, Knightsbridge, on January 13th 1900.

Shortly after this Mrs Ismay and some of her family went for a three months' holiday abroad. While staying at San Remo she had her first experience of motoring when they went for a picnic in two hired motor-cars. Not long after on their return to England, her second son, Jimmy, bought his first motor-car; later when her youngest son was discharged from the Army Mrs Ismay bought him a large Panhard-Levassor with tonneau body and the whole family began to take motoring seriously. Lottie who was the first to own a motor-car, bought herself a small three-wheeled one and engaged a chauffeur named Holly. In spite of an occasional breakdown, she was most adventurous for a young lady of 1900; she went as far from Liverpool as Edinburgh or London, a good record for those days when motor-cars were unreliable and the roads bad.

Mrs Ismay never owned a motor-car but continued to use horses, although she was not averse to a trip in one of her children's "horseless carriages", but even her drives with her carriage were not without incident as we see from her diary:-

August 29th, Monday, 1904. Ethel, the children and I drove in the carriage to tea at Hooton. We collided with a bicycle and I had to give a man a guinea.

October 31st, Monday, 1904. Went out for a drive in the afternoon. Williamson drove us. The horse was very restive, and shied running the best brougham into the hedge.

Bruce Ismay, however, never cared for motoring but his wife loved it; in 1905 she acquired her first motor-car, a large Mercedes with a Roi-de-Belge body. When her father and mother came to visit her in 1906 she took them for a tour abroad in it, she has toured the Continent regularly ever since except for the war years and has been as far afield as Yugoslavia.

J Bruce Ismay much preferred to travel by train, in a reserved compartment where he could have his papers spread around him, and work and think. He had the same attitude towards his motor-cars as he had with the ships of the White Star Line, the motor-car was just as much the responsibility of the chauffeur as the ship was that of the captain.

His chauffeur sometimes drove him faster than he would have wished and he often complained of this to his wife. But when she suggested that he should tell the chauffeur to slow down his reply was "No, he is in charge, and if he thinks we should go so fast it is not for me to interfere."

Years later, although his children all drove their own cars, he would never permit them to drive his, nor would he ever ride with them.

On January 19th, Saturday, 1901 Mrs Ismay writes:- "There is grave news about the Queen's health, I fear the end is not far off."

Queen Victoria died on January 22nd, at Osborne in the Isle of Wight, and the great Victorian era, of which Thomas Ismay's achievement was so typical, had come to an end.

Later in the year James's wife, Lady Margaret, died in childbirth, leaving Jimmy with two daughters. To help him get over his loss, he decided to go for a world tour, retire from the White Star Line and live in the South of England. Mr Morgan's offer to buy the White Star Line came most opportunely for him. Eventually, two and a half years later, he married again, a Miss Muriel Moreton, at Bembridge in the Isle of Wight, and the whole family travelled down for the wedding.

Meanwhile, Bower had been invalided out of the Army and returned home from South Africa in time to attend the wedding of his sister Dora to Joshua Fielden on December 12th 1901 at St Paul's Knightsbridge.

Five years later, early in August, 1906, Thomas Ismay's old friend and partner, William Imrie, died at his home, and Bruce lost a valued friend and adviser.

In the autumn Mrs Ismay went to stay with her daughter Ethel at 29 Cadogan Square, London SW1. She had been in ill health for some time suffering from Bright's disease and on April 9th, 1907 she died. Her body was taken back to Thurstaston and laid beside that of her husband.

When Mrs Ismay's will was published, it was known that she had been as generous as her husband; she left large sums to some of the charities which he had supported during his lifetime, and which he had named in his will. She also left £10,000 towards the building of the new Liverpool Cathedral; sometime before her death she had made arrangements to erect a permanent memorial to her husband's memory in the form of the Great East Window.

CHAPTER 12

Salvage of the 'Suevic', opening of the new Southampton route, loss of the 'Republic', building of the 'Olympic' and 'Titanic'

From the moment J Bruce Ismay assumed the presidency until his retirement, the International Mercantile Marine became an efficient concern. Of course, the White Star Line was foremost in his thoughts and remained the principal line of the combine, receiving his first consideration at all times.

In March 1907 the *Suevic* was returning home to Liverpool from Melbourne. She was scheduled to call at Plymouth, land some of her passengers, and then discharge her cargo in London, before proceeding to her home-port of Liverpool.

On March 17th she was approaching the Cornish coast and the Lizard light was calculated to be 138 miles away. Her course was set accordingly, and she proceeded at her full speed of 13 knots. By the time she had covered 122 miles by dead reckoning, she should have come within sight of the Lizard light, which is very powerful. However, she carried straight on, still at full speed, although a slight fog with drizzle of rain had come up.

At 10.25pm the chief engineer, who was on the deck, saw the light looming up very close and breakers on the port side of the ship; at the same time the look-out reported "Breakers ahead". The captain ordered the helm "hard-a-port", but it was too late and the ship struck the rocks at full speed. The engines were immediately put full astern to try to get her off, but she was firmly aground. There was danger of damaging her further in any attempt to drag her bows off the rocks, so it was decided to stop the engines and send up distress signals.

The signals were seen at once from the shore and lifeboats were immediately launched. At the same time the *Suevic* was lowering her own boats and all the passengers were safely carried ashore in these and in the lifeboats. They landed at the little Cornish fishing village of Cadgwith and the Great Western Railway organised a fleet of motor cars to take them to Helston, (a remarkable feat on the part of the railway company).

Meanwhile salvage vessels from Liverpool had been sent for and hurried down to examine the wreck. It was decided that the only thing to do, short of abandoning her as a total loss, was to cut off the bows and refloat the stern. This was a considerable undertaking in those days, as there was no such thing as oxyacetelene flame and the job would have to be done with small charges of dynamite. It was an undertaking which required great skill and precision, as the conditions were not at all favourable. Several divers were asked to undertake the work and all said it would take over a week.

Eventually a young man named Fabian who was employed by the Liverpool Salvage Company was found. He examined the wreck and declared he could do the job in twenty-four hours. He worked without stopping under great difficulties and eventually the bow of the *Suevic* was very skilfully parted from the stern, which riding free on the swell, helped the final break away.

The whole of the passenger accommodation and the engines and boilers were undamaged, and so she was cut in two abaft the bridge where the passenger accommodation was divided from the officers' quarters.

The *Suevic* was taken in tow by tugs, but they were only needed to steer her as she proceeded, stern first, under her own steam to Southampton, where she was dry-docked.

A new bow was built for her by Harland & Wolff in Belfast, and when finished was launched head on. It was a difficult operation to launch half a ship, but one which was successfully carried out. The new bow was towed round to Southampton, where it was joined to the stern. So precise was the engineering of the builders that no difficulty whatever was found in mating the two halves together again. It proved to be a job well worth doing as the *Suevic* saw many years service after this event. The owners advertised her first sailing for January 14th, 1908, whilst the new bow was still on the stocks which illustrates the complete

Olympic

confidence J Bruce Ismay had in his old friends at Harland & Wolff. She resumed her normal Australian runs and until 1914 ran regularly with no further trouble.

It is difficult to understand why such an experienced captain did not use the lead-line on approaching the Lizard, as this would have at once told him he was nearing the shore. He wished to take a four point bearing before altering course for Plymouth, but it seemed foolhardy in the extreme to remain on his course at full speed without sounding, when being so near the shore.

As the year 1907 opened, it was decided that in the future the fastest vessels of the White Star Line should run from Southampton instead of from Liverpool, as it was much nearer to London and the Continental ports. So in May the *Celtic* took an experimental voyage by this route. A month later, the *Adriatic* took the first sailing in the new regular service. Her partners were to be the *Oceanic,* the *Teutonic* and the *Majestic*. The *Celtic* would continue to operate the Liverpool service.

During this year, whilst the *Mauretania* was still building for the Cunard Company and the world could see the performance of the *Lusitania,* her sister ship, Mr and Mrs Bruce Ismay went one night to dine with Lord and Lady Pirrie at their London home, Downshire House, Belgrave Square. During that evening Ismay and his host, who both believed in the 'big ship' with great comfort and moderate speed, first discussed the *Olympic* and *Titanic* which were to be followed by a third, the *Britannic.* These three great new ships were for the Southampton mail service.

There and then, after dinner was over, they drew up rough plans of the three sisters. They were to be the last word in comfort and elegance, and although fast, the key word was to be safety and comfort for the passengers, combined with economy of operation. The plan for the future was as follows. The *Majestic* and *Teutonic,* which were now getting on in years, would be relegated to reserve. The big four, as they were known, *Celtic, Cedric, Baltic* and *Adriatic* would work the Liverpool service. The *Oceanic* would partner the *Olympic* and *Titanic* on the Southampton route until the *Britannic* was put into commission, and then would deputise for whichever ship was in for overhaul.

To raise the money to assist in building these new ships, early in 1908 the White Star Line issued £1,500,000 worth of additional shares, which were eagerly bought; at Harland & Wolff's yard in Belfast two gigantic slipways were built, in a place formerly occupied by three. Work commenced on the *Olympic* and shortly afterwards on the *Titanic;* the two sisters were built side by side and when both were on the stocks they must have presented a magnificent sight. Meanwhile the *Megantic* and *Laurentic* were building for the Canadian trade, the *Laurentic* being given a new type of machinery. This was a combination of a pair of reciprocating engines driving two wing propellers exhausting into a low pressure turbine which only drove ahead on the centre shaft, making the *Laurentic* a triple screw vessel. So satisfactory was this combination method of propulsion that it became standard Harland & Wolff practice for many years and was adopted for the *Olympic, Titanic* and *Britannic* as well as for many other large vessels built in the Belfast shipyard.

The White Star Line had always staunchly believed in the value of training officers under sail so J Bruce Ismay bought the 1,713 tons steel ship built by Connell of Glasgow in 1894 as an ocean going training school, and renamed her *Mersey.* She had the distinction of being the first sailing vessel to carry a wireless and under the command of Captain Corner voyaged all over the world until sold by H A Sanderson at the outbreak of the 1914-18 war.

It was about this time that Bruce Ismay decided that White Star employees should have a superannuation fund. In 1908 this was rather unusual, but he felt that many of the staff both ashore and afloat would be glad of a pension in their latter years. He therefore started a pension fund for the office staff which was to be operated through the Royal Insurance Company, the idea being that once the scheme was well established and satisfactory, it would be extended to the officers of the Line. It was always the intention to do this, but in view of the sinking of the *Titanic* in 1912 and the retirement of J Bruce Ismay just over one year later, the scheme for the officers never materialised; and it is sad to think that there are White Star officers who are now old men living in very, very reduced circumstances.

In 1909 wireless was still in its infancy, but its worth was proved on January 23rd, when the *Republic,* in thick fog was rammed by the Italian ship *Florida* off Sandy Hook. The *Republic* sent out distress signals and five vessels hurried to the scene. Amongst these rescuing ships was the *Baltic,* which tried to tow the *Republic* but the latter sank before reaching port. The *Republic* was the largest vessel to be lost at sea at that time, and although the *Florida* was only 5,000 tons and had been badly damaged in the bows, she took off the *Republic's* crew and passengers. These were transferred to the *Baltic* and the *Florida* herself managed to reach New York for repairs.

The following year the White Star Line and wireless again made front-page news, this time by the flight of a murderer to Canada.

Dr Crippen had poisoned his wife with hyoscin, dismembered her, and buried her in the cellar. He had then told neighbours that she had gone to America with another man. However, suspicions were aroused and the police were informed that she was missing, and Dr Crippen was interviewed. Inspector Dew of Scotland Yard examined the house, questioned the doctor and went away apparently satisfied. Crippen, however, panicked and taking his secretary, Miss Ethel Le Neve with him, fled to Antwerp, and there boarded the Canadian Pacific steamer *Montrose* for Canada, in the name of Robinson, with Miss Le Neve disguised as his son. After his flight the police dug up the garden at Hilldrop Crescent, Camden Town, where Dr Crippen had lived, and also excavated the cellar. Here they found the remains of Belle Elmore (the name Crippen's wife had adopted for the stage) and a tremendous hue and cry was raised after the fugitives.

The captain of the *Montrose* became suspicious of his passenger, Mr Robinson, as he and his 'son' were seen to walk about hand in hand in a very affectionate manner, and he wirelessed his suspicions to Scotland Yard. Inspector Dew left Liverpool for Canada aboard the *Laurentic,* which was a faster vessel, and came aboard the *Montrose* with the Pilot at Father Point. He arrested Dr Crippen and Miss Le Neve, and brought them back to England in the *Megantic* (the *Laurentic's* sister ship). Dr Crippen was tried at the Old Bailey, and sentenced to death, and Miss Le Neve was acquitted.

In connection with this event, an old White Star employee tells the following curious story. He was a steward aboard the *Megantic* some months later. Having completed his duties in the second-class cabins, he fell asleep on one of the bunks and had a terrible nightmare, waking in a cold sweat and shouting. One of his fellow stewards rushed in and asked what was the matter. When he was told of the dream he said "That is the bunk that Dr Crippen slept in when he was brought home to stand trial last year".

CHAPTER 13
Olympic's maiden voyage

The day the *Olympic* was handed over to her owners was a great one for Belfast, for also on that day, May 31st, 1911, the *Titanic* was launched. Bruce Ismay attended the launching accompanied by his daughter, Margaret; many prominent people including J Pierpont Morgan, had come specially from London. After seeing the *Titanic* safely launched the whole company of guests sailed away from Queens Island to Liverpool on board the *Olympic*.

The Press was full of the news of the two great sisters, which represented 90,000 tons of shipping. All credit was given to the White Star Line for their great undertaking, and also to Harland & Wolff for the building of these two ships, which together represented £3,000,000, an immense sum for those days. Added to this, the *Olympic* was some 15,000 tons larger than the previous world's largest liners, the Cunarders *Lusitania* and *Mauretania*.

On arrival in the Mersey, Ismay and his daughter disembarked and returned to Sandheys, and the vessel was thrown open for public inspection, the proceeds of which were given to local hospitals. She lay in the Mersey dressed overall and everyone on Merseyside was able to obtain a good view of her graceful lines.

Later the *Olympic* sailed down to Southampton, and on June 14th 1911, she set off on her maiden voyage to New York; she was still receiving enormous publicity and it was a great contrast when her sister sailed the following April. The *Titanic* received little publicity in comparison, partly no doubt owing to the coal strike which was in progress at the time.

Mr and Mr J Bruce Ismay travelled down to Southampton and went on the maiden voyage of the *Olympic*. From this experience Ismay devised a number of improvements which were to be incorporated into her sister ship the *Titanic*. One of these was the glass enclosed screen on B Deck, with self-contained suites and private promenade decks; the following letter to Ismay, Imrie & Company in Liverpool shows the meticulous attention he paid to the smallest detail.

9, Broadway, New York.
June 22nd, 1911.
To Messrs. Ismay, Imrie & Co., 30, James Street,
Liverpool.
Dear Sirs,

I was very pleased indeed to be able to send to you the following cable message on Wednesday last:- "Arrived at Lightship 2.24, docked at 10 a.m. Everything worked most satisfactorily, passengers delighted. Passage 5 days, 16 hours, 42 minutes, average speed 2 1.7; coal consumption given *3,540*, think it liberal estimate. Delayed by fog 1 1/2 hours. Daily runs 428, 534, 542, 525, 548. Single ended boilers not lighted. Communicate this to Pirrie, Harland, Belfast," which I now have to confirm.

Everything on board the ship worked most satisfactorily, and the passengers were loud in their praises of the accommodation and table.

The machinery worked excellently, and there was no hitch of any kind in connection with same.

The consumption has been extremely low, averaging, as far as I can make out, about *620* tons a day instead of *720* as anticipated, and we arrived here, with approximately, *1,300* tons of coal on board the ship. I am arranging to have the ship fully coaled for the return trip, including the reserve hunker, so as to reduce the quantity required to be taken at Southampton.

At no time during the passage were the engines working at full speed, the highest number of revolutions being 79 port and 81 starboard, at which speed the ship was practically quiet. On the passage home we expect to work her up to full speed. The five single ended boilers were not used at all during the passage out.

The most popular room on board the ship was, undoubtedly, the Reception Room, as it is always crowded after lunch, at tea time and after dinner and we cabled you, requesting you to communicate with Messrs. Harland & Wolff, asking them to order 50 additional cane chairs and ten tables for this room.

The after companion-way between the Lounge and Smoking Room on 'A' deck was practically not used at all, and I think we must again consider putting state rooms in this space; but I propose to watch this matter carefully on the voyage home to see what use is made of the accommodation for the large number of passengers on board.

The deck space, with the number of passengers on board going out, was certainly excessive, and I think, in another ship we might carry out the rooms on 'B' deck the same as those on 'C' deck.

I also cabled, asking you to arrange for a potato-peeler in the crew's galley, as it was felt desirable one should be placed there, and also one of Phillips water tube steam ovens for the bakehouse, of the largest capacity possible to increase the output, as experience shows that the oven at present in the ship is not capable of producing sufficient bread daily.

Finding that there were no holders for cigars or cigarettes in the W.C.s we cabled you, asking you to arrange to supply these, so that they can be fitted before the next voyage.

The only trouble of any consequence on board the ship arose from the springs of the beds being too "springy", this, in conjunction with the spring mattresses, accentuated the pulsation in the ship to such an extent as to seriously interfere with passengers sleeping, and we cabled, asking you to communicate with Pirrie that if he sees no objection, we would like to have lath bottoms fitted before the next voyage, and hope this can be arranged.

The trouble in connection with the beds was entirely due to their being too comfortable.

Finding that the service from the pantry to the saloon could be satisfactorily carried out through one door on each side, we have arranged to close the other doors, which will enable us to put in two additional tables in the Saloon, giving an increased seating capacity of eight people.

It came to my knowledge that some people had been down in the Engine Room during the passage from Southampton to Cherbourg. I therefore wrote to Mr. Bell in regard thereto, and herewith enclose you his reply. I am sure you will share my surprise that Mr. Willett Bruce and Mr. Blake should feel themselves justified in giving permission to the gentleman named to visit the Engine Room, and I shall be glad if you will ask them for their explanation for so doing.

The working of the tenders at Cherbourg with passengers and baggage was extremely unsatisfactory, in spite of the fact that the whole question had been very carefully gone into at a meeting held at Southampton on the 3rd May, when definite instructions were formulated for dealing with this important matter, and I cannot understand why Captain Beresford did not carry out same.

I was also extremely surprised that Captain Beresford should have felt himself justified in leaving the *Olympic* before all the baggage was on board the ship. He left in the *Nomadic* long before the baggage was transferred from the *Traffic,* it occurs to me that it is part of the duties of a Marine Superintendent to remain by the ship until all the baggage has been transferred, and I shall be glad if you will ask him why he did not do so.

I send you herewith copy of a memorandum drawn up by Mr. Andrews, which clearly states the manner in which the passengers and baggage should be embarked, and I should be glad if you will pass same on to Captain Beresford, requesting him to carry out same in future.

I am much obliged for your marconigrams of the 15th and 16th, and your cables of the 20th and 21st instant reading as follows:

Received June 15th. After full conference have agreed to give increase 10s. sailors and firemen *Teutonic* and *Baltic.* Hope to sign men on this afternoon.

Received June 16th. Baltic, Teutonic crews practically complete.

Have made statement 10s. advance given voluntarily your sanction before sailing.

Received June 20th, All well house, Tom better, labour situation still very unsettled, now experiencing trouble with stewards. Acting with Cunard Line, have had to give ordinary stewards £3 15s.

Received June 21st. Labour position Southampton very unsatisfactory, stevedores, coalies, crews all stopped work. Crews unwilling to accept Liverpool basis settlement. We think it is not desirable to make any further concessions Southampton, as will inevitably result upsetting Liverpool settlement. Are informing Southampton that unless we can get crew for *Adriatic* on Liverpool basis settlement, will blank round voyage. Think firm attitude necessary in order to clear position Southampton before *Olympic* returns. Do you agree?

We are advised employment outside crew Southampton will cause renewal Liverpool disturbance, and doubtful if any material number can be obtained. and confirm my cable to you of yesterday, reading:- Entirely share your views that Southampton steamers should not be given greater proportionate advance than crews Liverpool steamers. If sailing *Adriatic* would prejudice your despatching *Olympic* agree to blanking *Adriatic* sailing, sincerely trust, however, this will not be necessary, as it is expected that she will have 300 first-class passengers hence July 12th. You have full discretion deal with situation. Please keep us fully posted.

The *Olympic* is doing very well for Wednesday next, and I expect she will leave here with over 700 first-class passengers.

For your information, the following is copy of a cable I sent to Lord Pirrie immediately on arrival:- *"Olympic* is a marvel, and has given unbounded satisfaction.

Once again accept my warmest and most sincere congratulations. Will cable you full particulars speed, consumption later."

I was glad to receive your message at Cherbourg, reading: Telegram from Ballin begins confidential. Had meeting with Bosworth Berlin yesterday. Though for well known reasons not remaining in the Pool-east bound, agree not only to enter rate agreement, but binds itself, in order not to disturb working of Pool, to follow all advances of rates which Allan and Dominion Lines might be obliged to adopt for adjustment purposes. Bosworth further agreed in principle to make the same arrangement applicable to the British, Scandinavian, West bound traffic, provided Allan Line concur Bosworth undertakes to use his influence with Allan Line that latter remains in the Pool for Continental and East bound business. This is subject to the Royal Line remaining in the Pool, or if they should not remain agree to enter this separate agreement. And wired you copy of the reply I sent to Mr. Ballin, as follows:- Your confidential telegram received, and congratulate you on result of your interview with

Bosworth, which clears the ground very much, and leads me to be very hopeful that the meeting of the 10th July may prove successful.

We had meetings of the board and finance committee of the I.M.M. Company yesterday on board the *Olympic*. Messrs. Steele, Morgan Junior, Widener, Perkins and Waterberry being present, and they were all very much pleased with the ship.

I confirm the following cables which have passed between us in regard to the labour situation to-day:-

Received

No. 1. Are hopeful Southampton crews wages difficulty may be settled satisfactorily, but demand is being made for full recognition of Union here and Southampton by allowing officials on steamers. This would destroy any chance retaining free labour. Would like to resist this, even at risk stopping *Adriatic,* but have reason believe Cunard Line and others have conceded, therefore our position greatly weakened. Do you feel strong enough this point to justify risking rupture.

No.2. Notification to crew that unless they sign forthwith at rates offered, *Adriatic* would be laid up, has resulted in their now signing. As *Celtic, Megantic* also now signing, it will be difficult for Union attempt to enforce recognition of point this week.

Sent

Your two messages received. Very pleased learn rates offered are being accepted by crew *Adriatic, Celtic, Megantic.* Sincerely trust this ends matter, and that there will be no further trouble next week.

I was very pleased indeed to receive your second message, advising me that the notification of the crew of the *Adriatic* that unless they signed at the rates offered, the ship would be laid up, had the desired result, and that her crew, and that of the *Celtic* and *Megantic* were signing on, and agree with you that it will be very difficult for the Union to attempt to enforce recognition next week, and sincerely hope that the trouble is now ended.

Yours truly,
J. Bruce Ismay.

R.M.S. *Olympic* at Sea.
June 14th, 1911.
Mr. Ismay
Sir,
In reply to your inquiry regarding visitors to Engine Rooms, I beg to state that three gentlemen have been in Engine Room during the passage from Southampton all by Mr. Blake's instruction, viz. Mr. Van Eldon and two gentlemen connected with a French Steamship Company, whose names I do not remember, but whom Mr. Blake said had been sent to him by Mr. Willett Bruce.

Another gentleman presented himself this morning saying that Mr. Currie had instructed him to come to me, but I refused him permission on his verbal statement.

Your instructions shall be strictly obeyed.
I am, Sir,
Your obedient servant,
J. Bell,
Chief Engineer.

CHAPTER 14

Circumstances of Bruce Ismay's retirement

For some years previously Mr and Mrs Bruce Ismay had rented, as a London home, 27 Chesham Street, Belgravia, SW1 and it was here that their youngest son, George, was born. Bruce Ismay was so often in London now, which his wife infinitely preferred to Liverpool, that they began to look for a permanent home there. Mrs Ismay favoured one of the houses that stand in their own grounds in the Inner Circle of Regent's Park but her husband decided it would be better to be more centrally situated, so, in 1909 they bought 15 Hill Street, Mayfair. They then alternated between here and 'Sandheys' at Mossley Hill, Liverpool. It was in this house that he died 28 years later and from here that his eldest child, Margaret, was married in March, 1912, just before the *Titanic* sailed on her maiden voyage.

As has already been seen in this story the White Star Line was intimately connected with the Shaw Savill & Albion Company and in the autumn of 1911, as the *Titanic* lay completing at Queen's Island, J Bruce Ismay offered the chairmanship of the Shaw Savill & Albion Company to H A Sanderson. In November Sanderson wrote to Ismay saying he would be happy to accept the chairmanship and the letter continued:-

But this brings me to another point, and I feel I must be entirely candid with you, and that you should know all the facts before you are asked to give a decision.
You are, of course, aware that I have had it in mind for some time to retire from the position that I hold in Liverpool, and that when we were last in New York together, the period of my remaining service was referred to as of two or three years'

duration, and this fact has at least once been mentioned in conversation between us since that time. It was my intention, after the turn of the New Year, to intimate to you that I would like this period to expire with the next calendar year, 1912, but I feel that the Shaw Savill matter places an obligation upon me to disclose to you at once what I have in mind, for I realise, of course, that the knowledge of my approaching withdrawal might very reasonably cause your views to alter, as to my taking on the chairmanship, either temporarily or permanently, and I have, therefore, kept the matter quite open and subject to further review by your goodself.

I will not attempt to disguise the fact that having been identified with the White Star Line so long and so intimately, the prospect of terminating the connection causes me real distress, and I dislike to think of it; but, on the other hand, the strain of the Liverpool work is, I know, beginning to tell on me, and I want to arrange the remainder of my business career in a manner that will extend it as long as is possible and desirable, and it is not practicable to do so without asking to be relieved of my Liverpool work. We have good, loyal, able men under us, who, I am convinced will rise to the occasion if you will increase their reponsibilities, and I most earnestly hope that, upon reflection, you will not harbour the thought that I am, in any sense, deserting the ship prematurely, or that I am doing what is not right and fair by you and the company. That would not be doing me justice, I honestly believe, and were you to do so, it would cause me more unhappiness than I could possibly express in words.

Our friends in New York will not be surprised to learn of my intention to retire, as it was referred to at an interview which I had with Grenfell, on their behalf, in New York on the occasion already referred to, when you and I discussed the same subject, and I would like the fact to be communicated to them by your goodself as I feel that to be in every way the proper procedure. It only remains for me, consequently, to place the whole matter unreservedly in your hands, and to ask you and them to accept the assurance of my very great anxiety to so arrange matters that when my connection with the company ceases on the 31st December, 1912, I may leave with the knowledge that I do so with that goodwill and regard which I have consistently sought to deserve at your and their hands.

On January 10th, while at Southampton waiting to sail to New York aboard the *Olympic,* Bruce Ismay wrote to Sanderson; part of the letter read:-

I had a long and friendly talk with Grenfell last night, in regard to the wish you have expressed of retiring from the service of the I.M.M. Company at the end of the present year.

During our conversation, I told him briefly of what took place when you and I talked the situation over the other day in Liverpool, referring more particularly to your remark that during the whole of your business career you had never filled the premier position in the business in which you were engaged, and that this had caused you a certain sense of disappointment, and both Grenfell and I fully appreciate and realise your feeling.

I further stated that, had I left the I.M.M. Company a few years ago, as I had intended, you would have taken the position of President for a certain length of time, when you would have retired, having occupied the highest position in the service.

I repeated to Grenfell what I told you at our interview, namely, that I was prepared to resign the position of President at once in your favour, but that this apparently did not appeal to you.

I am very anxious to meet your wishes, and will gladly do anything in my power to enable you to complete your business career at the top of the tree, and, with this in view, I would ask you to seriously consider the following proposition, namely, that I will remain on as President of the I.M.M. Company until the 31st December, 1912 during which period I would practically make London my headquarters, coming to Liverpool, say, once a week, in order to attend to my duties as director of the Liverpool, London & Globe, the Sea Insurance Company, and the Protection Association, and you should take entire charge of and be responsible for the conduct of the Liverpool business, only referring to me matters of exceptional importance, and questions of policy; that you should take the chairmanship of Shaw, Savill & Albion Company and continue looking after the London business as you have done in the past.

In reply to this letter Sanderson sent the following cable to New York which Ismay received on his arrival there:

Consider proposal contained in your letter 10th most generous, and assuming you are not solely actuated by kindly consideration for me, I accept provided hankers in accord, in which event will do utmost justify your and their action. I attach particular importance your offer remain British Committee, and will endeavour to make your co-operation there as agreeable to yourself as it will certainly be helpful to company.

Later having had several discussions on the subject with all concerned in the Morgan Combine, Bruce Ismay sent the following cable to Sanderson:-

Would it be entirely agreeable to you, if my resignation took effect from the 30th June, 1913 instead of 31st December, 1912. Referring to your letter 13th have no intention mentioning proposed changes to anyone. Wish matter kept absolutely private for present.

Sanderson replied, also by cable:-

Please conclude any arrangements regarding your resignation which is agreeable and convenient to yourself and bankers, but if later date than December 31st next fixed prefer my resignation take effect then as arranged, and if thereafter bankers desire me take office will be very pleased fall in with their wishes all being well, and provided interval not sufficient put me out of touch with affairs.

On January 24th 1912 Bruce Ismay sailed for Southampton aboard the *Olympic* and on arrival in London he wrote to Sanderson explaining his point of view:-

It is my intention (subject always to the I.M.M. not giving me six months' notice to resign the presidency at an earlier date), to remain in my present position until the 30th June, 1913 instead of resigning on the 31st December, 1912, as indicated in my letter of the 10th ultimo. My reason for this is, that, in any circumstances, I can only look upon my prospective severance from the business with which I have been connected all my career with very mixed and doubtful feelings, and, perhaps selfishly, I am anxious to make it as easy as possible, which, after all, is not unreasonable. I feel that making such an entire change in my mode of life as that contemplated would come less hardly if made in the summer than in the winter, as in the former case, I should have good weather, long days, and my shooting to look forward to, which would give me occupation for some months and this would enable me to better prepare for the time when I should have little or nothing with which to fill up my time.

Forgive me for remarking that it is difficult to understand why you should be apparently anxious to assume the presidency on the 1st January, 1913, but doing so on the 1st July, 1913 has no attraction to you whatever. This, however, is not my business. I understand your position is as follows:-

If I remain as president of the I.M.M. Company until the 30th June, 1913 you wish to resign from all your positions on the 31st December, 1912, and if on the 1st July, 1913, all being well, and you feel that the interval during which you have been out of the business is not sufficient to put you out of touch with affairs, and our friends in New York wish it, you are prepared to accept the position of president of the I.M.M. Company.

If I have accurately stated your decision, and I think I have, let us see how it would work out from a business and personal point of view. The position would be as follows:-

I would, during the last six months of office, have not the least idea as to whether or not I was going to retire from business on the 30th June, 1913, as it must be obvious that, if you decided you did not wish to assume the position of president, I must continue to do so until such time as some other arrangement could be made, as I could not, for one moment, be a party to placing the I.M.M. Company in a difficulty, and (perhaps stupidly), I feel that if both you and I were to sever our connection with the company at the same time, it would do so.

Sanderson's answer to this was the following:-

I have for years looked forward to the 31st December, 1912 as the date on which I shall take the important step of retiring, and retirement, or altered conditions, such as you propose in your letter of the 10th January would alike give me the relief and change I need.

This idea did not appeal to J Bruce Ismay as he says:-

Of course, I cannot express any opinion as to how your proposition will appeal to our banking friends, this is a matter for them to consider, but it occurs to me that there are many serious difficulties in the way of their coming under such a commitment.

Has it occurred to you what people will say, and think, if the suggestion you make is given effect to, viz.:- that you resign from business on the 31st December, 1912, and I resign on the 30th June, 1913, and you succeed me on the 1st July, 1913? They would, I think, naturally draw the following conclusions:- "When Sanderson resigned, Ismay tried to carry on the business alone, failed, and had to resign, then Sanderson was brought

back to take the presidency although he had resigned from the company six months previously. Would this not be a very natural inference to draw from what has taken place?"

Please do not think I am trying to bring pressure to bear on you to remain with the company during the six months in question, as I do not wish to influence you in your decision, but no question such as that indicated in the previous paragraph would arise did you do so, and assume the office of president the day I resign without any interregnum.

Finally, two days later, after a further discussion between them a memorandum was issued and signed by them both.

The following is the result of my conversation with Sanderson in regard to retirement, and I understand the arrangement come to is entirely satisfactory to him, viz.:-

That I should remain as president of the I.M.M. Company and hold my present position until the 30th June, 1913 on which date I resign the presidency.

Sanderson to be granted six months' leave of absence from the 31st December, 1912. During this time he would act as chairman of the Shaw, Savill, Albion Company and of George Thompson, but be entirely relieved of all other work. He wishes it understood that during this time he would receive no remuneration.

Sanderson would resume all his duties on 1st June, 1913, or some time about this date, so as to get in touch with the business, and assume the office of president of the I.M.M. Company on the 1st July, 1913.

I would continue a member of the British Committee after the 30th June, 1913, and if thought desirable, would act as a director of Shaw, Savill & Albion Company, and George Thompson & Co., either prior or subsequent to this date.

Of course, it is understood that the above arrangement has been come to subject to its being agreeable to Messrs. J. P. Morgan & Co.

(signed) Bruce Ismay.

Dated London, 26th February, 1912.

This was followed by a letter from J Bruce Ismay to Charles Steele, the secretary of Morgan & Company, in New York, which read:-

It is abundantly clear that Sanderson has definitely made up his mind that unless he is to succeed me as president of the I.M.M. Company on the 30th June, 1913 he will absolutely retire from business on the 31st December next.

Further, he practically makes it a condition of remaining with the I.M.M. Company that he should be granted six months' leave of absence from the 31st December (without any remuneration), on the grounds that he could not continue in business for a day after the 31st December, being tired, and "wound up" to that date but for no longer; he also feels that rest will be beneficial, in view of his assuming the duties of president in July.

There is no reason, from my point of view, why the six months' leave of absence should not be granted.

I am anxious that Sanderson should obtain his wish as to holding the premier position in the business in which he is engaged before he retires from business, and the only possible way of giving effect thereto is by my resigning in his favour, and this I have expressed my willingness to do.

Of course, the 30th June, 1913 is a "FAR CRY" and much may happen between now and then, for this reason I suggest that whatever may be arranged should be kept absolutely private until the 31st December. No good purpose would be served by making any announcement, as it would only create a feeling of unrest, and the suggested changes may never come into force.

We can talk the whole situation over when I see you in April, as I hope to do.

On March 2nd just one month before the *Titanic* set out on her trials in Belfast Lough, Charles Steele wrote the following reply to J Bruce Ismay's letter:-

There must be something like mental telepathy in the world, for as I came down town I was thinking about the situation over there, and had just about decided to cable you making the suggestion which you had already thought of and adopted. The proposed arrangement is entirely satisfactory to me, and I hope is both to you and Sanderson. I quite agree there is no reason whatever why it should be made public at the present time, and I think it much better that nothing more should be said on the subject until the time arrives to act. I trust everything will run along smoothly now. There are lots of things that may happen before the 30th June, 1913.

When these arrangements were made and Bruce Ismay wrote those last words, he little knew that before all these carefully made plans could take effect, there would be a marine disaster of such magnitude that it would shake the whole world, the sinking of the *Titanic* on her maiden voyage in April 1912, and that he himself would have to face an ordeal of hate and calumny started by the newspapers such as few men have had to endure. One of the rumours started at the time of the *Titanic's* loss was that as he could not face public opinion he retired from his position in the IMM Company and White Star Line, withdrew to Ireland and became a recluse. This rumour has become a legend but, as can be seen from the foregoing correspondence, the *Titanic* affair had nothing whatsoever to do with Bruce Ismay's retirement which had already been arranged two months before the ship was put into commission.

CHAPTER 15

Titanic's maiden voyage

On April 2nd at 0.600 hours on a fine morning the *Titanic* left Queen's Island on her trials in Belfast Lough and after adjusting her compasses steamed towards the Isle of Man.

H A Sanderson was on board representing the White Star Line; Lord Pirrie wished to go on the maiden voyage himself but he was not well and his doctor would not let him make the voyage. The Hon. Alexander Montgomery Carlisle (Lady Pirrie's brother) had been their chief designer but had recently retired, so Harland & Wolff were represented by Thomas Andrews (Lord Pirrie's nephew). He was a brilliant young naval architect who had had a great deal to do with the construction of the vessel. He

Titanic

J Bruce Ismay pictured shortly before Titanic's maiden voyage

was Lord Pirrie's right-hand man, managing director of the firm, and was marked down to be Lord Pirrie's successor. He had with him some employees from the shipyard to deal with any adjustments that might be required to the machinery of the new ship on her first long voyage.

At 6pm the *Titanic* returned to Queen's Island and later left for Southampton, where she arrived at midnight on Wednesday, April 3rd.

Exactly one week later she was due to leave Southampton on her maiden voyage but during this week a great deal of work still remained to be done. Officials of the Board of Trade, thoroughly inspected and passed the life saving equipment, having the starboard lifeboats lowered into the water.

As the *Titanic* was advertised to sail on April 10th, the company was determined that she should do so. Unfortunately there was a coal strike on at the time, and in order to allow her to sail as advertised it was necessary to take the coal out of the *Oceanic* and the American liner *New York,* both of which were laid up in consequence.

Thomas Andrews wrote a letter to his wife, saying how delighted he was with everything, but that he still had a great deal of work to do, before the ship sailed on April 10th.

Mr and Mrs J Bruce Ismay motored down from Hill Street with their three children in the big Daimler Landaulette which was always used by Mrs Ismay for touring. It was one of the few occasions when Bruce Ismay undertook a long journey by car as he disliked motoring so much. They all stayed the night at the South Western Hotel, Southampton. He was in good spirits, having just a fortnight before seen his eldest daughter happily married, and now he was going on the maiden voyage of his latest ship. The improvements that he had suggested after travelling as a passenger on the maiden voyage of the *Olympic*, had been incorporated in the *Titanic*, and he was looking forward to seeing them in action.

He was sailing alone as it was the Easter holidays and his wife felt that as he was only going straight out and back in the new ship, she ought to spend her time with the children, who were not home for very long.

At 9.3am. on April 10th the family went aboard the *Titanic* as she lay in the Ocean Dock; at noon the liner sailed. Unlike her sister ship the *Olympic*, and contrary to what one would have expected for the maiden voyage of a ship of such size and magnificence, she put quietly to sea, with no great publicity. Mrs Bruce Ismay and the children watched her depart, and then set off on their motor tour of Devonshire and Wales.

As the *Titanic* passed the *New York* which was lying alongside the quay, the suction caused by her propellers drew the *New York* out from the side and for a moment a collision seemed inevitable. Mats were rigged, and the *Titanic* stopped dead while the tugs came and towed the *New York* back to her berth, and so an unfortunate incident was avoided.

In brilliant April sunshine, although the day was cold, the shining new ship, her gold band showing clearly on the black hull, crossed the Channel and reached Cherbourg about 6.30pm. She took on board additional passengers, and mails from tenders. At about 8pm the world's largest vessel left Cherbourg for Queenstown, where she arrived about 11.30 the following morning and took on board more passengers and mails from tenders; she left at 1.30pm for New York.

Fortunately, in view of what was to follow, she was by no means carrying her full complement of passengers - only 332 first class, 277 second class and 709 third class instead of 735 first class, 674 second class and 1,026 third class for which she had accommodation.

Most of the crew were from the *Olympic*, some from the *Oceanic*, and some from the *New York*. Many had only joined the vessel on the previous Wednesday morning, and were completely lost on board such a large ship. A great number of them were unacquainted with each other.

At Queenstown, Bell, who was the chief engineer, came to

Bruce Ismay's cabin, B56 on 'B' Deck, to discuss with him the coal which was to be consumed on the voyage. Ismay wished it to be conserved and the ship not forced at all. It was, however, arranged between them that a speed trial should take place on the following Monday morning, provided the weather was suitable. This conversation was afterwards to be twisted into a declaration that Mr Ismay had interfered with the navigation of the vessel, a statement which was quite untrue, as Ismay never intruded on the captain while at sea.

As with his father before him, Bruce Ismay believed in great prudence in navigation. He had already had a serious disagreement with his fellow directors over the length of passage of the *Olympic*. In order to make certain of a safe passage he had wished that the vessel should have an extra 24 hours at sea, but his co-directors had argued that the popularity of the *Olympic* would suffer from this, and the speed which she could make would be wasted, as a great many of the passengers wished to cross the Atlantic as quickly as possible. He finally gave way on this point in the case of the *Olympic,* when the vessel was on the Northern track. But now in the case of her sister ship he was adamant and the instructions which Captain Smith received before sailing were "Under no circumstances whatsoever is the *Titanic* to arrive before 5 a.m, on Wednesday morning at the Ambrose Light Vessel".

On the North Atlantic there are definite lanes, which the ships follow, called tracks. The Northern track, which is taken during the months of August to December, is approximately 200 miles shorter than the one used during the months of January till July. The Southern or longer track is taken because the ice floes or icebergs from the North coming down with the Labrador current break up and drift in the Gulf Stream, melting as they go, and presenting a serious menace to navigation.

The year 1912 was exceptional for the amount of ice about; the winter in the Arctic had been mild and the ice had come down earlier than usual. Many sailors at that time said they had never seen anything like it. The *Titanic* was on her proper seasonal course, which was the Southern track during the days of April 11th, 12th, 13th and 14th. She received a number of warnings of ice and icebergs, and these she acknowledged.

Out of courtesy to J Bruce Ismay, Captain Smith sent some

of these or any other wireless messages which he thought would be of interest to him. Quite often Bruce Ismay simply put them in his pocket unread, and returned them later.

The policy in those days was to keep a good look out in the vicinity of ice, and, provided the weather was clear to keep up a good speed; this was to ensure that the ship should answer more readily to the helm. After the *Titanic* catastrophe this practice was altered and vessels now reduce speed when ice is reported. The *Titanic* had been four days at sea, and everyone's high expectations of this new vessel had been realised. The trip had been smooth with no difficulties. It was Sunday night, April 14th, and there had been a half hour of hymn singing in the second-class library.

At 9.30pm a wireless message had been received from the Atlantic Transport liner, *Mesaba* belonging to the International Mercantile Marine Company reading:- "In latitude 42° N. to 41° 25' N., long. 49° to 50° 30' W. Saw much heavy pack ice and a great number large icebergs. Also field ice. Weather good, clear." Unfortunately this vital message never reached the bridge. In 1912 wireless was still in its infancy, and the range was not nearly so wide as it is today. The *Titanic* was in range of Cape Race, a shore station off Newfoundland and she would only be near for a short time. The passengers knew it was possible to send private messages and although a great many had been sent, there were still more to be transmitted. The two wireless operators had been, and were, extremely busy with this work and somehow the message from the *Mesaba* got overlooked, with tragic consequences.

These two wireless operators were employed by the Marconi Company; they had only recently completed their training, and each had to do a twelve hour watch. Phillips, the senior, was twenty-four and Bride was only twenty-two; they bore a tremendous burden of responsibility. After the accident they remained at their post even after Captain Smith had relieved them.

At 11pm they received another message, this time from the Leyland liner *Californian,* another IMM ship, bound from London to Boston. It read: "We are stopped and surrounded by ice". She was very close and practically blew Phillips' headphones off. He was very tired, still transmitting messages to Cape Race, and he interrupted "Shut up, keep out I am working Cape Race", and so this was another vital warning which did not reach the bridge. The *Californian* had stopped for the night, as she was on the edge of a gigantic icefield. She only carried one wireless operator and at 11.30pm he went off duty for the night.

She was held by the subsequent Court of Inquiry to have been not more than eight to ten miles from the *Titanic*. Passengers and crew in the sinking ship clearly saw the lights of a vessel approach quite close to them and then recede some time between 12.30 and 2am, and could not understand why this ship did not answer her distress signals, which she was giving continuously during this period over wireless and by Morse lamp: eight rockets had also been sent up at intervals. It was alleged at both the English and American Courts of Inquiry that this vessel was the *Californian,* and Captain Lord, her master, was severely criticised. However, this has never been proved conclusively and there is a possibility that it was another unidentified ship which approached the *Titanic* this fateful night. If this unknown ship had responded to the signals, she could probably have saved many, if not all, the lives that were lost.

The conditions which the *Titanic* encountered on this night were quite extraordinary. The sea was as calm as a mill pond and the night extremely clear, with no wind at all, except that made by the ship as she slipped through the water at 21 knots; the stars were brilliant, but there was no moon. First Officer Murdoch was on watch on the bridge, Captain Smith had retired to his cabin, being satisfied that all was well. He had left instructions that a sharp look-out was to be kept for ice and that if visibility worsened they were to slow down, and call him immediately.

Suddenly at 11.40pm the still night was shattered by three rings on the bell, giving the alarm from the crow's nest and at the same time a shout down the telephone "Ice ahead". The look-outs had seen, looming up in the darkness, a large iceberg on the starboard bow. Murdoch had seen it almost as soon and immediately rang "Full speed astern" on both wing engines and "Stop" on the centre turbine. At the same time he shouted to Quartermaster Hitchin, who was at the wheel, "Hard a starboard". The *Titanic*'s bows veered slightly to port and as the iceberg slid past on her starboard side the well deck forward was deluged with ice. Murdoch shouted the order "Close all watertight doors". At this moment Captain Smith appeared and quickly took in the situation. He sent the carpenter below to sound the ship and gave orders for the wireless operators to send out distress signals.

Some of the passengers felt a slight shudder, but none realised that from this moment the fate of the great ship was sealed, for part of the iceberg under the water had ripped her open in the bilges. The gash extended 300 feet, from just forward of the foremast to No 5 boiler-room. Five water-tight compartments were damaged. She was designed to float with her two largest compartments flooded, but no merchant ship that has ever been built could have sustained this blow and remained afloat.

At the speed at which she was travelling, this appalling damage was done in less than 10 seconds. This was proved from experiments made later with the *Olympic;* it was found to take her 37 seconds to go from "full ahead" to "full astern", during which time the vessel travelled 456 yards. As it has always been assumed that the iceberg was about 500 yards ahead when first sighted, the *Titanic* would have only just begun to slow down when she struck. It has been said that if she had struck head on she would not have sunk, as her bow would have been telescoped and only the smaller compartments damaged. However, as was said at the Court of Inquiry, it would have been very bad seamanship on Murdoch's part not to have tried to avoid the hazard ahead.

If there had been moonlight it would have reflected on the ice which the look-outs would have seen earlier; or if the sea had been rough the breakers round the berg would have been visible from a greater distance. The whole story is so incredible, everything that night went against her, it seems now almost as if the tragedy were destined to take place, to make the rules for safety at sea more rigid in the future.

One of the survivors, F Dent Ray, who was at sea for many years with several companies, and who was a first class steward on many White Star ships, including the *Olympic,* has always said that the *Titanic* was magnificent.

Everyone was delighted with her, especially Thomas Andrews, who had taken special instruments on board to put on the deck to measure the vibration from the engines to the propellers. He found there was practically none. He was worried about only three things. (1) The number of screws in the coat hooks on the cabin doors. (2) The galley hot press did not work properly, and (3) The pebble dashing in the Parisian cafe was too dark.

Dent Ray was thirty-two at the time of the disaster and had recently married. He had gone to bed early that night as he had had a tiring day waiting in the first-class dining saloon. As he lay in his bunk, covered with his overcoat because of the intense cold, he felt the ship give a shudder and thought that she had dropped a propeller, but as he knew this was not a matter that concerned him, he turned over and prepared for sleep. Suddenly he was roughly awakened by a fellow steward who shouted to him to get up as the ship was sinking. Ray thought it was a joke, but his mate told him they had struck ice and put some, which he had taken off the deck, into Ray's bunk to prove his point.

At that moment the second steward, Dodd, arrived and ordered them all up on deck. As Ray went out into the passage known as 'Scotland Road', (through which it was possible to drive a four-in-hand) he noticed a slight tilt down to the bows. He went up the back stairs to the boat deck, where he saw crowds of people in strangely assorted clothing, and the covers being removed from the lifeboats. The *Titanic* lay dead in the water, all way having been taken off her; the safety valves of the boilers were blowing off steam and the noise was deafening. It was so cold that he almost stopped dead in his tracks and decided that some warmer clothing was essential, so he went back to his quarters to put on some more clothes and the overcoat his wife had given him just before the voyage. He knew then that the ship was going to sink. Water had reached the foot of the service doors to the grand staircase from 'Scotland Road'. As he passed the purser's office on his way back up the grand staircase, he noticed that they had the safes open and were taking out the jewellery. He had been detailed as an oarsman to row in boat number 13 on the starboard side, so he made his way there. On the way he met another steward, who said to him "You're not going are you?, you're safer here". But Ray replied, "I am. I'm detailed to row that boat". He never saw that steward again, nor did he ever see Dodd again.

The crowds of people who had been near the boats when he came on deck the first time had all disappeared, except those who were already sitting in the lifeboat, which was full to capacity (one of the few which were). One of the difficulties the crew encountered was to try and persuade people to get into the boats. The ship was thought to be "unsinkable" and nobody dreamed that she would actually go down. The majority believed they would be safer, and warmer, in the *Titanic* than to be lowered 70 feet in a small boat, and cast loose in mid-Atlantic on a freezing cold night. There were boats for only about 1,000 people but Ray says that even if there had been enough for every soul on board, they still would not have gone. As it was, it took the whole two hours before she finally sank, to lower those that there were. He took his place in the boat and they were lowered away. (For details of the adventures of Lifeboat 13, see Lawrence Beesley's book 'Loss of the R.M.S. *Titanic*' which has an excellent account).

From the boat it could be seen how down at the head the *Titanic* was. As she sank lower, her stern rose higher in the air. Suddenly all the lights went out, came on, then went out again, this time for good. Ray says that just before she sank she stood almost perpendicular, with her bow submerged, her stern and propellers pointing to the sky. There was a terrific noise like thunder, which it can only be assumed was caused by the engines leaving their beds, and smashing through the bows of the ship, wrecking everything in their way. (Engines which at that time, together with those in the *Britannic* and *Olympic* were the largest turbine engines ever made). After this, there was an awful moaning, the deep cry of many souls struggling in the icy water.

Everyone in the lifeboats knew that there were many people left on board; the pumps and dynamos were kept going until the end. The engine room staff perished to a man and a memorial to their heroism stands in Southampton. But it was not until the survivors in Lifeboat 13 were safely on board the *Carpathia,* and a roll was called, that they realised what a terrible loss of life there was, over 1,500 people. The *Carpathia* having picked up the *Titanic*'s distress signal (the *Titanic* was the first ship to use the new SOS signal, which had only recently come into being) had steamed at top speed (her usual speed was 14 knots but on her dash that night to save life she made 17 1/2 knots). She reached the scene of the tragedy in time to pick up all the lifeboats, but tragically not in time to save the wretched people who were flung into the icy water as the ship went down. Some of them floated for three or four hours, before they died of exposure. Few of the passengers actually drowned, as they mostly all had on life jackets; if the ship whose lights they could see so near, had answered the distress signals, hundreds of lives could have been saved.

Earlier the same evening Bruce Ismay had dined quietly with Dr O'Loughlin, a man he knew very well, as the doctor had been with the White Star Line for over 30 years. After dinner he had gone back to his cabin and read for a while before turning in, and was asleep when the actual collision occurred. He was awakened by the jar, and like Ray, he thought that the ship had dropped a propeller. He got out of bed and went into the corridor to see what had happened, but the steward he questioned knew nothing. He knew sufficient about ships and their ways to realise it was something serious, so he put on a pair of trousers and an overcoat over his pyjamas and went for the first time to the bridge. There Captain Smith told him they had struck ice. He asked the captain whether the ship was seriously damaged. The reply was "I am afraid she is." Bruce Ismay then went below and on the main stairway met Bell, the chief engineer, from whom he learned that the pumps would keep the water out for a time. He returned to the bridge and saw Captain Smith again who, with Thomas Andrews, had carried out an inspection of the ship and ascertained the damage. They must have quickly told Mr Ismay how seriously the *Titanic* was damaged and that she could not last the night.

When the captain gave orders for the lifeboats to be uncovered and swung out, Bruce Ismay, dressed just as he was, did everything he could to assist in getting the boats out and putting the women and children into them.

In all he helped to fill and lower lifeboats 3, 5, 7 and 9 on the starboard side. Chief Officer Wilde and First Officer Murdoch were in charge of lowering the boats of the starboard side, and Fifth Officer Lowe was helping them; Bruce Ismay was nearly beside himself with anxiety for the passengers. Knowing how little time there was, he was urging Lowe to hurry, shouting "Lower away. Lower away." Fifth Officer Lowe did not know Bruce Ismay and thought he was just an over excited passenger and vented his overwrought nerves with "If you'll get the hell out of the way, we can get on with the job". The chairman of the line turned and walked away, completely squashed as he had been so many times before when his father spoke severely to him.

Finally at 1.40am Chief Officer Wilde was lowering the last boat, C collapsible on the starboard side. It was almost full and was actually being lowered away. There were no more passengers, either men or women in sight, and Wilde ordered Mr Ismay and a Mr Carter, who was also helping, to get into the boat. Bruce sat with his back to the stern of the boat, pushing the oar away from him, with his back to the *Titanic*. He could not bear to see her end.

About five hours later, at 6.15am, he climbed on board the Cunard *Carpathia*. By this time he was completely shattered; it was he who had the *Titanic* and her sister ship built, and he was overwhelmed by the tragedy.

He was put into the doctor's cabin and it was while he was being treated there that the rumours started, chiefly by the talk of two women, first class passengers, both of whom had lost their husbands and were having to sleep on blankets in the saloon. The chairman of the line being cared for in the privacy of the doctor's cabin was more than they could bear. Bruce Ismay only got into the lifeboat when he thought that all the women had been taken off and when he heard that there were still some left aboard he was inconsolable, and collapsed completely.

To make matters worse he also learnt that his butler, Fry (who had accompanied him as his valet), and his secretary, Harrison were also missing. He had not seen either of them after the collision as he had been on deck helping to load the boats. He felt he was responsible for their presence on the ship and this upset him even more. When he finally got home to England one of the first things he did was to ensure that their widows received a generous annuity for life.

Lightoller describes Ismay's position in full in the verbatim American Inquiry; he was the second officer on board the *Titanic* and the senior one to survive, having had a miraculous escape. He was thrown into the water when the ship went down, was sucked against an engine room grating, then blown clear by the force of air coming from it; he managed to swim to an upturned lifeboat to which he clung all night until picked up with about 30 survivors by one of the lifeboats and so transferred to the *Carpathia*.

Lightoller:- "I may say that at that time Mr. Ismay did not seem to be in a mental condition to finally decide anything. I tried my utmost to rouse Mr. Ismay, for he was obsessed with the idea and kept repeating that he ought to have gone down with the ship, because he found that women had gone down. I told him that there was no such reason; I told him a very great deal; I tried to get that idea out of his head, but he was taken with it; and I know that the doctor tried too; but we had difficulty in arousing Mr. Ismay, purely owing to that, wholly and solely, women had gone down in the boat and he had not. You can call the doctor of the *Carpathia* and he will verify that statement."

On board the *Carpathia* the officers all knew that an inquiry would be held, once they got back to England, and so they met for a consultation. They were afraid the *Titanic* crew might go off in other ships, or run into trouble in New York. (The pay of all men stopped from the moment the *Titanic* sank.)

So, knowing the *Cedric* was in New York and due to sail for Liverpool, they wondered if it would be possible to hold her until the *Carpathia* arrived. Lightoller went to see Ismay in the doctor's cabin and explained the situation. He was only just able to take it in, but he did finally grasp what was being said. So a cable was sent to the White Star offices in New York, signed 'Yamsi'. This was Bruce Ismay's personal signature which he used to distinguish his private messages from those of Ismay, Imrie & Company. He asked for the *Cedric* to be held, until the arrival of the *Carpathia.*

The first rumour that reached America was that the *Titanic* had been damaged in collision with an iceberg and was being towed to Halifax by the Allan liner *Virginian* and that all on board were safe. It was not until late in the afternoon of April 15th that P A S Franklin (the vice-president in the United States of the International Mercantile Marine Company) received the news that she had sunk at 2.20am and that there was a terrible loss of life.

As the *Carpathia* was returning to New York with the survivors the US decided to hold its own inquiry before the crew of the *Titanic* had time to return to England.

Meanwhile, as Bruce Ismay lay in the doctor's cabin on board the *Carpathia,* his wife and children had reached Fishguard, in Wales, on their motor tour. It was here that Mrs Ismay received the dreadful news. She told the chauffeur to make straight for 'Sandheys' and all along the roads on this beautiful April day with the gorse out in full bloom, she kept saying to herself "It cannot be true, it cannot be true".

Immediately on returning from her honeymoon on the Continent, his elder daughter Margaret was greeted by her aunt in London with the terrible news; she went at once to 'Sandheys' to join her mother and there the family, always united and devoted, gathered to wait anxiously for further information. On hearing that her husband was safe, Mr. Ismay immediately cabled that she would join him and would have taken the first available boat. She packed a bag and sent him some clothes but Mrs Sanderson urged her not to go, saying that she would only pass him in mid-ocean. But it was to be nearly a month before he came home.

As soon as the *Carpathia* docked, Senator Smith, who was appointed by Congress to hold an inquiry into the cause of the accident, stepped on board and was shown straight to Doctor McGhee's cabin to see Bruce Ismay. He quickly explained the purpose of his visit when Bruce Ismay immediately said he would do anything he could to help the Senator. Although he was disappointed that he was not able to return to England and his family, he placed himself entirely at Senator Smith's disposal.

The surviving officers of the *Titanic* were extremely annoyed when they heard that there was to be an inquiry in the United States, particularly Fourth Officer Boxhall. They took the view that their ship was British and that the accident which had befallen them had occurred on the high seas, not even in US territorial waters, and they regarded the inquiry as unwarrantable interference. These complaints reached the ears of Mr Ismay who immediately sent a message asking them please to co-operate, and give the United States Senate every possible assistance at the inquiry. He pointed out that neither they, nor the White Star Line, had anything of which to be ashamed; in fact he welcomed the facts being made known.

Before going to the Ritz Carlton Hotel where he was to stay for the New York Inquiry, Mr Ismay gave the following statement to the Press:-

"In the presence and under the shadow of a catastrophe so overwhelming my feelings are too deep for expression in words. I can only say that the White Star Line, its officers and employees will do everything humanly possible to alleviate the suffering and sorrow of the survivors and of the relatives of those who have perished. The *Titanic* was the last word in shipbuilding. Every regulation prescribed by the British Board of Trade had been strictly complied with, the master, officers and crew were the most experienced and skilful in the British service.

"I am informed that a committee at the United States Senate has been appointed to investigate the circumstances of the accident. I heartily welcome the most complete and exhaustive inquiry and any aid that I, or my associates, or our builders or navigators can render is at the service of the public and the Governments of both the United States and Great Britain.

"Under the circumstances I must respectfully defer making any further statement at this time."

But unfortunately the American Press was hysterical, a great disaster at sea had occurred, 1,500 people, some of them known the world over, had lost their lives but the chairman of the company had been saved. As with all disasters a scapegoat had to be found. Ismay had never been popular with the Press owing to his abrupt and autocratic manner and they had already heard of his wish to go back to England in the *Cedric*. They made this sound as though he was running away.

The newspapers began to pillory him before he had even appeared to give evidence before the American Senate. He was accused of interfering with the navigation of the vessel, that he wanted to break the record for an Atlantic crossing, of jumping into the first lifeboat and even that he dressed up in women's clothes.

One paper ran a banner headline 'Ismay In Wreck Grill', another showed a photograph surrounded by fingers pointing at it in a sensational manner, headed 'THIS is J. Bruce Ismay'. Another reported that when J Bruce Ismay was aboard a vessel of the White Star Line, the captain of the ship was no better than a cabin boy and that therefore Ismay was to blame for the disaster. But perhaps the cruellest of all was a full page cartoon, which depicted Mr Ismay in a lifeboat, watching the sinking ship, and captioned 'THIS IS J. *BRUTE* ISMAY', and underneath was written "We respectfully suggest that the emblem of the White Star, be changed to that of a 'Yellow Liver', and, underneath the picture was written 'A Picture that will live in the public memory for ever, J. Bruce Ismay safe in a lifeboat while 1,500 people drown'."

Bruce Ismay was no coward. Very far from it. He knew that he would have to face an angry and indignant public. As it was he survived to give valuable evidence which has had a great bearing on drastically altering the rules and regulations of navigation and ensuring that it is practically impossible for such a calamity to occur again.

The first thing he did on reaching his hotel in New York was to issue instructions that no vessel belonging to the IMM Company was to put to sea without enough lifeboats for everybody on board. The owners were already having difficulty with the stokers on the *Olympic,* who were threatening to go on strike until the situation with the lifesaving equipment was completely overhauled.

The following morning, April 19th, he appeared at 10.30 before the Senate to give his evidence. He was the first witness to be called; in all he was called three times, the second and third times were after the inquiry had moved to Washington. He was fairly treated at this inquiry and not condemned in any way, but sections of the Press continued to cry out against him in the United States. Survivors from the *Titanic* were interviewed also and when some of them (and these were many) refused to give their story of the tragedy, they were quoted just the same, out of the reporters' imagination.

One of the charges levelled against the White Star Line was that the steerage passengers were kept locked below deck, whilst the first and second class passengers escaped in the lifeboats. The basis for this charge was that the gates between the steerage and other classes had to be kept locked under the American Immigration Laws and there was delay in opening them when the *Titanic* struck ice, as whoever had charge of the keys could not immediately be found. In fact there is some doubt as to whether some were ever opened; however, the steerage passengers had their own access to the decks. One of the main difficulties the crew experienced in getting them up was in explaining what had happened, as there were so many different races few of them spoke English. Also it was difficult to persuade them to leave their belongings which in many cases were all that they possessed in the world. The treatment of these third-class passengers was thoroughly examined during both the following inquiries and it was decided by both Courts that no more could possibly have been done for them.

The British Press were more sympathetic but Bruce Ismay received enormous publicity and the famous murder case involving Seddon the poisoner was relegated to the back pages. The magazine *John Bull* at that time run by Horatio Bottomley (himself to be the subject of a scandal later, owing to his embezzlement of money from war widows during the Great War) carried a scathing article about his escape; the *Daily Mirror* printed a large photograph of J Bruce Ismay headed 'The Most Talked of Man in all the World', the *Daily Sketch* also published a large photograph of Mr Ismay headed 'Mr. Bruce Ismay sends home a Defence of his Action'.

In order to try to help the British public to understand Bruce Ismay's position in view of the terrible articles which were appearing in the United States papers, Bruce Ismay sent a cable to the London *Times* explaining his conduct. (The full statement is printed at the end of this chapter).

Meanwhile, as the Press continued its outcry against J Bruce Ismay and the inquiry was progressing in Washington, the cable ship *Mackay Bennett* was sent from America to the scene of the disaster to search for the bodies of people who had died of exposure in the freezing cold water when the *Titanic* went down.

On April 30th the *Mackay Bennett* returned to her pier at Halifax, Nova Scotia. In her search she had found 306 of the *Titanic's* dead; many were buried at sea but she brought home the bodies of 190 amongst which were those of J J Astor, the well-known millionaire, and Millet, the famous American painter. The identified bodies were handed over to relatives and given a proper burial.

Finally on May 5th, 1912, Bruce Ismay left America on board the *Adriatic* bound for Liverpool where he had to face another official inquiry which also completely cleared his name. But, when mud is thrown, some of it sticks and Bruce Ismay lived the rest of his life under the shadow of doubt.

His wife has been heard to say "The *Titanic* disaster almost ruined our lives."

Statement issued by Bruce Ismay on 21st April, 1912:

When I appeared before the Senate Committee Friday morning I suppose the purpose of the enquiry was to ascertain the cause of the sinking of the *Titanic* with a view to determining whether additional legislation was required to prevent the recurrence of so

horrible a disaster. I welcomed such inquiry and appeared voluntarily, without subpoena, and answered all questions put to me by the members of the committee to the best of my ability, with complete frankness and without reserve. I did not suppose the question of my personal conduct was the subject of the enquiry although I was ready to tell everything I did on the night of the collision.

As I have been subpoenaed to attend before the committee in Washington to-morrow, I should prefer to make no public statement out of respect for the committee, but I do not think that courtesy requires me to be silent in the face of the untrue statements made in some of the newspapers.

When I went on board the *Titanic* at Southampton on April 10th, it was my intention to return on her. I had no intention of remaining in the United States at that time. I came merely to observe the new vessel, as I had done in the case of other vessels of our Line.

During the voyage I was a passenger and excercised no greater rights or privileges than any other passenger. I was not consulted by the commander about the ship, her course, speed, navigation or her conduct at sea. All these matters were under the exclusive control of the captain. I saw Captain Smith only occasionally, as other passengers did; I was never in his room; I was never on the bridge until after the accident; I did not sit at his table in the saloon; I had not visited the engine room or gone through the ship, and did not go or attempt to go, to any part of the ship to which any other first-class passenger did not have access.

It is absolutely and unqualifiedly false that I ever said that I wished the *Titanic* should make a speed record or should increase her daily runs. I deny absolutely having said to any person that we would increase our speed in order to get out of the ice floe or any words to that effect.

As I have already testified, at no time did the *Titanic,* during the voyage attain her full speed. It was not expected that she would reach New York before Wednesday morning. If she had been pressed she could probably have arrived Tuesday evening.

The statement that the White Star Line would receive an additional sum by way of bounty or otherwise, for attaining a certain speed, is absolutely untrue. The White Star Line receives from the British Government a fixed compensation of $70,000 per annum for carrying mails, without regard to the speed of any of its vessels, and no additional sum is paid on account of any increase in speed.

I was never consulted by the captain or any other person nor did I ever make any suggestions whatever to any human being about the course of the ship. The *Titanic,* as I am informed, was on the southernmost westbound of transatlantic steam ships. The tracks, or lanes, were designated many years ago by agreement of all the important steamship lines, and all captains of the White Star Line are required to navigate their vessels as closely as possible on these tracks, subject to the following standing instructions:

"Commanders must distinctly understand that the issue of these regulations does not in any way relieve them from responsibility for the safe and efficient navigation of their respective vessels, and they are also enjoined to remember that *they must run no risk which might by mry possibility result in accident to their ships. It is to be hoped that they will ever bear in mind that the safety of the lives and property entrusted to their care is the ruling principle that should govern them in the navigation if their vessels, and that no supposed gain in expedition or saving if time on the voyage is to be purchased at the risk of accident. The Company desires to maintain for its vessels a reputation for safety and only looks for such speed on the various voyages as is consistent with safe and prudent navigation.* Commanders are reminded that the steamers are to a great extent uninsured, and their own livelihood as well as the Company's success depends upon immunity from accident; no precaution which ensures safe navigation is to be considered excessive".

The only information I ever received on the ship that other vessels had sighted ice was a wireless message received from the

Baltic which I have already testified to. This was handed to me by Captain Smith without any remark as he was passing me on the passenger deck in the afternoon of Sunday, April 14th. I read the telegram casually and put it in my pocket. At about ten minutes past seven, while I was sitting in the smoke room, Captain Smith came in and asked me to give him the message received from the *Baltic* in order to post it for the information of the officers. I handed it to him and nothing further was said by either of us. I did not speak to any of the other officers on the subject.

If the information I received had aroused any apprehension in my mind - which it did not - I should not have ventured to make any suggestion to a commander of Captain Smith's experience. The responsibility for the navigation of the ship rested solely with him.

It has been stated that Captain Smith and I were having a dinner party in one of the saloons from 7.30 to 10.30 Sunday night and that at the time of the collision Captain Smith was sitting with me in the saloon.

Both of these statements are absolutely false. I did not dine with the captain nor did I see him during the evening of April 14th. The doctor dined with me in the restaurant at 7.30, and I went direct to my stateroom and went to bed at about 10.30. I was asleep when the collision occurred. I felt ajar, went into the passage way without dressing, met a steward, asked him what was the matter and he said he did not know. I returned to my room. I felt the ship slow down, put on an overcoat over my pyjamas and went up to the bridge. I asked Captain Smith what was the matter and he said we had struck ice. I asked him whether he thought it serious and he said he did. On returning to my room, I met the chief engineer and asked him whether he thought the damage serious and he said he thought it was.

I then returned to my room and put on a suit of clothes. I had been in my overcoat and pyjamas up to this time. I then went back to the boat deck and heard Captain Smith give the order to clear the boats. I helped in this work for nearly two hours as far as I can judge. I worked at the starboard boats helping women and children into the boats and lowering them over the side. I did nothing with regards to the boats on the portside. By that time every wooden lifeboat on the starboard side had been lowered away and I found that they were engaged in getting out the forward collapsible boat on the starboard side. I assisted in this work and all the women who were on this deck were helped into the boat. They were I think third class passengers. As the boat was going over the side, Mr. Carter, a passenger, and myself got into it. At that time there was not a woman on the boat deck nor any passengers of any class, so far as we could see or hear the boat had between 35 and 40 in it, I should think, most of them women. The rest were perhaps four or five men, and it was afterwards discovered that there were four Chinamen concealed under the thwarts in the bottom of the boat. The distance that the boat had to be lowered into the water was, I imagine, about 20 feet. Mr. Carter and I did not get into the boat until after they had begun to lower away. When the boat reached the water I helped to row it, pushing the oar from me. This is the explanation of the fact that my back was to the sinking steamer. The boat would have accommodated certainly six or more passengers in addition if there had been any on the boat deck to go. These facts can be substantiated by Mr. E. E. Carter of Philadelphia, who got in at the time that I did and was rowing the boat with me. I hope I need not say that neither Mr. Carter or myself would for any moment have thought of getting into the boat if there had been any women to go in it, nor should I have done so if I had thought that by remaining on the ship I could have been of the slightest further assistance.

It is impossible for me to answer every false statement, rumour, or invention that has appeared in the newspapers. I am prepared to answer any questions that may be asked by the committee of the Senate or any other responsible person. I shall therefore make no further statement of this kind except to explain the messages which I sent from the *Carpathia*. These messages have been completely misunderstood. An inference has been drawn from them that I was anxious to avoid the Senate committee's inquiry which it was intended to hold in New York. As a matter of fact when despatching these messages I had not the slightest idea that any inquiry was contemplated and I had no information regarding it until the arrival of the *Carpathia* at the Cunard dock in New York on Thursday night when I was informed by Senators Smith and Newlands of the appointment of the special committee to hold the inquiry. The only purpose I had in sending these messages was to express my desire to have the crews returned to their homes in England for their own benefit at the earliest possible moment, and I also was naturally anxious to return to my family, but left the matter of my return entirely to our representatives in New York.

I deeply regret that I am compelled to make my personal statement when my whole thought is on the horror of the disaster. In building the *Titanic* it was the hope of my associates and myself that we had built a vessel which could not be destroyed by the perils of the sea or dangers of navigation. The event has proved the futility of that hope. The present legal requirements have proved inadequate. They must be changed, but whether they are changed or not this awful experience has taught the steamship owners of the world that too much reliance has been placed on watertight compartments and on wireless telegraphy, and they must equip every vessel with lifeboats and rafts sufficient to provide for every soul on board, and sufficient men to handle them.

April 21st, 1912.

CHAPTER 16

The inquiries and the aftermath

On May 9th Mrs Bruce Ismay, her maid, Bower Ismay and Mr Concannon (one of the managers) sailed from Southampton in the *Oceanic* for Queenstown, there to await the arrival of the *Adriatic* with J Bruce Ismay and those members of the crew who had remained in the United States for the inquiry, including the surviving officers Lightoller, Pitman, Boxhall and Lowe. The remainder of the *Titanic*'s crew had come home in the Red Star Line steamer *Lapland* some weeks previously.

On Saturday morning at 7.30 on May 11th, 1912 the *Adriatic* was due alongside the Princes Landing Stage, and absolutely dead on time she steamed alongside. Bruce Ismay waited till nearly all the first class passengers had gone, and so he was one of the last to come down the gangway, accompanied by his devoted wife and his brother, Bower. Henry Concannon, who had disembarked shortly before, handed the following written statement to members of the Press, who were there to meet the *Adriatic* and obtain a statement from Mr Ismay. The statement read as follows:-

"Mr. Ismay asks the gentlemen of the Press to extend their courtesy to him by not pressing for any statement from him. First he is still suffering from the very great strain of the *Titanic* disaster and subsequent events.

Again because he gave before the American Commission a plain and unvarnished statement of fact, which has been fully reported; and also because his evidence before the British Court of Inquiry should not be anticipated in any way. He would, however, like to take this opportunity of acknowledging with full heart, the large number of telegraphic messages and letters from public concerns, and businesses and private friends conveying sympathy to him and confidence in him, which he very much appreciates in this, the greatest trial of his life."

Amidst cheers Mr and Mrs Ismay got into their car, and then motored to 'Sandheys'. As always, he was thinking of others, and the day after his return he wrote the following letter to Lord Derby:-

Sandheys,
Mossley Hill, Liverpool.
May 12th, 1912.
Dear Lord Derby,

The terrible disaster to the *Titanic* has brought prominently to my mind the fact that no permanent fund exists to assist the widows of those whose lives are lost, while they are engaged upon active duties upon the mercantile vessels of this country. The need for such a fund has been emphasized by some remarks made by your Lordship on the occasion of the Liverpool Bluecoat dinner.

The Mercantile Marine Service Association has administered with entire satisfaction the Liverpool Seamen's Pension Fund and the Margaret Ismay Fund, which were established some years ago by my father and mother to provide pensions for Liverpool seamen and their widows, but neither of these funds covers the object I have in view.

If under the administration of the same body and on the outlines of the enclosed memorandum a fund were initiated to meet the cases to which I refer, I should be happy to contribute £10,000 and my wife £1,000 thereto.

I need scarcely add that sufferers from the *Titanic* disaster would be eligible equally with others for the benefits of the proposed fund, so far as this is necessary to supplement the general assistance of the public.

Yours truly,
J. Bruce Ismay.

The memorandum referred to is as follows:-

The object of the fund is to provide pensions for the widows of those who lose their lives at sea while engaged upon active duties in any capacity whatever upon a merchant vessel registered in the United Kingdom.

"No pension to exceed £20 per year and it will be continued or discontinued at the absolute discretion of the committee.

The fund shall be vested in the name of the Mercantile Marine Service Association, who will have complete discretion in selecting those who are to receive the pension and in fixing its amount from time to time."

Lord Derby's reply is below:-

Derby House, Stratford Place, W.
Telephone No. Gerrard 5185
14.5.12
Dear Mr. Ismay,
I only got your letter late yesterday afternoon, and as I had to preside over a dinner I was unable to answer it last night.

I now beg to thank you and Mrs. Ismay most sincerely for the generous offer you make. Needless to say, I gratefully accept it and will communicate with the Mercantile Marine Service Association and inform them of your desire that they should administer the fund.

I only hope others will see fit to follow your generous lead and that then will be thus formed in this country a national fund which will go some way to alleviate those cases of distress which anybody connected with a seaport town is brought into contact with only too often, and for the relief of which no fund at present exists.

I hope I may have the pleasure of seeing you in Liverpool on Friday and thanking you personally for your generosity.

Yours sincerely,
Derby.

This is now known as the Mercantile Marine Widows' Fund. On the 31st December, 1958 it totalled £23,652. Pensions paid during 1958 amounted to £780.

The treatment that Bruce Ismay received from the American Press had aroused the sympathy and indignation of a great number of people all over the world, and he received hundreds of letters expressing these sentiments, which are still in existence. Below are two of these which give an idea of the great esteem in which Bruce Ismay was held by all who knew him, even those of only slight acquaintanceship. Amongst these letters was one from a doctor in Kent, who did not know him at all, and took the trouble to write and express his feelings:-

Eagle Cliff, Greenhithe, Kent.
May 13th, 1912.
Dear Sir,
I am very pleased to see that the people of Liverpool had the decency to give you a hearty welcome after the callous and heartless way you were treated in America.

After behaving in the very brave way you did when the *Titanic* was sinking you deserve the sympathy of everyone, instead of which you appear to have been treated in a manner which must have been repugnant to any fair-minded person.

The consciousness that you have done your duty will help to make you forget the terrible ordeal through which you have passed, and to ignore the rantings of certain journalists who ought to know better.

Believe me, Sir,
Yours faithfully,
Alistair McGregor, M.D.

The following day a letter arrived from an Army officer who was a survivor from the Castle liner *Drummond Castle* which had been lost some years previously:-

THE JUNIOR CONSERVATIVE CLUB
43 & 44, Albemarle Street, Piccadilly, W.
May 14th 1912.
To Bruce Ismay, Esq.
Dear Sir,
It is some years since I had the pleasure of meeting you as a fellow passenger and I think it only right to express to you my utter disgust at the unjustifiable attacks which have been made upon you.

Perhaps I can more fully appreciate your feelings than most, because I happen to be one of the survivors of that terrible disaster the *Drummond Castle*. I had joined the ship at Madeira a few days earlier.

On the morning she ran on the reef I happened to be on deck.

To this fact I owe my life. Together with the ship's doctor who happened to have been called to attend a patient and some of the deck hands I managed to keep afloat until picked up in an exhausted condition. Imagine my feelings when a few days later I saw an account which was headed 'Army officer swims for his life. Women and children perish.'

This, of course, was literally true. I swam for my life and they perished. But even if I had not been able to swim they would still have perished and I am convinced that it was only put in this offensive way because I had strictly observed the rule which forbids officers furnishing statements to the Press which are of a sensational character and likely to bring them into notoriety.

Probably had you been ready to fill columns with 'copy' you would not have been attacked.

However, I am glad to see the Liverpool people received you decently and so long as you enjoy the confidence and esteem of your fellow townsmen you can afford to disregard vapid utterances of journalists, who probably have never been on an ocean liner in their lives and have therefore no conception of the size of such a vessel nor the great difficulties in saving life under such circumstances.

I am very glad to think you had the good fortune to be among the survivors and there is no reason why you as a passenger should have sacrificed your life needlessly.

The captain, of course, is in a different position and in the present instance all honour to the brave fellow who obviously did his utmost and upheld the best traditions of the Mercantile Marine.

You have probably received a number of letters and I would not have added to your trouble only that I, myself, have passed through a similar experience.

I am, dear Sir,
Yours sincerely,
Colin Catchcart (Captain R.E.)

The British Inquiry into the *Titanic* disaster had already opened at The Scottish Hall, Westminster, and a few days after arriving back in Liverpool, Mr and Mrs Bruce Ismay travelled down to their London home, 15 Hill Street, where they stayed during the time Bruce Ismay was required as a witness to give his evidence.

This was conducted in a very different manner from the United States inquiry which had been ordered by Congress and was conducted by people who knew little about shipping. They received a great deal of criticism on this account from the British Press, but, although Senator Smith and his colleagues may have asked some odd questions, they achieved their object in probing into the true causes of the tragedy.

The British inquiry was presided over by Lord Mersey of Toxteth, and the various interested parties were represented by the most eminent counsel of the day. Sir Robert Finlay KC, MP, appeared for the White Star Line and Mr Clement Edwards MP appeared on behalf of the Dock, Wharf, Riverside and General Workers Union of Great Britain. Mr W D Harbinson appeared for the third class passengers.

The Court had been sitting 15 days when Bruce Ismay took the stand. His evidence lasted exactly 11 days, but the attitude of some of the counsel, particularly the last two mentioned, (who tried to make him a scapegoat for the whole affair) affected him deeply, and was something he never forgot.

It is interesting to compare the different way the two inquiries were conducted in relation to Mr Ismay. At the United States inquiry he was asked the following questions:-

Senator Smith. Not desiring to be impertinent at all, but in order that I may not be charged with omitting to do my duty, I would like to know where you went after you boarded the *Carpathia,* and how you happened to go there.

Mr. Ismay. Mr. Chairman, I understand that my behaviour on board the *Titanic,* and subsequently on board the *Carpathia,* has been very severely criticised. I want to court the fullest inquiry, and place myself unreservedly in the hands of yourself and any of your colleagues, to ask me any questions in regard to my conduct; so please do not hesitate to do so, and I will answer them to the best of my ability. So far as the *Carpathia* is concerned, Sir, when I got on board the ship I stood with my back against the bulkhead, and somebody came up to me and said, "Will you not go into the saloon and get some soup, or something to drink?". "No," I said, "I really do not want anything at all". He said, "Do go and get something." I said, "No. If you will leave me alone I shall be very much happier here." I said, "If you will get me in some room where I can be quiet, I wish you would." He said, "Please go into the saloon and get something hot." I said, "I would rather not." Then he took me and put me into a room. I did not know whose the room was, at all. This man proved to be the doctor of the *Carpathia*. I was in that room until I left the ship. I was never outside the door of that room. During the whole of the time I was in this room, I never had anything of a solid nature at all; I lived on soup. I did not want very much of anything. The room was constantly being entered by people asking for the doctor. The doctor did not sleep in the room the first night. The doctor slept in the room the other nights that I was on board that ship. Mr. Jack Thayer was brought into the room the morning we got on board the *Carpathia*. He stayed in the room for some little time, and the doctor came in after he had been in, I should think, about quarter of an hour, and he said to this young boy, "Would you not like something to eat?" He said, "I would like some bacon and egg"; which he had. The doctor did not have a suite of rooms on the ship. He simply had this one small room, which he, himself, occupied and dressed in every night and morning.

Senator Smith. Did he keep his medicine and bandages there?

Mr. Ismay. No, Sir, no. He kept them in the dispensary; in the surgery.

Senator Smith. Right near this room?

Mr. Ismay. I have no idea where it was. As I tell you, I was never outside of that room from the time I entered it.

Senator Smith. In view of your statement, I desire to say that I have seen none of these comments to which you refer. In fact, I have not read the newspapers since I started for New York; I have deliberately avoided it; so that I have seen none of these reports, and you do not understand that I have made any criticism upon your conduct aboard the *Carpathia*.

Mr. Ismay. No, Sir. On the contrary, I do not say that anybody has. But I am here to answer any questions in regard thereto.

Senator Smith. What can you say, Mr. Ismay, as to your treatment at the hands of the committee since you have been under our direction?

Mr. Ismay. I have no fault to find. Naturally, I was disappointed in not being allowed to go home; but I feel quite satisfied you have some very good reason in your own mind for keeping me here.

Senator Smith. You quite agree now that it was the wisest thing to do?

Mr. Ismay. I think, under the circumstances, it was.

Senator Smith. And even in my refusal to permit you to go you saw no discourtesy?
212

Mr. Ismay. Certainly not, Sir.

Senator Smith. Do you know of any unfair or discourteous or inconsiderate treatment upon the part of the committee of any of your officers connected with this investigation?

Mr. Ismay. No, I do not.

In his summing up made on May 28th, 1912 before the United States Senate, Senator Smith made the following remarks concerning J Bruce Ismay:-

"Among the passengers were many strong men who had been accustomed to command, whose lives had marked every avenue of endeavour, and whose business experience and military training especially fitted them for such an emergency. These were rudely silenced and forbidden to speak, as was the President of this company, by junior officers, a few of whom, I regret to say, availed themselves of the first opportunity to leave the ship."

And later Senator Smith said:-

"I think the presence of Mr. Ismay and Mr. Andrews stimulated the ship to greater speed than it would have made under ordinary conditions, although I cannot fairly ascribe to either of them any instructions to this effect.

The very presence of the owner and builder unconsciously stimulates endeavour, and the restraint of organized society is absolutely necessary to safety."

Contrast this with the British inquiry when Clement Edwards in cross examination of J Bruce Ismay put the following questions to him:-

18848. You were one of those, as the managing director, responsible for determining the number of boats? - Yes, in conjunction with the shipbuilders.

18849. When you got into the boat you thought that the *Titanic* was sinking? - I did.

18850. Did you know that there were some hundreds of people on that ship? - Yes.

18851. Who must go down with her? - Yes, I did.

18852. Has it occurred to you that, except perhaps apart from the captain, you, as the responsible managing director, deciding the number of boats, owed your life to every other person on that ship? It has not.

The Commissioner: I do not think that is a question to put to him; that is an observation which you may make when you come to make your speech. It is not a question for him.

Mr. Edwards: I thought the witness ought to have an opportunity of answering before I attempted to make the observation.

The Commissioner: You will make that observation, if you think it worth while, when the time comes.

18853. (Mr. Edwards - To the witness). According to your

statement you got into the boat last of all? - I did.

18854. So that if a witness says that you, in fact, got into the boat earlier and helped the women and children in, that would not be true? - It would not.

18855. I suppose you know that it has been given in evidence here by Brown?- Yes.

The Commissioner: What evidence?

18856. (Mr. Edwards). The evidence of Brown was that Mr. Ismay got into this particular boat some time earlier. On page 223, at Question 10520, the question was: "Was Mr. Bruce Ismay taking any part in connection with that boat? - (A.) Yes, he was calling out for the women and children first. He helped to get them into that boat, and he went into it himself to receive the women and children". That is not true? - No, it is not.

18857. Now, it has been given in evidence here that you took an actual part in giving directions for the women and children to be placed in the boats. Is that true? - I did, and I helped as far as I could.

18858. If you had taken this active part in the direction up to a certain point, why did you not continue and send to other decks to see if there were passengers available, for this last boat? - I was standing by the boat; I helped everybody into the boat that was there and, as the boat was being lowered away I got in.

18859. That does not answer the question. You had been taking a responsible part, according to the evidence and according to your own admission, in directing the filling of the boats? - No, I had not; I had been helping to put the women and children into the boats as they came forward.

18860. I am afraid we are a little at cross purposes. Is it not the fact that you were calling out "Women and children first?" and helping then in? - Yes, it is.

18861. Is it not the fact that you were giving directions as to the women and children getting in? - I was helping the women and children in.

18862. Please answer my question. Is it not the fact that you were giving directions in helping them? - I was calling for the women and children to come in.

18863. What I am putting to you is this, that if you could take an active part at that stage, why did you not continue the active part and give instructions, or go yourself to other decks, or round the other side of the deck, to see if there were other people who might find a place in your boat? - I presumed that there were people down below who were sending the people up.

18864. But you knew there were hundreds who had not come up. That is your answer, that you presumed that there were people down below sending them up? - Yes.

18865. And does it follow from that that you presumed that everybody was coming up who wanted to come up? - I knew that everybody could not be up.

18866. Then I do not quite see the point of the answer? Everybody that was on the deck got into that boat.

The Commissioner: Your point, Mr. Edwards, as I understand is this: That, having regard to his position, it was his duty to remain upon that ship until she went to the bottom. That is your point?

Mr. Edwards: Yes, and inasmuch ...

The Commissioner: That is your point? .....

18867. (Mr. Edwards). Frankly, that is so; I do not flinch from it a little bit. But I want to get it from this witness, inasmuch as he took upon himself to give certain directions at a certain time, why hedid not discharge the responsibility even after that, having regard to the other persons or passengers? - There were no more passengers to get into that boat. The boat was actually being lowered away.

18868. That is your answer? - Yes.

In announcing his judgment Lord Mersey said "An attack was made in the course of the inquiry on the moral conduct of one of the passengers, namely, Mr. Bruce Ismay. It is no part of the business of the Court to enquire into such matters, and I should pass them by in silence if I did not fear that my silence might be misunderstood. As to the attack on Mr. Bruce Ismay, it resolved itself into a suggestion that, occupying the position of managing director of the steamship company, some moral duty was imposed upon him to wait on board until the vessel foundered. I do not agree. Mr. Ismay, after rendering assistance to many passengers, found 'C' collapsible, the last boat on the starboard side, actually being lowered. No other people were there at the time. There was room for him, and he jumped in. Had he not jumped in he would merely have added one more life, namely, his own, to the number of those lost."

In spite of these remarks by Lord Mersey, Bruce Ismay's conduct was criticised, and criticised severely; at both inquiries witness after witness was asked "Did you see Mr Ismay?" or "What was Mr Ismay doing?"

Bruce Ismay wished to make a public statement about his escape from the *Titanic,* but unfortunately he was not supported by his colleagues. He was not popular with them, owing to his autocratic manner, and also the petty jealousies which sometimes occur when the eldest son becomes head of his father's firm. Their attitude was that he had given the White Star Line quite enough bad publicity already with the adverse Press he had received for his part in the affair, and they would not have been sorry to see him retire.

Mr Sanderson wrote to him urging him to do nothing about a statement to the Press, and below is an extract from Mr Ismay's reply:-

"I have not yet decided what I am going to do in regard to communicating with the Press, and am much obliged with your advice, which is to do nothing. I am afraid we look at the position from entirely different points of view; you have not been attacked, whereas I have, so you can easily afford to sit still and do nothing."

In view of Lord Mersey's statement Bruce Ismay decided, however, not to issue a statement.

Unfortunately apart from the official inquiries, very few people know the exact circumstances in which Bruce Ismay left the *Titanic,* as afterwards, rightly or wrongly his wife took the attitude that it was best forgotten, that it was bad for him to talk about it and she would never allow the subject to be discussed. There was one occasion, however, when he began to talk to his sister-in-law about his escape. He told her that one of the officers had urged him to get into the boat. There were no other passengers near, the boat was actually being lowered away and the officer had told him that he must go, as his captain would need his evidence at the inquiry which was bound to follow. That officer was Chief Officer Wilde who lost his life that night, and whose evidence if he had lived would have been of great value to Ismay. Bruce Ismay did not tell this story at the inquiries, however. Possibly he felt it would sound as though he were trying to make excuses for his escape. This story is borne out by the affidavit of Weikmann, the barber (see Appendix B) in which he says he heard Chief Officer Wilde order Mr Ismay to get in.

As far as J Bruce Ismay was concerned he was never the same again. He had always been very shy, so much so that few people on board the *Titanic* knew who he was. For once he had come out of his shell, and working with the crew, had done all he could to assist in getting the passengers into the boats. So he was heartbroken to come home to face all the calumny of the Press and public, and he seldom again entered the head office of the White Star Line, 30 James Street, Liverpool.

After attending the British inquiry he went to his brother Bower's house in Perthshire, Scotland, at Dalnaspidal, to recover from his ordeal. Whilst there he received the following sympathetic letter from his son Tom.

Sandheys,
Mossley Hill, Liverpool.
Dearest Father,
This is just a line to tell you how sorry I am that I did not see more of you to-day, and to tell you that I quite realise what an ordeal you had to go through, and how deeply I feel for you, however, I very much hope that the worst is over now, and that you will never again be misjudged and your words misinterpreted as they have been in the present Inquiry.

I hope you will be benefited by your stay at Dalnaspidal and not be worried by any anonymous communications.

I hope you will have fine weather and be able to get some fishing.

Evelyn and I went to the cricket ground this afternoon. It rained a good deal, though some of the games were very close being mostly finals.

I hope you did not meet much rain on your run up to Carlisle, and that you will not be recognised as I know how you must hate to be before the public eye especially under the present trying circumstances.

I know this letter is very badly expressed, but I hope, you

will realise that the spirit in which it is written is none the less sincere for that.

With hopes that your stay in Scotland will be a complete rest I will close.

I am always your loving son,
Tom.

When Lord Mersey's findings into the *Titanic* disaster and his public statement which completely exonerated Bruce Ismay from all responsibility or blame were published, Bruce Ismay received hundreds more letters congratulating him on Lord Mersey's judgment. Amongst these was a touching letter from a young surgeon who had recently married a stewardess who was a survivor from the *Titanic*. He said he owed his wife's life to Mr Ismay, who had replied to the girl when she had refused to enter the boat owing to her position as a stewardess, "You are all women now", and with this he had put her into the boat.

It was while he was at Dalnaspidal that he first heard of The Lodge at Costelloe in County Galway in Ireland. It had just come on the market, and a friend of his knew how much he liked fishing recommended it to him as the finest salmon fishing in all Ireland. He had previously rented fishing in various parts of Scotland, but now the idea of a place of his own, away from the public eye appealed to him very much. Without seeing the property, acting on the advice of his friend he bought it. But it was not until he retired from the presidency of the International Mercantile Marine and the White Star Line that he visited it.

In July the vice president of the International Mercantile Marine, P A S Franklin, came over to England on a visit and after seeing Bruce Ismay, he returned to America aboard the *Olympic;* while aboard the *Olympic* he wrote to Bruce Ismay.

This letter shows most clearly what high regard Franklin had for his chief:-

August 7th, 1912.
On board R.M.S. *Olympic,*
Personal & Confidential.
My dear Mr. Ismay,

In a few minutes we will be in Queenstown but I did not want to leave without again endeavouring to express to you how deeply I appreciated your very frank and generous treatment of me, and I am certainly very much indebted to you.

You have always been most courteous and kind to me, and it was always a great pleasure and honour to me to serve under you, and whenever I was with you, I learned something every minute and my deep regret always was that I did not have the opportunity of being more with you.

Before travelling on this steamer I had no idea what a splendid, comfortable and marvellous steamer she is but all the time I cannot help thinking of your goodself - the man that had the nerve, and ability to order and plan her, and then of what has happened, and it all seems too cruel, but I suppose there was some good reason for it.

My time was most limited after leaving Lord Pirrie's on Tuesday, but Mr. Sanderson told me briefly regarding his future position, and expressed his and also Mr. Grenfell's regret that I had not been previously informed, and I said that I had felt hurt about that, but that you had explained that you had requested that it be kept quiet. Mr. Grenfell later called me on the telephone and I said practically the same thing. Mr. Sanderson was extremely nice and I told him that as long as I remained with the I.M.M. Company I would serve under him and with absolute loyalty, and to the best of my ability, but he must appreciate that recent developments made it clear that I could not expect to get much higher in the company and that therefore should in the future, in my own country, something offer that seemed better than present conditions I would naturally have to consider it.

I felt it was only fair and right for me to say that, although I have nothing more in my mind than when I talked to you, but I do feel a little blue about my future.

My talk, with him was most hurried.

I am sorry we did not get further in the tonnage talks, but I hope the new *Adriatic* and *Minnei* will be ordered in October / November.

I believe if our banking friends had been further pressed they would have agreed then and there, but I felt that I said too much as it was.

I suppose it is too much to expect that you will be out in New York this winter, but I do hope to see you soon.

I can only say that I *regret exceedingly* that you have decided to go out of the business and wish it were otherwise.

Your position regarding the *Titanic* is improving every day and the more thinking people consider it the better it will be, and you certainly have absolutely nothing to reproach yourself with. You were saved for some good purpose and must take advantage of it.

Please give Mrs. Ismay my very kindest regards and accept the same, and *many, many* thanks for your goodself.

Most sincerely yours,
P. A. S. Franklin.

It was not long after this letter was written that the *Olympic* returned to Belfast for major alterations. She had been designed to remain afloat with her two largest compartments flooded but by building a new skin inside the vessel and raising the bulkheads this number was increased to six. The cost of this work was approximately £250,000 and she did not return to the Southampton service until early in 1913 when she was probably one of the safest vessels afloat.

Bruce Ismay had given his word to H A Sanderson in March 1912, before the *Titanic* sailed, that he would retire in his favour. But he now desired very much to stay on as chairman of the White Star Line and his wife too wished him to carry on as before. So in October 1912 he communicated with Morgan & Company with regard to his future plans and below is the copy of the correspondence which passed between J Bruce Ismay, the directors of the Morgan Combine and H A Sanderson:-

22, Old Broad Street, London E.C.
October 23rd, 1912
To J. Bruce Ismay, Esq., 30, James Street, Liverpool.
PRIVATE & CONFIDENTIAL
My dear Ismay,
Referring to your express desire to make some public announcement in the immediate future as regards your plans, I have had a talk with Mr. J. P. Morgan, Junior, and also cabled to Mr. Morgan in America in reference to our conversation of last Friday. They are both of opinion that if a new man is to take over the presidency of the I.M.M. Company it would not be advisable

for his predecessor to accept a seat on the boards of the operating companies.

As president you have been in absolute control of all the companies forming the I.M.M. Company, and you have, as was only natural, by your ability and strong personality overshadowed the other managers, and to a certain extent they have looked to you for guidance in all matters great and small. On your retirement several of these junior men will have to be promoted to more responsible positions, and I think it will be easier for these men, as also for the incoming president, to assert their independence if their former chief is not on the boards with them.

My partners and I hope that you will continue to act as a director of the I.M.M. Company, and also remain a member of the British committee. I hope to have more frequent meetings of the latter and thus to have the benefit of your advice on all general questions of policy. In our conversation in January last you expressed yourself as willing to remain on this committee and I hope that you will not change your decision.

Yours sincerely,
E. C. Grenfell.

Copy of Mr Ismay's reply to Mr Grenfell's letter of October 23rd, 1912:

October 28th, 1912.
Many thanks for your private and confidential letter of the 23rd inst. contents of which have been read with some measure of disappointment, as I had hoped after what I said to you, that our friends would have been willing that I should continue a director of the White Star Line at any rate; I really do not care one iota about the other companies, but you will appreciate I am bound to have a good deal of sentiment in connection with the White Star Line.

I quite understand junior men will be promoted when I go and rightly so, but I cannot see how my remaining a director of the White Star Line will in any way hamper matters. At present there are only three directors, therefore four vacancies on the board; why not fill them up and so promote some of the juniors? I cannot think my being on the board would in any way interfere with the incoming president, but if it would do so this ends the matter.

I wish you would reconsider the matter, only so far as the White Star Line is concerned.

It is good of you and your partners wishing me to remain a director of the I.M.M. Company and also a member of the British committee. Perhaps you will kindly let my decision remain in abeyance for a little time, as I want to carefully consider the matter.

I do not propose making any announcement before the end of December, unless anything unforeseen arises.

22, Old Broad Street, London.
November 21st, 1912.
To J. Bruce Ismay, Esq., 30, James Street, Liverpool.
PRIVATE & CONFIDENTIAL
My dear Ismay,

I was absent yesterday when your letter of the 18th arrived. Since receiving yours of the 28th ulto, I have had a further discussion with Mr. J. P. Morgan, Junior on the question of your retaining your directorships of the constituent companies of the I.M.M. Company, after your retirement from the presidency. I fully appreciate your desire from sentiment to remain on the board of the O.S.N. Company, and I much regret that, after further consideration, I do not see my way to alter the opinion expressed to you in my letter of the 23rd October.

I understand you wish to let your decision as regards the directorship of the I.M.M. Company, remain over until the end of next month.

Yours sincerely,
E. C. Grenfell.

Copy of Mr Ismay's reply to Mr Grenfell's letter of November 21st, 1912:

I am in receipt of your letter of the 21st instant, the contents of which are duly noted.

You are correct in understanding I wish to let my position as regards the directorship of the I.M.M. Company and continuing as a member of the British committee remain over until the end of next month, and presume this is agreeable to those concerned.

>38, Leadenhall Street, London, E.C.
>November 29th, 1912.
>To J. Bruce Ismay, Esq., Sandheys,
>My dear Bruce,
>I dined with Grenfell last evening, and had the desired opportunity for discussing with him the directorship matter of which he spoke last Wednesday. The result has convinced me that I was correct in concluding that the decision they have reached is to be attributed to a considered and settled policy, and not to any personal feeling towards yourself.
>I gathered the impression from Grenfell's remarks that they would not be disposed to depart from the line that has been suggested, and I hope upon reflection, you will agree with the view I expressed to you, i.e., that, as retiring President, your name might very properly be expected to appear amongst the directors of the controlling company (I.M.M. Co.), and that this expectation could hardly apply in the case of any of the boards of the subsidiary companies, not even excepting the P.S.N. Co.
>A shocking wet day here.
>Yours sincerely.
>Harold A. Sanderson.

Copy of telegram from Mr Ismay to Mr Grenfell dated December 30th, 1912:

>If you and your associates desire me to continue a director of the I.M.M. Co. and a member of the British committee after my presidency ceases I shall be glad to do so.

Another person who was extremely upset by the loss of the *Titanic* was J Pierpont Morgan, the man who had first thought of the large American shipping trust which was known as the International Mercantile Marine. Alone of all Pierpont Morgan's undertakings which had proved successful to a large extent the International Mercantile Marine was a failure; he received a lot of unfair criticism over the *Titanic* and died in Rome, in March 1913 a disappointed man.

It was about this time early in 1913 that the first Atlantic ice patrol was started. Run by the United States Government this patrol was inaugurated owing to the loss of the *Titanic*.

Patrol boats go out to chart the icebergs and the Governments of all nations using the North Atlantic pay a proportion towards the cost of this scheme.

On June 30th 1913 Bruce Ismay retired from the presidency of the International Mercantile Marine and from the chairmanship of the White Star Line; he went to The Lodge at Costelloe, County Galway and was amazed to find it so primitive. It had no electricity, no bathroom and the only water supply was a well. It was not a big house nor did it stand in large grounds; there was a short drive, and a small garden in the back and front. However, it had a lovely position, flanked by the laugh on the West and the river at the garden door; the fishing was excellent. So they put up with the inconveniences for the summer, but as soon as they returned to London, Bruce Ismay instructed a firm to make the house habitable during the winter. During the 1920s the original house was burnt down, and in 1927 Bruce Ismay had it entirely rebuilt.

The Lodge at Costelloe after it was rebuilt in 1927

CHAPTER 17

*The White Star Line under Harold Sanderson,
the war years and after*

When J Bruce Ismay reluctantly retired from the White Star Line, on June 30th 1913, the original name of the firm disappeared; he had made an arrangement with the International Mercantile Marine Company, when they bought the White Star Line, that when he retired the name of Ismay, Imrie & Company would become his exclusive property.

On taking over the presidency of the I.M.M. and chairmanship of the White Star Line H A Sanderson reorganised the whole of the White Star management. The new managers were Henry Concannon, E Lionel Fletcher and A B Cauty. He was not, however, president for long, as, with J Bruce Ismay gone and the *Titanic* affair still on everyone's mind, the Morgan Combine began to go down hill again; it was decided that it would be better if the president were an American, so P A S Franklin was appointed and H A Sanderson resigned; he remained as chairman of the White Star Line.

Thirteen months after J Bruce Ismay retired the Great War broke out and the company faced many fresh problems. By 1915 the Morgan Combine Was in financial difficulties, and it was only the abnormal wartime demand for tonnage and the skilful management of the Public Receiver which enabled it to keep going.

In August 1914, the training ship *Mersey* was sold because her captain and officers were needed for more important wartime duties; the *Oceanic, Teutonic, Celtic* and *Cedric* were immediately taken over by the Admiralty as armed merchant cruisers.

The *Oceanic* became attached to the Tenth Cruiser Squadron, but unfortunately her life was short. Whilst patrolling the North West Approaches on September 8th 1914, she went ashore off Foula Island in fog. All hands were saved but it was impossible to get the vessel off, although some of her guns and fittings were saved. She remained stranded there for nine years, battered by the winds and tides, but she was so soundly constructed that in 1924 the salvage company engaged on work with the scuttled German Fleet at Scapa Flow also managed to salvage a considerable quantity of material from the *Oceanic.* For such a magnificent vessel it was a sad end.

The *Teutonic* also served in the Tenth Squadron but the Admiralty bought her outright in 1915. Later, as the war drew to a close, she returned to White Star management, and was used for trooping between Britain and Egypt, as were also the *Celtic* and *Cedric.*

The *Adriatic* and *Baltic* continued to work for a time between Liverpool and New York but later both were used as troop transports. (The *Adriatic* had the nickname 'Queen of the Munitions Fleet'). To USA declared war on Germany, and for the rest of her life she carried a plaque commemorating this event.

But the *Olympic* gave the most spectacular war service of all.

When war broke out her prestige was high indeed. She was on a voyage to New York at the time, from where she returned to the Clyde, as Southampton was immediately abandoned as a port on declaration of war. On a later voyage, on her way back to the Clyde she took in tow the battleship HMS *Audacious* which had been mined; all the crew were taken aboard, but the battleship sank whilst under tow.

In the following September the *Olympic* became a troop transport, carrying British troops to the Mediterranean. Later she carried troops between Canada and the US and Great Britain and was nicknamed 'The Old Reliable' by the services with whom she became very popular.

In May 1918, carrying United States troops on her 22nd trooping voyage she was attacked by a submarine U.103 in the Atlantic, which she rammed and sank, no mean feat for such a large vessel.

On finishing her war work, the *Olympic* was handed back to her owners and was immediately sent to Belfast to be refitted, arriving there on August 12th, 1919. She had given magnificent

Britannic, which became a hospital ship during the Great War

service running non-stop for five years and the opportunity was taken of converting her to oil firing, thus being the first large Atlantic liner to be oil fired. Her refit took over six months and cost more than £500,000; when it was completed she was almost a better ship than when she was originally built in 1911.

The *Britannic* was the third sister ship of the *Olympic* and *Titanic* class, and her construction had been held up during the inquiry into the *Titanic* disaster. She was given two feet more beam than her two sisters and served as a hospital ship in 1915. She never sailed in the fleet of her owners; mined in November 1916, in the Aegean Sea, she sank with the loss of 21 lives. So, of the three great ships, built with such high hopes, only the *Olympic* remained.

During the war Mr and Mrs Bruce Ismay continued to live at Hill Street; as a director of the companies in which he was still interested, he did all he could to help the Allied cause. He made frequent trips to Liverpool in connection with this work and usually stayed at Sandheys, until he disposed of the property in 1920. When the war ended he felt he wanted to do something to help the Merchant Service, as he knew only too well what they had been through. So often they were overlooked whilst all credit was given to the Navy. So in 1919 he gave £25,000 in War Loan Stock to the Mercantile Marine Service Association in Liverpool, to found a fund to be known as the 'National Mercantile Marine Fund' to mark his admiration of the very "splendid and gallant manner in which the officers and men of all ranks in the British Mercantile Marine have carried on during the War".

The primary object was to make grants and pensions to "necessitous masters and seamen of all ranks, who have served at sea on British Merchant vessels at any time during the Great War". It also made provision for the widows and children of such seamen. Preference was to be given to applicants and dependents of masters and seamen who sailed out of Liverpool or in Liverpool owned ships, or who had their homes in the port of Liverpool. The pension was not to exceed £50 per year nor a grant to exceed £10.

His Majesty, King George V, sent the following telegram to the secretary of the MMSA:

"The King has learnt with much pleasure of Mr. Bruce Ismay's generous gift to the National Mercantile Marine Fund. His Majesty feels sure that this tribute to the splendid services rendered by the officers and men of the British Mercantile Marine will be much appreciated".

Mr Gersham Stewart, MP, sent the following letter to J Bruce Ismay:-

Dear Sir,

I was recently asked by the Mercantile Marine Service Association to become their honorary treasurer, and as I hope to be of use to them in the House of Commons, I accepted their invitation.

You may perhaps imagine my feelings in reading in to-day's papers the announcement of your magnificent gift of £25,000 for the purpose of founding a National Mercantile Marine Fund. It gives me a profound pleasure to express to you in the first letter I have written on behalf of the M.M.S.A., my deep gratitude for this great gift. It is indeed an auspicious commencement for 1919.

All merchant seamen will be immensely gratified at such a recognition of the services of our 'Unofficial Navy'.

With all good wishes for the New Year,
Believe me, very truly yours,
Gersham Stewart.

The original fund of £25,000 has been added to over the years, and today it stands at £60,220, out of which pensions to the value of £2,073 were paid in 1958.

After the war was over, Mr and Mrs Bruce Ismay settled down to a normal life again, a life that became almost routine, right up to 1937 when Bruce Ismay died.

Every Sunday night would find him on the evening train to Liverpool, in a reserved compartment with the blinds drawn down and with a cold supper packed for him at home, so that he did not need to use the dining saloon. If it was fine, summer or winter, he walked to Euston station, the car carrying his luggage. He always stayed in Liverpool at the LNWR hotel and when there attended board meetings of the Liverpool London and Globe, Sea Insurance, etc.

He sometimes visited St George's Hall for a concert in the afternoon, as he was very fond of music. He always took two seats, the second one for his hat and coat. On Wednesday evening he was back in London in time for dinner. Whilst he was away Mrs Ismay frequently gave parties for bridge, or dancing, but never when he was at home; he had always been shy and the *Titanic* affair had certainly not helped him to overcome this.

However, he enjoyed giving small dinner parties, not more than eight guests at a time; these were for his intimate friends, of whom he was genuinely fond and whom he had mostly known for a long time. With these friends he was a genial and entertaining host. Mrs Ismay kept a good table, but his dinner was always the same, cold turkey, which he loved. This was well known to his family and friends; on one occasion, when his daughter Margaret knew he was coming to stay with them in Scotland, she went to a lot of trouble to obtain and cook a turkey for him. For the rest of the party there was pheasant, but when he was told that there was turkey especially for him, he said "Turkey, I don't want turkey, I have that every night at home, I would like some of that pheasant." This was typical of Bruce Ismay, unpredictable and contrary.

He was kind and generous in a quiet unobtrusive way. Not long after the war was over, a friend came to stay. She was not well off and her husband had been killed in France. Mr Ismay heard that the YMCA were arranging for widows to visit their husbands' graves and thought that she would like to go.

So one evening on going to her room, she found an envelope on the dressing table enclosing a cheque for the fare and a note saying "I have made it for two, as I feel sure you would like to take somebody with you." Naturally she was very grateful but he always disliked being thanked.

He always enjoyed being in the open air, and when in London, he often walked in the parks. Sometimes he took business papers with him to study at his leisure on one of the park benches; he enjoyed talking to people he met there, particularly the 'down and outs' who told him their troubles. Whenever he could he helped them, with advice and often with money, although he never disclosed his identity.

Another of Ismay's favourite relaxations was watching processions and although he usually had seats offered to him, he would usually arrange for a friend to accompany his wife, whilst he himself stood amongst the crowd in the street. He did this in 1935 to watch the jubilee procession of George V, and thoroughly enjoyed his kerb-side view.

Mr Ismay never accompanied his wife on her continental tours, as he hated motoring, but they occasionally went on holiday together. Once, while staying at Gleneagles Mrs Ismay heard that a young man was giving flights in an aeroplane. Always eager for some new experience, she asked her husband to accompany her, but he refused to have "both feet off the ground" and suggested that she took Smith with her; the butler was delighted and they went for an hour's flight in the open cockpit of a small biplane. In spite of her husband's remark, spoken with a twinkle in his eye, "I hope you break your necks", they thoroughly enjoyed themselves and returned safely full of the pleasures of flying.

One day not long after the war Bower Ismay was travelling from his home in Northamptonshire to attend a meeting of trustees of the T H Ismay Trust Fund, which was usually held at 15 Hill Street. Bruce Ismay, with his mania for punctuality, was annoyed when his brother did not arrive. After a while he became worried and asked Smith to telephone Euston Station; he was told that a gentleman had been found unconscious in a first-class carriage and taken to The Royal Free Hospital. It was Bower, suffering from sleepy sickness which he had contracted during his service in Africa. He died on May 25th 1924, at his home, a comparatively young man. It was a great blow to Bruce as he and

Bower had always been very close in spite of the difference in years.

On January 1st, 1923 the LNWR was to become a constituent of the LMSR; Mr Ismay who had always been greatly interested in railways received the following letter:-

THE LONDON NORTH WESTERN RAILWAY COMPANY
Chairman's Room,
Euston Station, London, N.W.
November 27th, 1922.
My dear Ismay,
I have pleasure in informing you that you have been selected by the committee appointed for the purpose as a member of the board of the new company to be known as the London Midland & Scottish Railway.

The first meeting, which will be an informal one, will be held in the board room at this station on Friday, 15th December, at 2.30 p.m. and luncheon will be served in the dining room at 1 o'clock.

I hope you can arrange to be present.
Yours faithfully,
C. A. Lawrence.

At the first informal meeting of the board of directors it was proposed that J Bruce Ismay as a director of the new company should serve on the following committees:-

Shipping
(Duties to deal with all matters relating to the company's shipping interests).

Traffic
(To superintend conduct of all business relating to passenger and goods traffic over the company's lines both from operating and commercial points of view, and to receive officers' reports on matters of importance and general interest.)

Rolling Stock
(To take charge of all matters connected with the rolling stock, including the construction, purchase and repair of engines,

carriages, wagons, road vehicles and electric plant and power houses, and the supervision of the company's workshops connected therewith. To supervise generally all matters related to mechanical plant.)

Stores
(To superintend the purchase, examination and issue of all stores, including coal and coke, and the disposal of surplus and scrap material.)

Of all the various boards of directors which Bruce Ismay served on during his long life the work that he enjoyed most was that which he called his railway work. As with everything he did, he put his whole heart and soul into it, and on several occasions he was offered the chairmanship of the London, Midland and Scottish Railway, but he always refused to take this position. He was quite determined that never again, after the *Titanic,* would he come prominently before the public eye.

While Bruce Ismay was thus continuing his life in Hill Street, his connections severed with the White Star Line, its managers were busy trying to get the line into some sort of shape again and to restore the magnificent service for which they were famous before the war. This was not going to be easy, because the only vessel for the Southampton service was the *Olympic;* her sister ship had been lost eight years before in the worst disaster in marine annals. As we have seen the *Britannic* had been lost in the Aegean, and so it was decided to lay down a new vessel of 40,000 tons, which was to be named *Homeric.*

Fortunately the 'Big Four', as they were always known, *Celtic, Cedric, Baltic* and *Adriatic* had survived the war and after a major overhaul, would revert to their old employment LiverpoolNew York, but their speed made them quite unsuitable for the express service from Southampton.

In 1919 the *Adriatic* reopened this service running in conjunction with the Red Star liner *Lapland;* they were joined in 1920 by the reconditioned *Olympic.* After she had completed her refit at Queen's Island, she was opened for public inspection at half-a-crown a head and between three and four thousand people visited her. The proceeds were given to various hospitals.

A fortnight after she was on exhibition her sister ship the

Titanic came into the news again. It had been decided, before the outbreak of war to erect a memorial to Thomas Andrews and those of Harland & Wolff's workpeople, who lost their lives in her and to some of the Crew who were also Belfast men; the memorial was to be placed in front of the City Hall in Belfast. It had not been possible to transport the marble from Italy during the war, and it was finally unveiled by the Lord Lieutenant of Ireland on June 26th, 1920. It was the third *Titanic* memorial to be erected in the United Kingdom, the first is at Southampton and the second at Liverpool.

After the *Olympic* had been on view for two days she sailed to Southampton with a large party on board as guests of the White Star Line, including H A Sanderson and Lord Pirrie. A dinner was held on board and in his speech Mr. Sanderson referred to the *Olympic* as "the one ewe lamb of the White Star Line" and said that "owing to world conditions he could not see such a large vessel being built for some time to come."

The White Star Line were now faced with the problem of having no other vessel to run in conjunction with the *Olympic* on the Southampton service of comparable speed and size. The 40,000 tons vessel which was to be called *Homeric* had been laid down at Harland & Wolff, but they needed a ship at once. Lying at Danzig was an uncompleted vessel named *Columbus* of 34,000 tons which had been launched just before the war for the Norddeutscher Lloyd Line. She had been taken over with all other German tonnage by the Shipping Controller as part of war reparations.

The International Mercantile Marine bought her for the White Star Line and Harland & Wolff sent technicians and workpeople over to help complete her in the traditional manner. She was renamed *Homeric* (the projected vessel laid down at Harland & Wolff's was dropped) and throughout her career she held two records; she was the world's largest twin screw vessel and the largest to be propelled by reciprocating engines. Though a fine ship she did not compare with those White Star liners built by Harland & Wolff, but she acquired a reputation for being one of the steadiest ships on the North Atlantic; she made a wonderful cruising liner in her later years.

When first taken over by the White Star Line her speed of 18 1/2 knots was inadequate for the Southampton express service and after two years she went to Belfast for conversion to oil firing; when she came back into service her speed was increased to 19 1/2 knots, and it was found that passengers could reach London from New York 24 hours faster than before.

At the same time a gigantic vessel was lying in a partially completed state in the River Elbe at Hamburg, this was the third of Albert Ballin's (the head of the Hamburg American Line) giant ships, which he had planned as an answer to the White Star Line's *Olympic, Titanic* and *Britannic* and also to the Cunard Company's *Lusitania, Mauretania* and *Aquitania.* She was named *Bismarck;* the other two were the *Imperator* (which later became the Cunard Line's *Berengaria)* and the *Vaterland* (which later became the United States Line *Leviathan).*

The only lines which could consider operating the *Bismarck* were the White Star and the Cunard companies. The Cunard Company was already operating the *Imperator,* so as to avoid outbidding each other the vessels were bought by both lines and remained in joint ownership for ten years.

The *Bismarck* was only surrendered to the British after lengthy legal wrangling. As she lay completing in the Elbe, technicians from Harland & Wolff went over to assist in fitting her out ready for sea. Before leaving Hamburg there were rumours that she would never reach Britain, but would suffer the same fate as the German Fleet at Scapa Flow and be scuttled by her crew; however she reached Southampton safely.

She was renamed *Majestic* and with *Olympic* and *Homeric* maintained the Southampton service. When she sailed on her maiden voyage May 10th 1922, she was the world's largest vessel and was considerably larger and faster than any that the White Star Line had previously owned.

Not long after she entered the Atlantic mail service she made the fastest crossing of her career averaging 24 1/2 knots; but she had a weakness in her construction. In order to make her public rooms more spacious the uptakes from the boilers had been taken up the sides and joined to the base of the funnels on the boat deck instead of going up through the centre of the vessel as was usual; on one voyage she cracked down one side and was only held together by expert seamanship in trimming the ballast.

Each of the 'Big Four' was sent to Belfast in turn to be reconditioned before returning to its old employment of Liverpool

- New York. The *Adriatic* was used for cruising between voyages and frequently visited the Mediterranean.

At the same time as the White Star Line was beginning to get into some sort of shape again another White Star liner was figuring in the news; this was the 15,000 ton *Laurentic* (the first ship Harland & Wolff had built with reciprocating engines and exhaust turbine) and aboard which Inspector Dew had travelled to Canada to arrest the murderer Dr Crippen and Miss Le Neve.

In 1917 she sailed from Liverpool to Halifax carrying gold bars worth £5,000,000. She struck a mine off Malin Head on the West coast of Ireland and sank; 354 out of the total of 475 officers and men lost their lives. After the war, gold was in short supply and so it was decided to try and salve the bars. The *Laurentic* had sunk in an exposed part of the coast and had been battered by the sea for five years, lying in twenty fathoms of water. However, she was located and found to be lying at an angle of 45 degrees on the bottom. During suitable weather the Admiralty divers, at a cost of about £130,000 managed to salvage nearly all the gold, between the years 1921 to 1924. The story of the *Laurentic* is one of the greatest salvage stories of the sea.

The White Star Line were always pioneers and not long after the war they decided to use the liner *Vedic* on the LiverpoolNew York service as third class only. The idea was popular for a time as it meant that all passengers had unrestricted access to all decks. But the American Immigration laws put an end to it.

In 1923 the *Doric* was commisioned for the Liverpool-Montreal service and was the only vessel ever built for the White Star Line to be propelled by geared turbines; she voyaged steadily between Liverpool and Montreal until 1932.

In 1924 Lord Pirrie set off on a tour of South American ports in the Royal Mail Steamer *Arlanza* to study the harbour facilities, etc, on behalf of the Royal Mail Steam Packet Company. He transferred to the *Ebro* and it was aboard this ship that he collapsed and died on June 7th 1924.

He was considered to be one of the greatest shipbuilders and captains of industry of his time and had played an extremely important part in the affairs of the White Star Line ever since the death of T H Ismay nearly 25 years before. It was he who had been so much in favour of the White Star Line joining the Morgan Combine in 1902. His body was taken to New York and was brought back to Southampton on board his favourite ship the *Olympic* and from there to Belfast and buried in the city cemetery. On a panel of his tomb is a four funnel steamer with this inscription:-

R.M.S. *Olympic* 45,439 tons for the White Star Line, built by Harland & Wolff 1911.

As the middle of the 1920s approached, the IMM wished to dispose of the White Star Line and all its foreign holdings, but no buyers were forthcoming. They ordered their last ship from Harland & Wolff for the Oceanic Steam Navigation Company. This was *Laurentic (II)*, the only ship to be built by Harland & Wolff to a fixed price. She was a most unsatisfactory vessel in every way, being completely out of date before she was launched. For some reason she was coal fired while her furnishings were not up to White Star Line standards because Franklin would not allow a penny more to be spent on her than was absolutely necessary.

CHAPTER 18
(contributed)
Sale of the White Star Line to the Royal Mail group, the amalgamation of the Cunard and White Star Lines, the death of J Bruce Ismay

The Morgan Combine - the gigantic international shipping trust which was formed in 1902 - had never been the success envisaged, so it did not come as a surprise when towards the close of the First World War, the IMM Company intimated that it was prepared to dispose of all its foreign flag holdings. This soon led to confidential negotiations with many prominent British interests some of whom appeared anxious to play a part in regaining British control of many companies, especially the White Star Line.

Talks extended over several months and ultimately a syndicate headed by Lord Pirrie and Sir Owen Phillips (later Lord Kylsant) made an offer of £27 million for all the British flag tonnage and other assets which included cash accumulations of £11 million.

All parties concerned reached agreement, the necessary documents were prepared and printed, meetings arranged in London to finalise the matter, and the whole scene set for final completion when, at the last moment, a cablegram was received from New York announcing that the President of the USA (Dr Woodrow Wilson) had vetoed the transaction for reasons of state.

No purpose would be served by going into all the circumstances which brought this decision about but for the time being negotiations were called off, much to the disappointment of the British interests involved.

Discussions were revived again, and in 1926 an offer was made by a syndicate in London headed by Sir Frederick Lewis who was chairman of Furness, Withy & Co Ltd. These negotiations also proved abortive owing principally to the attitude adopted by the IMM Company in connection with the terminals at New York as well as the general strike in Britain which made the outlook extremely uncertain.

Within a few months of the Furness negotiations terminating it was suddenly announced that Lord Kylsant, as chairman of the Royal Mail Steam Packet Company, had completed the purchase of the ordinary share capital of the Oceanic Steam Navigation Company Limited (which was better known under its trading name of White Star Line). At that time, Lord Kylsant was regarded as the leading shipowner in Great Britain; he also had interests in shipbuilding, oil installations, port development and other activities embracing some 60 different companies. The news of his latest acquisition was received with great satisfaction by the British public.

It also had the effect of what was known as the Kylsant Group becoming the largest shipowners in the world with well over two million tons of shipping.

The Royal Mail had many problems of its own without embarking on the acquisition of the OSN Company for the sum of £7 million, which was certainly an extravagant figure to pay having regard to the prevailing circumstances. Possibly Lord Kylsant had many reasons for embarking upon this somewhat hazardous venture and it is reasonable to assume that the close connection which had existed between the White Star Line and Harland & Wolff since 1869 was the principal reason for his haste in dealing with a situation which was undoubtedly causing him much concern.

It was well known that an understanding existed whereby Harlands carried out all building and heavy repair work on a 'cost plus basis' for the White Star Line and many of the other important companies in the Royal Mail Group. By 1924, Lord Kylsant had acquired control of Harlands and upon the death of Lord Pirrie, he took over the chairmanship - another vast empire to add to his many commitments.

In the long association between the two companies, no formal contract for the building of a new ship was ever made, nor was a price agreed upon, an arrangement which prevailed until 1927. In common with other shipowners, the White Star Line was seriously concerned at the ever-increasing costs of building new ships as well as the heavy outlay involved in extensive repairs, and, in placing an order for the second *Laurentia,* it was stipulated that a 'fixed price' must be quoted, otherwise the ship would not be built. A few months later, the company, after reviewing all the circumstances, decided to terminate its long-standing arrangements with Harlands and the necessary six months' notice to do so was duly despatched on the authority of the White Star Line directors.

Alarmed at the action of its most important customer and no doubt somewhat apprehensive that other companies might act similarly, Lord Kylsant evidently reached the conclusion that the time had arrived to obtain control of White Star, which soon became an established fact.

Upon taking over the chairmanship of his new purchase, his first action was to arrange for the withdrawal of the notice which had been given to Harlands some months previously. Unfortunately, as events subsequently turned out, this decision proved of little benefit to the famous shipbuilders.

Undoubtedly there were other reasons which prompted Lora Kylsant and his colleagues, but whatsoever they may be attributed to, the fact remains that it was a most unfortunate day for White Star Line when it became a member of the Royal Mail Group.

The first question which obviously arose was how did Royal Mail propose to raise the necessary funds to meet the cost of acquiring the White Star Line? Lord Kylsant's first idea was to issue further debentures of Royal Mail Steam Packet Company, but financial interests stipulated that, in such an event, a substantial proportion of the proceeds of the issue would require to be ear-marked to reduce indebtedness to the company's bankers. He thereupon changed his ideas and decided to form an entirely new company which was duly incorporated in January, 1927 under the name of White Star Line Ltd. Its purpose was to take over the contract entered into by Royal Mail for the purchase from the IMM Company of the ordinary share capital of the Oceanic SN Company. The use of the well-known trade name of White Star Line for this new company was strongly resisted by the American vendors as they claimed that until a substantial part of the purchase price had been paid it was unreasonable for the purchasers to make use of the goodwill value attaching to White Star.

These difficulties were eventually overcome and in January 1927 White Star Line Limited made an issue of £2.5 million in 6.5 per cent preference shares of £1 each. The issue was subscribed to the extent of £9 million and six months later, a further 2.5 million shares were issued. These two issues of preference shares totalling £5 million were guaranteed as to capital and dividend by the Royal Mail Steam Packet Company, an action which, unfortunately, considerably accelerated the serious financial problems which beset Royal Mail.

Upon the new company being formed, there was also issued £4 million of ordinary share capital which was entirely subscribed for by companies within the Royal Mail Group and upon which only 2/- a share was called and paid up, so that, upon incorporation, the total amount of ordinary capital paid up was only £400,000.

Much might be written concerning the unfortunate history of White Star Line Ltd., as it had a short and eventful history from the date of its promotion in 1927 until April 1935 when it was wound up. In this short space of eight years, the ordinary and preference shareholders in addition to other financial interests unfortunately lost over £11 million.

To turn back to the affairs of the Oceanic Company, it soon became obvious that, in addition to the slump in trade, great difficulties lay ahead as the Royal Mail Steam Packet Company was due to repay substantial amounts to the Treasury for facilities granted to it under the Trade Facilities Act. The first repayments of these fell due in 1929 and 1930, and this led to an approach by Lord Kylsant for an extension of the maturity dates of certain of these loans.

In considering the application, the Advisory Committee (of which Lord Plender, an eminent chartered accountant, was chairman) came to the conclusion that the various companies were so interlocked and there was so little information available as to the real financial position, that an independent report should be prepared regarding the affairs of all the major companies in the Royal Mail Group. It was under these circumstances that Sir William McLintock, another well-known chartered accountant, was instructed to examine the position of the various companies. This investigation was completed in April 1930 whereupon the Advisory Committee reached the conclusion that, whilst they were anxious to be of real assistance, this purpose could not be achieved merely by postponement of the maturity dates of the TFA loans. They intimated to Lord Kylsant that, in their view, the whole of the banking and financial interests concerned in the Royal Mail Group should be consulted.

The outcome of such consultations was a decision of the financial interests involved to continue their facilities or accommodation conditional upon the voting control of all the companies in the group being vested in three trustees who became known as the 'Voting Trustees'. The Oceanic company being a member of the group unfortunately became involved in all these difficulties and although the company continued to carry on its day-to-day activities in the years 1931, 1932 and 1933 the company had considerable difficulty in meeting its commitments due to the depression in shipping.

There is little doubt that the acquisition of the famous Oceanic Company was a tragedy, both for it and the Royal Mail Group. The financial position of the latter was such that it was very doubtful whether they were justified in agreeing to pay such an extravagant price as £7,000,000 to obtain control-indeed, it is well known that another well-known shipowner at that time who was also anxious to purchase the entire share capital assessed the value at exactly half this figure. Nor was Royal Mail in a position to guarantee the preference share capital and the annual interest thereon of the new company, a decision which caused grave misgivings in financial circles. The eventual failure of the Royal Mail Steam Packet Company in February, 1936 was mainly attributable to these unfortunate transactions and in this connection it is of interest to recall that the position disclosed a total deficiency of over £22,000,000.

The reaction on the Oceanic Company was just as serious as immediately Lord Kylsant became chairman, which he did within a matter of days, he embarked upon a policy of obtaining the maximum financial assistance for Royal Mail to the unfortunate detriment of Oceanic from whom excessive dividends were extracted at a time when the money would have served a more useful purpose had it been retained by the company. In the year

1930, the Oceanic operated at a loss for the first time in its history of 61 years, a regrettable state of affairs which was repeated in the years 1931, 1932 and 1933.

The magnitude of the losses incurred during these four years, coupled with the fact that many vessels required extensive improvements or complete replacement, made it abundantly clear that the future of Oceanic was in great jeopardy unless new finance was forthcoming. Lord Kylsant had been removed from the chairmanship of Oceanic and a new board of directors appointed, but the damage had been done and the future of the company rested with the Treasury and financial interests.

The Oceanic was not the only North Atlantic company to be in difficulties. Its friendly rival for over half a century, the Cunard Line, was also having problems in connection with the 81,000 ton *Queen Mary* which had been laid down by John Brown & Co Ltd, Clydebank, at the end of 1930, only to be suspended by the end of 1931. The long delay in proceeding with the completion of the ship raised considerable agitation throughout the country and the Government was urged to arrange the necessary finance to enable work to be resumed and the vessel completed.

HM Treasury eventually agreed, but the offer was conditional upon Cunard and White Star getting together with a view to merging their respective fleets in the North Atlantic. The proposal met with considerable opposition from those interested in White Star, the International Mercantile Marine Company going so far as to seek an injunction to restrain the proposed merger agreement being carried into effect.

However, all the many difficulties were eventually disposed of and a new company was formed in 1934 under the title of Cunard White Star Limited. The capital of the new venture was fixed at £10,000,000, of which 62 per cent was allotted to Cunard and 38 per cent to Oceanic interests. The Treasury undertook to provide:-

£3,000,000 to complete the *Queen Mary*
£1,500,000 as working capital
£5,000,000 to build the *Queen Elizabeth*
being a total of £9,500,000.

All these loans were duly repaid within a few years after the completion of the two ships.

The board of directors was fixed at ten, of whom six were to represent Cunard and four Oceanic interests. The first fleet of the merger company consisted of 25 ships, as follows:-

Cunard: 15 ships - 329,257 tons - average 21,951
Oceanic: 10 ships - 285,680 tons – average 28,568.

Within a few years, all the Oceanic ships were scrapped or disposed of - the one exception being the *Britannic* which, remained in commission until late 1960, operating under the White Star flag and funnel colours.

The completion of the merger foreshadowed the end of the Oceanic Company; within a short period, its remaining interests in the Australian and New Zealand trades, property, office furniture and everything capable of being turned into cash, was disposed of. Eventually, in 1937, all that was left of a great empire was a small office in Cockspur Street which was shut when a few carpets and chairs came under the auctioneer's hammer to close an era which will long live in the memories of those who have a love of ships, upon which depends the security and prosperity of our great country.

It was indeed a sad ending to the efforts of two outstanding gentlemen and those privileged to serve the company during its wonderfully successful career covering a period of some sixty-five years.

At the same time as Lord Kylsant was negotiating to buy the shares of the Oceanic Steam Navigation Company, Dawpool began to figure in the Liverpool and Wirral newspapers; once again it was put up for sale and this time it was decided that if it did not make a substantial figure it would be demolished and sold piecemeal. All the fittings, both inside and out, were the finest it was possible to procure. Catalogues were prepared to this effect, and in 1926 it was offered for sale as a whole. The highest bid was £5,900; it was decided to sell all the interior fittings, then the exterior, the tiles and the lead, and finally the fabric. The conditions of sale stipulated that the site had to be cleared completely within six months. A large hotel in Llandudno bought some of the doors and panelling; a Birkenhead cinema bought a fireplace which can still be seen in the vestibule. The house had been so well built that the only way the contractors were able to demolish the main walls was with explosives. Ultimately the site was cleared and part of T H Ismay's work and memories were swept away; today of the great mansion only the terrace remains. In place of the house there are now three large modern self-contained houses, standing in their own grounds. Some of the original materials were used in the building of these.

One of the last photographs of J Bruce Ismay ever taken

As the negotiations between the Cunard and White Star Lines were progressing in 1933 Sandheys was sold, the buyers being the Liverpool Corporation. They could see no future for such a house in the present Liverpool, so it went the same way as Dawpool; not a trace of the house or grounds remain, the whole area being covered with small modern houses. It is only by looking at an old Ordnance sheet that the site can be found.

As the Cunard and White Star Lines were being merged into Cunard White Star Ltd Bruce Ismay, now aged 70 years, was retiring from his various directorships. His health was beginning to fail and he began to be more troubled by pains in his legs. In 1936, while at The Lodge, Costelloe, Co Galway, he was so ill that John Smith, his former butler and faithful friend, was sent for. He had retired some twelve months previously, but there was nothing he would not do for his old employer.

As soon as John Smith arrived, the packing started, and The Lodge was closed up again until the next year, but Bruce Ismay never visited the house again. Back in London, at 15 Hill Street, he underwent an operation in his own bedroom, his right leg being amputated just below the knee; it was touch and go whether he would lose the left one also.

Smith looked after him all the time and never left him. When he was better, he withdrew more and more into himself. He had always been shy, as we have seen and now he was in a wheel chair and could only walk on crutches, he never again visited the theatres and concert halls which he loved.

During the summer of the following year, Mr and Mrs Ismay went to stay near Sunningdale.

In October they were back in Hill Street; on the 14th, Warr, the butler, went to draw Bruce Ismay's bath. In spite of his disability Bruce Ismay remained as independent as possible, and with the use of various pulleys and gadgets which he had rigged up, he preferred to bath and dress without assistance.

When Warr returned to the room, he was horrified to see that his employer had collapsed and was unconscious in the big armchair at the foot of the bed. It was no easy matter to move somebody who weighed 17 1/2 stone, and who was 6ft 4ins tall, but with assistance he was able to get him back on to the bed. J Bruce Ismay had suffered a stroke which had taken his sight and his speech. He had two nurses to attend him and his devoted wife never left his side, but three days later at 1.30pm he died, never having regained consciousness.

The following day in the City of Liverpool, the flags flew at half mast, as they had done for his father and mother before him. Bruce Ismay died on a Sunday and on the following Monday morning Frank Bustard went to his office in Cockspur Street as usual. On arrival he was amazed to find that a mirror which Bruce Ismay had given him many years before was shattered into a thousand pieces.

Bruce Ismay was buried in Putney Vale and a memorial service was held at St Paul's, Knightsbridge. Representatives of Harland & Wolff, Cunard White Star, and all the other companies with which he had been associated, attended the service.

Just short of a month previously, on September 20th, the first of the three giant ships which J. Bruce Ismay had so enjoyed planning, the *Olympic,* left Jarrow where she had been for the last two years having been taken there for scrapping. The hulk was towed to Inverkeithing in Scotland for final demolition.

Today, 24 years after his death, only one of Bruce Ismay's ships remains in commission. His name and that of his father are practically forgotten; I can only hope that this book pays but a small tribute to two great men, who did so much for their country and its Mercantile Marine.

EPILOGUE

As the last years of J Bruce Ismay's life drew to a close, he received a letter from a certain Dr Crera, a medical practitioner who lived in Maryport, He was interested in local history, and particularly in Thomas Ismay, whom he regarded as "one of Maryport's greatest sons". He spent every spare moment he could manage from his busy practice gathering together all the information he could find. He felt a memorial should be erected to him and he wrote and told J Bruce Ismay that it was proposed to put up a plaque on Ropery House which would read:-

'In this house lived through his boyhood Thomas Henry Ismay,
Born in Maryport, 7th January, 1837
Founder of THE WHITE STAR LINE'

Unfortunately J Bruce Ismay died about one month before the plaque was unveiled and never saw the newspaper cuttings which Dr Crera sent him.

APPENDIX A

Rules and Regulations of the White Star Line

WHITE STAR LINE - OCEANIC STEAM NAVIGATION COMPANY LTD.

REGULATIONS for the Safe and Efficient Navigation of the Company's Steamships

GENERAL RULES

1. Instructions to be attended to. The Company's commanders and officers are particularly enjoined to make themselves not only acquainted, but familiar with the following rules and regulations.

2. Responsibility of Commanders. The commanders must distinctly understand that the issue of the following instructions does not in any way, relieve them from entire responsibility for the safe and efficient navigation of their respective vessels; and they are also enjoined to remember that, whilst they are expected to use every diligence to secure a speedy voyage, they must run no risk which might by any possibility result in accident to their ships. It is to be hoped that they will ever bear in mind that the safety of lives and property entrusted to their care is the ruling principles that should govern them in the navigation of their ships and no supposed gain in expedition, or saving of time on the voyage, is to be purchased at the risk of accident. The Company desires to establish and maintain for its vessels a reputation for safety, and only looks for such speed on various voyages as is consistent with safe and prudent navigation.

3. Authority of Commanders. The officers, engineers, and all others borne upon the ship's books, are subject to the control and orders of the commander, and all on board, of every rank, must be careful to respect his authority. Leave of absence in all cases, is only to be granted by the commander or commanding officer for the time being, and the return to duty must be reported in a like manner; it being understood that in no case, when the ship is in a foreign port, are the chief and second officers to be absent from the ship at the same time, and that a junior officer is always to be on board.

4. Respect due to officers. Every superior officer is to exact, upon all occasions, from those under him, unequivocal and respectful compliance with his orders, and it is expected of all that they will not neglect the usual exterior mark of respect, either when they address or are addressed by a superior officer.

5. Watches. The watches must be equally divided, and the ship is never to be left without an officer in charge of the deck, either at sea or in harbour; and no officer is, on any occasion, to leave the deck during his watch, nor until he is relieved of his duty; and officers are expected, when performing the duties of the ship, or when at their different stations, to preserve silence among the men, and to see that orders from the bridge or upper deck are executed with promptitude, and without confusion or noise. At sea, when the officer of the watch believes his ship to be running into danger, it is his duty to act, at once, upon his own responsibility; at the same time, he must pass the word to call the commander. The first and second officers should never give up charge of the bridge during their watch excepting in clear weather and open sea, when they may be relieved for their meals by the third and fourth officers, but at no other time, unless with the express permission of the commander.

6. Watch in dock, Liverpool. In dock, at Liverpool, an officer is always to be on deck with the quartermaster as a day watch, until relieved by the night officer, one quartermaster and one watchman.

7. Watch in dock, abroad. In port abroad, an officer of the ship is always to be on the upper or spar deck, in charge, together with the two quartermasters in the day-time. At night the watch is to be kept by an officer and two quartermasters.

8. Anchor watch. In harbour, when the ship is at anchor, the watch, night and day, is to consist of a junior officer, two quartermasters and four seamen.

9. Junior officers. The junior officers must exert themselves to afford every assistance in the navigation of the ship, by perfecting themselves in the practice of solar and stellar observations, both for the correction of the compasses and ascertaining the position of the ship.

10. Junior officers. In ships carrying third and fourth officers, those officers are not to have charge of a watch at sea except at the discretion of the commander.

11. Log and observations for position of ship. The log to be regularly hove, and the ship's position to be ascertained each day by solar observation when obtainable. The chief officer is required to work up the ship's position as soon after noon as practicable, and then to take it to the commander in the chart-room, where he will see the place of the ship pricked on the chart, so as always to keep himself posted as to steamer's position and course.

12. Compasses. The compasses should be carefully watched, and any difference that may be observed between the local deviation and that shown by the table of corrections to be noted in the compass-book kept for the purpose.

13. Night order book. The commander to enter in the night order book the course to be steered, and all other necessary instructions.

14. Nearing the land and heaving the lead. A wide berth to be given to all headlands, islands, shoals, and the coast generally; and the commanders are particularly enjoined, on all occasions when nearing the land or in places of intricate navigation, to take frequent cross-bearings of any well-marked objects that may be visible and suitable for verifying the position of the ship. Should the weather be unsuitable for cross-bearings the engines should be eased, and, if necessary, stopped occasionally, and casts of the deep sea lead taken. The steam-whistle to be sounded during the prevalence of fogs, and the fact recorded in the log book.

15. Boats, fire-hose, pumps, etc. A crew to be appointed to each boat, which, with the tackling, is required to be kept in good order and ready for immediate service. The ship's company to be exercised at their stations occasionally, in working the pumps, fire-hose, and handing along buckets, etc., so that the crew may be kept in proper training and the stores in efficient order, in case of fire or other accident.

16. Lights. The side and mast-head lights to be particularly attended to and always ready, and when in use to be placed according to Government regulations. All lights, except such as the captain or executive officer shall suffer (or the law requires), are to be put out every evening at 10 o'clock in forecastle and steerage, at 11 o'clock in the saloon, at 11. 15 p.m., in the smoke rooms, and at 11.30 o'clock in the sleeping berths or state rooms.

17. Fires. No fire to be allowed in the galleys after 10 o'clock p.m., unless with the express permission of the commander.

18. Sounding the wells, etc. The holds and fresh water tanks to be sounded twice a day by the carpenter, who is also required to turn the cocks in the water-tight bulkheads every 24 hours; pump gear to be examined, and everything kept in order for immediate use. A sounding book must be kept by the carpenter, and each examination recorded. The chief officer to inspect the book daily and initial it.

19. Inspection of ship by commander. The commander is expected to make a thorough inspection of the ship, at least once in every 24 hours, accompanied by the purser and surgeon. 11 a.m. would probably be found the most convenient hour for this duty. In the engine room inspection, the commander should be attended by the chief engineer only.

20. Spirit-room. The spirit-room is, under no circumstances, to be opened except during the day, and then only in the presence of the purser. No light is to be taken into the spirit-room on any pretext whatever. The key of the spirit-room to be kept by the purser.

21. Smoking. Smoking by the officers when on duty is strictly prohibited, and is allowed only in their own cabins or on the main deck, but on no account in any of the companion ways. Smoking by seamen, firemen, stewards, and others, allowed only on the main deck, forward of the main mast, when off duty.

22. Parcels, etc., not to be carried by ship's compnny, No parcels or goods of any description are to be carried by the ship's company for any person whatsoever.

23. Smuggling. The ship is to be searched for contraband goods before entering any port, and the result entered in the official log book. The chief of each department to conduct the search, accompanied by the purser. Any person detected in smuggling will be dismissed the service, any fines incurred being deducted from the wages due to the offender; and the heads of the different departments will be held responsible for those people immediately under their orders.

24. Signal lights. Rockets and blue or green lights, especially company's private signals, to be always kept at hand, ready for night signals, but on no account to be stowed in the powder magazine.

25. Flags. In port, from the 21st day of March to the 21st day of September, the ensign and company's signal to be hoisted at 8.30 a.m., and from the 22nd day of September to the 20th day of March, at 9 a.m., and hauled down at sunset. In stormy weather, small flags must be substituted.

26. Punishment. No man to be confined or punished in any way, when the commander is on board, without his order, and the punishment must be registered in the official log book. In the absence of the captain, the offender is to be confined, if it be necessary, but at no time in port, without acquainting the peace authorities of the port; if at a wharf, or in dock, the police are to be called promptly.

27. Uniform. The uniform prescribed by the company is to be worn on board, at all times, by the officers (the engineer on watch excepted). The crew (consisting of the seamen, firemen, and stewards), excepting firemen on duty, must always wear it on Sundays, at sea or in port; also on the days of sailing from or arriving in port, each one of the crew being compelled to provide himself with a uniform.

28. Divine Service. Divine service is to be performed on board every Sunday, weather permitting.

29. Report on officers. The commanders are required to give a faithful and conscientious report of the conduct, qualifications, and sobriety of officers, engineers, and petty officers, individually, at the end of each voyage.

30. Rules of the road. The commanders and officers of the several ships are strictly enjoined to make themselves perfectly familiar with the rules of the road, as issued by the Board of Trade, a copy being attached hereto for general reference.

31. Change of commanders. When any change of commander takes place, the officer relieved must hand to his successor this Book of Instructions, the copy of mail contract (if any), and all other ship's papers, especially those relating to the compasses and chronometers.

32. Log-Book. The log-book is to be kept by the chief officer, who is required to write it up daily from the log-slate, and submit it for the commander's inspection and signature.

33. Log-slate; directions for keeping it. The log-slate to be carefully written up, by the officer in charge of the deck, every watch, at sea or in port, and the particulars noted below punctually attended to:-

- (i) Courses (in degrees) by standard compass.
- (ii) Courses (in degrees) true.
- (iii) Speed of ship by log.
- (iv) Direction and force of wind.
- (v) Barometer and thermometer.
- (vi) Revolutions of engines.
- (vii) Number of inches of water in the wells.
- (viii) Remarks upon the weather, and other particulars; such as, what sail set and when taken in, if any and what signals are made, vessels met or spoken, especially those belonging to the company.
- (ix) The true bearings and distance of any land or lights in sight, particularly cross-bearings.
- (x) When and what soundings are obtained.
- (xi) Lunar or stellar observations, azimuths, or amplitudes.
- (xii) Time of arrival and departure from any place, with the ship's draught of water.
- (xiii) Time when passengers (and mails, ifany) are landed and embarked.
- (xiv) Any births or deaths that may occur on board, and in the latter case time of burial.
- (xv) When and for what purpose boats leave the ship and return.
- (xvi) When the anchor is let go at any port or place, the depth of water, the number of fathoms of cable veered to, and crossbearings taken to determine the exact position of the ship.
- (xvii) How the hands of watches are employed during the day.
- (xviii) The exact quantity of coal and water received at the respective ports, and the expenditure each day.
- (xix) Any case of collision or touching the ground, or other accident, to be carefully noted, giving the name of the officer of the watch, and the names and stations of the men on the look out.
- (xx) Any case of misconduct among the crew (required by the Merchant Seamen's Act), particularly in reference to forfeiture of wages.

- (xxi) When the ship's company are exercised at their stations.
- (xxii) When Divine service is performed, or why omitted.
- (xxiii) The names of all persons on the sick list to be entered each day at noon.
- (xxiv) The ship's reckoning, up to noon each day, both by observation and account, complete.

34. Log-book. The log, when completed by the chief officer, is to have its correctness certified by the officer of each watch, and to be placed before the commander daily for his inspection and signature.

35. Log-book. A leaf must never be removed or closed up in the log-book, nor an erasure made under any circumstances, but all errors are to be cancelled by ruling a line through them, with the initials attached.

36. Log-book. At the end of the voyage the log-book must be signed by the commander and chief officer, and then delivered over to the managers of the company.

37. Engineer's log-book to be examined by the commander. The commander is required each day to examine and sign the engineer's log-book, and shall be responsible for any omission that may occur in the same. The commander is likewise enjoined to pay special attention to the daily consumption and remaining stock of coal.

38. Tracks. It is not desirable to specify in these instructions any particular route to take between Liverpool and New York, as commanders must, in a great measure, be left to their own judgment in the matter, and be guided by circumstances; but the following may be taken as a guide, as emanating from officers of great experience in the Atlantic trade:-

"We consider the best and safest track to take in crossing the Banks of Newfoundland, say, from the middle of March to the middle of December, is to strike the Flemish Cap, and then shape a course to take the ship about 35 miles south of Virgin Rocks. The remaining three months we think it prudent to take the southern passage, as the field-ice is then forming on the edge of the banks".

Note:- During the month of November and half of December, the passage via Cape Race may be taken with safety, there being little fog there at the time.

Sable Island. This island should always be passed to the westward, as strong currents, fogs, and great local attraction are known to exist in the channel, between the island and the main, rendering the navigation extremely hazardous.

Skerries. The commanders are required invariably to pass to the northward, or outside this group of rocks, the channel inside being considered too narrow and dangerous to admit of large steamers being navigated through in perfect safety.

Course down channel. In leaving Liverpool, after passing the Skerries, it is usual in all steam-ship lines to steer for the Stack; with the Stack abeam and close aboard, shape a course for the Saltees Lightship; this will take a steamer about four miles south of the fair way of steam-ships, and ships, with a fair wind, bound to Liverpool.

39. Special reports. Commanders are required to furnish the managers with a special report, in writing, of any unusual occurrence which may have taken place on board, or in connection with their ships - such as accidents to life or limb, misconduct or mismanagement on the part of, or any serious complaint against, any of the company's servants, or anything requiring an entry in the official log of the vessel.

40. This book is to be returned to the company's office in the event of the holder leaving the service.

STEAMERS' NIGHT SIGNALS

WHITE STAR LINE - Green light, rocket throwing two green stars, and green light in succession.

APPENDIX B

AFFIDAVIT MADE BY A H WElKMAN

Senator Smith:
I also received the following affidavit made by A. H. Weikman, who was a barber on the *Titanic* which covers his observations.
April 24th, 1912.

Mr A H Weikman:
I certify that my occupation on the *Titanic* was known as the saloon barber. I was sitting in my barber shop on Sunday night, April 14th, 1912, at 11.40 p.m., when the collision occurred. I went forward to the steerage on 'G' deck and saw one of the baggage masters, and he told me that water was coming in in the baggage room on the deck below. I think the baggage man's name was Bessant. I then went upstairs and met Mr. Andrews, the 'builder', and he was giving instructions to get the steerage passengers 'on deck'. I proceeded along 'E' deck to my room on 'C' deck. I went on the main deck and saw some ice laying there. Orders were given, 'All hands to man the lifeboats', also to put on lifebelts. "Who gave the orders?" "Mr. Dodd, second steward".
I helped to launch the boats, and there seemed to be a shortage of women. When I was on 'E' deck I met the Captain returning from 'G' deck, who had been there with Mr. Andrews, and the Captain was on the bridge at that time. I did not think there was any danger. "What happened after the orders were given?" "Instructions were given to get the passengers into lifebelts and get on deck from all the staterooms." "Did you see Mr. Ismay?" "Yes. I saw Mr. Ismay helping to load the boats." "Did you see him get into a boat?" "Yes; he got in along with Mr.

Carter, because there were no women in the vicinity of that boat." This boat was the last to leave, to the best of my knowledge. He was ordered into the boat by the officer in charge, I think that Mr. Ismay was justified in leaving in that boat at that time.

I was proceeding to launch the next boat when the ship suddenly sank at the bow, and there was a rush of water that washed me overboard, and therefore the boat was not launched by human hands. The men were trying to pull up the sides when the rush of water came, and that was the last moment it was possible to launch any more boats, because the ship was at an angle that it was impossible for anybody to remain on deck. "State further what you know about the case." "After I was washed overboard I started to swim, when there was a pile of ropes fell upon me, and I managed to get clear of these and started to swim for some dark object in the water. It was dark. This was about 1.50 a.m. towards the stern." "How do you know it was 1.50 a.m.?" "Because my watch was stopped at that time by the water." "Did you hear any noise?" "Yes; I was about 15 feet away from the ship when I heard an explosion." "What caused the explosion?" "I think the boilers blew up about in the middle of the ship. The explosion blew me along with a wall of water towards the dark object I was swimming to, which proved to be a bundle of deck chairs, which I managed to climb on. While on the chairs I heard terrible groans and cries coming from people in the water." "Was it possible to help them?" "No; it was not. The lifeboats were too far away." "Do you think if the lifeboats were nearer they could render any assistance?" "Yes; had the lifeboats remained close to the *Titanic* they could have taken 10 to 15 or maybe 20 more passengers in each boat. There was a great number of people killed by the explosion, and there was a great number that managed to get far enough away that the explosion did not injure them, and these are the people that I think could have been saved had the lifeboats been closer." "Did you see the ship go down? I mean the *Titanic.*" "Yes; I was afloat on some chairs about 100 feet away, looking towards the ship. I seen her sink." "Did you feel any suction?" "No; but there was some waves come towards me caused by the ship going down, and not enough to knock me off the chairs." "How many lifeboats were there on the *Titanic?*" "About 18 or 20, and four collapsible boats, and the best equipment possible to put on a ship." "Do you think there were enough lifeboats?" "No".

"Do you know anything about the watertight doors?" "Yes; she had self closing doors of the latest type and they all worked, to the best of my knowledge." "How fast was she going when she struck that iceberg?" "I think about 20 knots. I was told by Mr. Ismay that she was limited to 75 revolutions several days before."

    A. H. Weikman.

    Subscribed and sworn to on this 24th day of April, A.D. 1912.

ACKNOWLEDGEMENTS

I am extremely grateful to the under-mentioned for the assistance they have given me in compiling this history.

My special thanks are due to Mrs J Bruce Ismay, who put the entire family papers at my disposal, for answering so many of my questions, for her own personal reminiscences, and her very many kindnesses to me. Mrs Ronald Cheape (Bruce Ismay's elder daughter) for her encouragement and help, and for introducing me to members of her family. Charles Drage has been exceedingly kind in allowing me to reproduce so many family photographs, and for lending me his grandfather's diaries written when T H Ismay was a young man, also those of Mrs T H Ismay. Without the help of these people this book could never have been written. Frank Bustard, a former employee and eventually Passenger Traffic Manager of the White Star Line, and the last apprentice to serve under J Bruce Ismay. Mrs Cavendish, Commander J Boxhall, Lawrence Beesley, Dent Ray, A Pugh and J Windibank, all *Titanic* survivors, for lending me various papers connected with the *Titanic* and for giving me their personal memories of the night of April 14th 1912. The management of Messrs Harland & Wolff, Belfast, with whom I spent two very pleasant days, for their great assistance in supplying information, and reproducing plans and illustrations of White Star vessels. Messrs Alexander Stephen of Lint House, Glasgow, for information regarding the *Angelita*. The Surveyor's office, Wirral Urban District Council, and the Librarian, Birkenhead Public Library, with reference to Dawpool. The City Surveyor's office, Liverpool, with reference to Sandheys. The Publicity Department, Mersey Docks and Harbour Board, with reference to Merseyside 50 years ago. The late H M Alderson Smith and his son, Alderson Smith, the Ismay family solicitors, for turning out old family papers, and allowing me to see them. Mrs K Simpson of Maryport, niece of the late Dr Crera, for her great assistance in obtaining for me from the Cumberland County Council archives all Dr Crera's papers relating to Maryport, and the early history of Thomas Ismay, also the Chief Archivist, T Grey, Cumberland County Council, for lending various papers, and Miss Carol Clarke for her assistance in this matter. Mrs. Scott, the present occupier of Ropery House, Maryport. The late R J A Shelley, late Publicity Department, White Star Line, Mr Cook and Miss Steinley, late of the White Star Line, now employed by the Cunard Steam-Ship Company in Liverpool. Roger Pain of Heathfield, Sussex, for reproducing family photographs. Gilbert H Fabes of Rye, Sussex, and John Harkness of Chelsea, for obtaining so many reference books for me. E W Paget-Tomlinson, Keeper of Shipping, Liverpool Public Museum. Captain T M Goddard (Captain of HMS *Conway* in my day), for his assistance, also for his first-hand account of *Oceanic* at Foula whilst he was on board. Captain F J Durrant of Rea Towing Co, Liverpool, for suggesting various lines of enquiry. George Dickinson, Editor of 'Sea Breezes', and his staff. C Mayes, assistant manager of Ship Dismantling, Messrs T W Ward of Sheffield, for his assistance in finding out all about the last days of the *Olympic*.

A W H Pearsall of the National Maritime Museum at Greenwich, who made available to me Bruce Ismay's evidence from the US *Titanic* Enquiry. Mr. Pearsall has also provided many helpful leads. The secretary of the Royal Insurance Company, Liverpool. The secretary of the Training Ship *Indefatigable*. The Librarian at the Liverpool Public Library. J B Thornhill, Librarian Sussex County Libraries, Seaford, for his great assistance in managing to procure for me the verbatim report on the *Atlantic*. Roy Bruce of Cranbrook, Kent, and his sister, Miss Doris Bruce, of Great Crosby, Liverpool, for their assistance in trying to obtain more information about Mrs T H Ismay's father, Luke Bruce. W Goffey of Hill, Dickinson & Co, Liverpool, for having J Bruce Ismay's evidence at the British *Titanic* enquiry reproduced. Mrs D Martindale, Croft House, Brampton, who lent me all her papers which deal with Croft House School, when Thomas Ismay was there as a boy. The late Captain S S Richardson of Beau Maris for his reminiscences of days when he was employed by the White

Star Line. W L S Harrison, the Secretary of the Mercantile Marine Service Association, who has been most helpful in supplying figures and facts about the various charitable funds founded by the Ismay family; he has also given me information about certain White Star vessels. The Librarian, Southampton Public Library, the manager, Odeon Cinema, Southampton; the Editor, 'Southampton Echo'; and L J Little, for their assistance in endeavouring to trace the whereabouts of August H Weikrnan and his family. Mrs Bruce Ismay's private secretary, for writing to various companies for me. Mrs Mary Quirke, whose husband designed the new Lodge, at Costelloe, rebuilt after being burned down, who has known the Ismay family since 1918, for her personal reminiscences of J Bruce Ismay spanning 20 years.

Mr and Mrs J Bruce Ismay's former butler, J Smith, who was J Bruce Ismay's devoted servant and friend for 25 years, and his former chauffeur, the late W Bungay, who was also with the family for over 20 years, for their personal reminiscences of J Bruce Ismay from 1912 until his death. Members of the photographic department, National Maritime Museum. The Libriarians of both the Brighton and Hove Public Libraries.

There are many other people who have helped me in various ways and I would like to take the opportunity of thanking them. I apologise if I have unknowingly infringed anyone's copyright. My wife, Margaret, has been of the very greatest possible assistance with her help and encouragement, also my mother-in-law, Mrs Marjorie Clews.

Lastly, Captain Charles Birchall who has taken such care and interest over the production of this book.

www.ingramcontent.com/pod-product-compliance
Lightning Source LLC
LaVergne TN
LVHW041611070426
835507LV00008B/185